STAY **SOLID**!

A **RADICAL HANDBOOK**
FOR YOUTH

EDITED BY MATT HERN &
THE PURPLE THISTLE CENTRE

AK Press Publishing & Distribution
Edinburgh | Oakland | Baltimore
2013

STAY **SOLID**!
A **RADICAL HANDBOOK** FOR YOUTH

Edited by Matt Hern and The Purple Thistle Centre

All essays © 2013 by their respective authors, unless otherwise noted
This edition © 2013 AK Press (Edinburgh, Oakland, Baltimore)

ISBN: 978-1-84935-099-0
e-ISBN: 978-1-84935-100-3
Library of Congress Control Number: 2012937709

AK Press
674-A 23rd Street
Oakland, CA 94612
USA
www.akpress.org
akpress@akpress.org

AK Press UK
PO Box 12766
Edinburgh EH8 9YE
Scotland
www.akuk.com
ak@akedin.demon.co.uk

The above addresses would be delighted to provide you with the latest AK Press distribution catalog, which features several thousand books, pamphlets, zines, audio and video recordings, and gear, all published or distributed by AK Press. Alternately, visit our websites to browse the catalog and find out the latest news from the world of anarchist publishing:
www.akpress.org | www.akuk.com
revolutionbythebook.akpress.org

Printed in the United States on recycled, acid-free paper.

Cover image: Cristy C. Road | www.croadcore.org
Cover and interior layout by Kate Khatib | www.manifestor.org/design
With grateful appreciation to Michelle Fleming

All proceeds from the book go to support the **Purple Thistle Centre**:
www.purplethistle.ca

Chapter Icons provided by **The Noun Project** | www.thenounproject.com

Family: **Jens Tärning**, from The Noun Project
School: **Saman Bemel-Benrud**
Community: **Arturo Molina**
Money: **Øystein W. Arbo**, from The Noun Project
Skills: **Thibault Geffroy**, from The Noun Project
Sex: **Marcelo da Silva**, from The Noun Project
Drugs: **Andrew Rockefeller**, from The Noun Project
Media: **Luis Prado**, from The Noun Project
Relationships: **Luis Prado**, from The Noun Project
Travel: **Jakob Vogel**, from The Noun Project
Class and Class Struggle: **Edward Boatman, Jay Demory, Tristan Sokol, Shirlee Berman & Doug Hurdelbrink**

Race: **Chiara Cozzolino**, from The Noun Project
Gender: **Joel Burke**, from The Noun Project
Disability: **Aynne Valencia**, from The Noun Project
Indigenous Struggles: **Chris Cole**, from The Noun Project
Ecocide: **Fabio Grande**, from The Noun Project
Immigration: **Roger Cook & Don Shanosky**
Cops & Courts: **Stephen West**, from The Noun Project
Mental Wellness: **Andrew J. Young**, from The Noun Project
Your Physical Body: **Boris Matusovski**
Getting Old(er): Unknown Designer

Table *of* Contents

"To be hopeful in bad times is not just foolishly romantic. It is based on the fact that human history is a history not only of cruelty, but also of compassion, sacrifice, courage, kindness.

What we choose to emphasize in this complex history will determine our lives. If we see only the worst, it destroys our capacity to do something. If we remember those times and places— and there are so many—where people have behaved magnificently, this gives us the energy to act, and at least the possibility of sending this spinning top of a world in a different direction.

And if we do act, in however small a way, we don't have to wait for some grand utopian future.

The future is an infinite succession of presents, and to live now as we think human beings should live, in defiance of all that is bad around us, is itself a marvelous victory."

—Howard Zinn

INTRO: SOLID!

WHAT IS THIS BOOK?

Hey thanks for picking this up! And welcome to our radical handbook.

This book is written directly to you. Especially if you're a youth, and even more especially if you're a youth with some radical ideas about yourself, your politics, and your world. It's also most definitely for anyone who considers themselves an ally: parents, neighbours, teachers, friends, relatives.

This book is a collection of ideas and stories, information, advice, and encouragement to stay solid and build a good life in a crazy world. We're pretty confident that what you'll find in here is an argument for a different, better kind of world. So much of our culture insists that you give up your ethics, forget your dreams, do what you're told, eat the dominant ideology, accept that the world sucks, and believe that oppression is natural.

We want to fight this. We want you (and us!) to stay radical, keep asking hard questions, keep resisting, keep fighting the good fight, and keep trying to be a good person leading a thoughtful, generous, fun life.

We want to talk about having real values and an ethical worldview, about how to keep doing the things that really matter to you. We really believe that you don't have to have a boring, depressing, defeated life—not now, not ever. We all have to compromise all the time and that's a good thing, but we want to support and exhort you to hang on to your best values and build a good life, not one that you meekly accept because you can't think of a different way.

And hey, a note here right from the beginning: throughout the book the contributors sometimes sound like they are talking to you, and that's awesome, because the book is intended to talk directly to teenagers. But we're not talking at you. We want it to be very clear—super clear—totally clear—right off the hop that we're not perfect people looking down on ignorant kids and showing them how to lead a good life. Very freaking far from it! We are talking to youth (many of the editors and contributors are youth, the rest of were once), but we are also talking to ourselves, our friends, our families, and each other, trying to articulate what a good life might mean.

The good life is not a thing. It's not a place. It's not something you can achieve. There's no good life that looks like a secular heaven/nirvana, and believe us when we say that none of us are there. We're all—and I mean all of us, not just people who have written something in here—trying to figure out what that might mean. There is no Truth in this book and none of it is gospel, it's just a bunch of solid people trying to understand how we can live the best lives possible.

The world is very fucked up in lots of ways, but this book is built on an explicitly active and hopeful premise: that there is a lot worth fighting for, and that you can scrap long and hard while still being a good person, having a lot of fun, giving and receiving a lot of love, and having a good time.

WHAT DO YOU MEAN "RADICAL"?

By radical we are talking about a left/socialist/anarchist/anti-capitalist world-view. Labels mostly suck though, so it's more accurate to say that we are people who are dissatisfied with the world as it is and are looking to contribute to a better, fairer, more ecological, more equitable world. We're speaking to kids who are asking themselves the same kinds of questions we are: how do we build a life that is dignified, fun, sustainable, meaningful, creative, and is a force for good?

Don't worry if you're not interested in naming your political beliefs with an 'ism'—or aren't sure what you think about those traditions. What you name yourself is a lot less important than how you act, what you're struggling for, who you support, and what you speak up for.

WHO ARE YOU GUYS?

My name is Matt Hern and I have coordinated the editorial collective that put this book together. In 2000 I founded the Purple Thistle—an independent youth-run community centre in East Vancouver—with seven teenage pals. Now we're over a dozen years old, have a couple of hundred regular low-income youth participants, and run a big resource centre that is full of classes, supplies, events, workshops, gardens, and tools, where everything is free for everyone. It is a very cool project that has inspired all kinds of work around the world and one that we're really proud of. Do check us out at www.purplethistle.ca.

When I was asked to put this book together it struck me right away that it would be a lot more fun to do with a bunch of Thistlistas. It also struck me we could organize the book in the same way that we organize the Centre. The whole Thistle project is based on a horizontal model where there are no bosses and all decisions are made by a collection of collectives. We don't vote, nor do we have a formal consensus procedure, and the whole project is held together by a youth collective. You can read a lot more about us on our website—but do come hang out, call or write us. We're always glad for visitors.

Once I had decided on this approach I put the call out and gathered a terrific group of twelve people as an editorial collective: an awesome crew, all of whom are part of the Thistle in one way or another: you can see their photos and bios on the Editors page. Then we figured out broad chapter topics to work with, everyone took one or two chapters, I picked up the left-overs, and off we went.

WHAT'S WITH THE SCRAPBOOK STYLE?

This has been a complicated book to figure out how to write. We want to speak directly to youth, but even that is a hellaciously broad category: you readers might be anywhere in the world, you might be 13 or 19 or a lot older. You might be in school or university, working or looking for a job or trying not have to get a job, traveling or in jail. You might be living in a village, a huge city, a suburb, or a farm. You might be straight, queer, bi, or some combination thereof. You might be native, African, Islander, white, Latino, Arab, Asian, a combination thereof, or identify as something else. And on and on and on. We don't know what language you speak at home, what challenges you're facing, what you feel proud and/or angry about.

To compound that, we are trying to write about a lot of things in here. We have broken the book up into 21 topics—even these don't come close to covering everything and these 21 are each ridiculously huge. How do you put together a single short chapter about Race? In some ways it is an impossible task. But I think these editors have done a fantastic job and each chapter is a really interesting, exciting, and challenging piece of writing.

So how do we speak to all of you? Well, we don't. We say our pieces and trust that you will find a lot in here that you'll like. I have asked each person who is curating a chapter to make an argument. Not to try to put together a chapter that tries to say everything to everyone about the topic—but to have each chapter make an argument, to suggest a specific way to think about the topic, and to present some great, thoughtful, inspiring, provocative writers. Hopefully we will pique your interest, get you thinking, challenge you, and give you some ideas for further thinking and reading.

Because there are so many editors and so many contributors, the book has emerged as a scrapbook of ideas. Each chapter has an introduction (sometimes written by the editor of the section, sometimes by me, mostly by the two of us together) so that the book flows as one larger argument and you can read the book from beginning to end if you like. But it should also work well to just read each chapter individually and out of order. You can also just read individual contributions. With any luck there will be lots to grab your attention and plenty of ideas, links, and resources for further reading and exploration.

WHAT ARE YOU HOPING FOR?

We're hoping that whoever you are, wherever you are, whatever you're doing, you will find something in here to challenge you. The book has so many voices there is lots in here that even I, and every editor, will argue with, and lots that you won't agree with. And that's great: this is not a blueprint for how to lead your life. We really want you to think of this book as a beginning, not an end in itself. We're hoping that this book can get you started, give you some ideas, and with luck introduce some new ways to think about things and give you energy to hang on to your best hopes for a better world.

The book is support, encouragement, guide, explanation, exhortation, manual, and advice in more or less equal parts: a call for you to be proud and live a good, honourable, powerful, and radical life. Thanks a lot for reading it and do get in touch with us, any of us. We'd be thrilled to hear from you.

1. FAMILY

Our families are the source of most of our troubles or our greatest strength and support. And very possibly both. Or maybe neither. But for all of us, especially youth, figuring out our family is one of our first and most persistent tasks.

Over the last couple of decades the idea of the "family" as a unit of strength and support has been co-opted by right-wing reactionary forces: think of the term "family values" for example, or extremist Christian groups like "Focus on the Family" that are deeply homophobic, racist, anti-feminist, anti-sex—and pretty much horrible on everything. At the same time, for many good folks, their family hasn't been a source of strength but a place of oppression, resentment, weirdness, and possibly abuse.

So it's understandable that "family" gets a bad name and that many people are antagonistic to the idea due to their own lousy family experiences and/or because it seems to stand for so many regressive values. But "family" is far too important to give up on, and there are other ways to think about it.

There are many types of families. The conventional nuclear family is one plausible rendition, but only one among many, many others. Family can be your biological parent(s), siblings, aunts, uncles, grandparents, and cousins. But it can also be found or chosen. The love and care shared by people who are in a family unit (and we're going to define that as the people who have always, always got your back) instead of smothering and shutting down life choices, can be used as a deep source of confidence. Families can be the safety net that lets you walk the tightrope, all the while keeping close enough to be able to call you on your mistakes and get you to consider your choices. It's your job as a teenager to differentiate yourself, to become your own person, but your family will always be part of who you are. Be grateful to the people who have taken care of you: it's a lot of work.

Whatever family you get born into is the hand you were dealt. If your family is a mess, or abusive, or weird, or not that supportive, it is not your fault and it is not your fate. It is also possible that your family situation just won't work. If your biological family is abusive you don't have to take that. You can find your own family. It might take some time, and you might have to look for a while, and you will surely have to work hard to build those relationships, but it is very possible.

No matter what your family is like though, it is worth trying really hard to make it work. Respect all the people in your family for who they are. But whether your family is the crew you were born into, a chosen group of people, or a combination thereof—they are the rock for you to work from: they will always be part of who you are. Knowing that there are people who will always love and care for you allows you to take risks of all kinds, and maybe counter-intuitively, really be yourself.

OTHER STUFF TO CHECK OUT:

- **TRACKS**, Louise Erdrich

- **MAUS**, Art Spiegelman

- **SONG OF SOLOMON**, Toni Morrison

- **SMOKE SIGNALS** (movie)

- **A COMPLICATED KINDNESS**, Miriam Toews

- **"THIS BE THE VERSE,"** Phil Larkin (poem)

- **FAMILY MATTERS**, Rohinton Mistry

- **TO KILL A MOCKINGBIRD**, Harper Lee

- **HOUSE ON MANGO STREET**, Sandra Cisneros

EIRLYS RHIANNON is a sometime singer, writer, and gardener with an-archist tendencies, who aims to keep her obsessions with lists and edible flowers in balance. She tries not to be a wanker. www.eirlysrhiannon.com

I assumed it would get easier, but it didn't.

With each passing year, any increase in power or status was offset by fear of having something to lose. When I lost power and status, the liberating sense of freedom was offset by fear that society might have me disappear entirely.

Passing seasons brought fragments of sparkled wisdom, but also the graft of learning the value of mundane things: being on time; budgeting; how to make a cheap meal into a feast. These things buy time, which I give to my inner child and inner teenager whenever I remember. They, in turn, paint my pictures, write my songs, play with my plants, and make my life rich. When I forget, I'm poor.

My parents said that family would matter more as I got older. Right in one way, but they misjudged how widely I would need to define "family." The hardest thing to learn has been how to love my ancestors while hating their actions. I had to find chosen family, and unconventional heroes, or I would not be whole. My born family knows me best, but also does not know me at all. They may never be on my side. I have to recognise that this will never stop being painful.

But life is pain and life is love and life is a constant healing. It's picking the seam undone with my best friends over a cup of tea or a beer, laughing, and then sew-ing it up differently. And doing that again. And again. And again.

Image by aly de la Cruz.
ALY D. is a young queer brown immigrant settler who lives on unceded Coast Salish Territories. She's also an artist-activist who's all about social change through art, youth liberation, and decolonial love. She has been a long time thistler, and currently is a mentor at the Purple Thistle.

KELSEY SAVAGE is a member of the 2009 Vancouver Youth Slam team and is one sixth of the insanely brilliant Candelabra Collective poetry group. She taught herself to beatbox by mimicking others, a process accompanied by months of awkward sounds. She also has a laugh that can shatter glass.

Christmas Is Far Away

Which holidays were you taught to celebrate?
This is for the holidays you don't. And the ones you do.
This is for the boxes that line the attics of houses you only knew one floor to.
This is for the ones that are filled with broken ornaments.
This is for the times you tried to move those boxes out of the way only to find shards of dust and tinsel.
This is for the decorations you never made it to.
How many holidays do you still celebrate?
This is for the homes you make it back to.
For the Thanksgivings that find your laundry.
This is for the partners you've introduced your parents to.
For the names they know of. And the ones they don't.
This is for the over-the-kitchen-countertop smiles your parents are sharing when they hear your voice on the phone and whisper, "I think there's someone..."
This is for the holidays you're happier without.
How much do you still talk to your parents?
This is for those offended by the question, "How's your family?"

This is for your definition of family.

This is for when they ask after your mother and you reply that both your dads are doing fine.
This is for those of us still naive enough to believe everyone had siblings.
Everyone had a yard.
Everyone had a car.
Everyone's life looked like yours.
This is for the holidays you still celebrate.
This is for the things we don't get days off work for, but still celebrate.
This is for the paint colour of your childhood home.
And for the home you have now.
This is for you. Because I love you.
This is for the person you love.
Because I'll probably love them, too.

ELDON HAY is a Professor Emeritus of Religion at Mount Allison University and a United Church minister. The first president of PFLAG (Parents and Friends of Lesbians and Gays) Canada, he also leads local chapters in Atlantic Canada, where he is highly respected for his thoughtful perspective on human sexuality. He was invested as a member of the Order of Canada in 2004 for this work.

The lives of some families can be rudely interrupted when one of its members—normally a teenage son or daughter—comes to the slow realization that they are homosexual. Such a discovery can be very difficult, even traumatic, for the young woman who realizes she is lesbian, or bisexual, or transgender. Similarly for the man, awakening slowly or quickly to the realization that he is gay, bisexual, or transgender. The normal expectations of growing up—getting along with friends of a different sex, dating—are challenged and undermined. To this challenge there is frequently fear and self-disgust at the new discovery. In some difficulties, youth turn to school, or church, or home. But in this situation all those avenues of support and assistance may be blocked off. "It's bad enough to find out I'm gay, but it'd be even worse if my parents knew."

Somehow or other, a father or mother may find out. Perhaps they suspect it. Sometimes, the youngster blurts the news out inadvertently. Again, youngsters may tell someone whom they can trust—a friend, an older member of the family, a particularly sympathetic counselor. If that encounter or sharing goes well, the circle may be enlarged. But each step is fraught with difficulty. A parent may erupt with hurt, anger or grief. Frequently a number of feelings are co-mingled.

How can we be different? How safe is it to be different?

PFLAG started on this continent several decades ago, earlier in the USA, slightly later in Canada. A small group of parents were looking for assistance and support. Parents and Friends of Lesbians and Gays was the result. From a handful of parents, the organization has blossomed.

I heard about PFLAG a short time after my son came out to me, back in the mid-1980s. At that time, my immediate reaction was fear: I was afraid my son would die of AIDS. I read, I thought, I prayed. And I contacted PFLAG. Laurie and Mary Jones, who had been two of the pioneers in Ontario, answered my request. And soon a PFLAG group started in two neighbouring communities, I facilitated both chapters.

Parents came. Not many at first. But they came. Sometimes very ashamed and hurt. Confused, angry. Why did this happen to me? To our family? We listened to each other, we became less ignorant about our gay, lesbian, bisexual children.

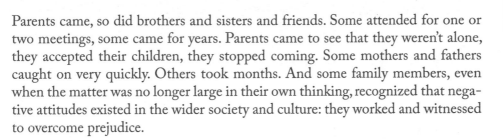

In the early days, we had no knowledge about transgender persons—that, too, came later.

Parents came, so did brothers and sisters and friends. Some attended for one or two meetings, some came for years. Parents came to see that they weren't alone, they accepted their children, they stopped coming. Some mothers and fathers caught on very quickly. Others took months. And some family members, even when the matter was no longer large in their own thinking, recognized that negative attitudes existed in the wider society and culture: they worked and witnessed to overcome prejudice.

From the outset, some gays and lesbians attended. They were invaluable. As a straight parent, I was able to hear from a gay teenager what he was feeling, what he was going through. My own son lived in a distant city, but a fellow gay was enlightening me in the small town where I lived.

That was one of the motives for starting a PFLAG group in a small town. I couldn't help Ron, my son, a thousand miles away. But I could perhaps make a small circle of acceptance and love. And others were doing the same. As the circles broadened and expanded, more and more places became safe spaces.

The work is not done, for homophobia and transphobia still exist.

On February 1, 2003, at a meeting held in Toronto, PFLAG Canada was formally created as an organization that would provide a national voice and act as a clearinghouse for information, peer counseling and public education. The name "Parents, Families, and Friends of Lesbians and Gays" was dropped, so that PFLAG Canada was no longer an acronym but simply a name in itself.

Now PFLAG Canada has more than 70 Chapters and Contacts across Canada, with representation in nine Canadian provinces. Throughout this period of growth, PFLAG Canada has not lost its connection to its roots. It was born of a need by parents to help themselves and family members deal with, understand, and accept their non-heterosexual children and the new world they are thrust into when their children "come out." Today, PFLAG Canada is the only national grassroots organization that deals with sexual orientation and gender identity issues from a **family perspective**, providing support, education, and resources. We rely on our network of compassionate volunteers across Canada to open their hearts and homes, give freely of their time and be there to listen to people in their time of crisis.

MIRIAM CHING YOON LOUIE is kimchee/chowfan member Oakland village band. Loving timbre of each instrument. Leaflet or poem. Hourglass drum or novel chapter.

To you, young artist

this is vein
that knife will kiss to ink
songs zinging thru your heart
oxygen red charcoal blue I dare you
to eat fear get vulnerable so your blood
can howl moon free

this is pus
bubbling stinky yellow sore itchy bitching
tumor squashing organs scar knit trauma tight
then swallowed my peeps carry ours
heart liver backhumps for feed revenge
suicide pepper shrimp sauce spiced
you know how you like your wounds
seasoned just chillax—scars be paper
upon which you will scribble your story

this is hair
guillotine straight does yours
froth July rent party twisty midnight
salt strands binding you me peasant
slave stubborn mustard seeds
who love & hurt ones we love
from braids swaddled holocaust
museum glass cases let us make
brushes to paint our stories

this is song
our fate to sing if ancestors don't kick
our ass for pissing away their gifts
if work work play play to hone blood
letting skills if keep drenching selves
bucket for drown self-bullshit-pity
if let our stories mix blood whether
your peeps like to season yours with
saffron or rum, finish what you start
young artist, let your blood
sing let your hair
lasso planets

WALKER BANERD was one of the first students to graduate with a high school diploma from the (in)famous Vancouver alternative public school Windsor House. He recently graduated from the Professional Communication program at Royal Roads University. Walker is also a musician, a swing dance instructor, and a proponent of the Oxford comma.

When we are young, we approach family the way we approach most things: passively. Family, like school, like our day-to-day lives, like the entire world we are born into, is something that happens to us. Most people don't start consciously shaping their own definition of family until adulthood. Why not do this when we are young, in the time of our lives where family exercises the greatest influence over us?

Growing up, I was lucky on two counts. I had a biological family that never let me down, and an extended community that could have picked up their slack if they had. I had teachers who were at times like aunts and uncles, a vice-principal who resembled a fifth grandparent, and family friends whom I still consider kin. So when I say that young people should shape their own families, I mean that they should have some agency in the process that I happily chanced upon. If your biologicals don't have your back, replace them. It won't take away their ability to bring you down, and you still have to live with them, but the distinction of family in your mind is something that they must earn. Be aware of the people in your life that support you, and perhaps more importantly, call you on your b.s. Maybe these people are related to you, and maybe they aren't, but they are true family.

The great thing about acknowledging your closest friends as family is that these friendships become so much richer. Familial relationships have an unequaled depth, because you can always be honest with family; they won't stop being family because they disagree with you. If you have friends that you treat like family, you won't hold anything back. You will be exposed to opinions and philosophies that are different from your own and you will be a richer person for it. Unlike friends, you don't even have to like them. But I guarantee that as the years go by, you won't be able to help but love them.

IVAN COYOTE was born and raised in Whitehorse, Yukon Territory. An award-winning author of six collections of short stories, one novel, three CDs, four short films and a renowned performer, Ivan's first love is live story-telling, and over the last thirteen years she has become an audience favourite at music, poetry, spoken word, and writers festivals from Anchorage to Amsterdam.

We pick up the rings next week. We drop off the cheque for the florist tomorrow. My custom suit is hanging in my closet, and her dress is nearly finished. It is really happening. We are getting married.

I have learned a lot about what other people think about marriage over the last few months. Next to birth and death, I think it is one of the most ritualized things we do as humans, and people have strong feelings about it. They have ideas. I quickly learned that whenever one of my friends confessed that they were surprised I was getting married, it was because they thought my marriage would mirror what their idea of marriage looks like. Which it often does not. My sweetheart and I have worked really hard to build the kind of relationship that we could live happily in, and this rarely involved tracing the blueprints of others.

This does not mean I am not open to hearing advice about the topic. In fact, last week I called around the family, as I do, and asked them for any words of marriage wisdom. My grandmother is 92, and she had a miserable marriage, followed by a passionate love affair, so I was interested in what she had to say, having lived through the extremes.

She told me to "foster the ability to really talk to each other. You don't want to know all of his secrets, but honour the ones that he does tell you. And respect each other. Respect is almost a bigger word for love."

Respect turned out to factor big in my family. My Uncle Rob told me to "make sure to marry your best friend. Respect her. You can love all kinds of stuff: you can love ice cream, you can love your new shoes. Love is the most misused word in the world. When you respect something, you take care of it. Respect her, and take care of her. Be her best friend. And remember, everybody fucks up. Especially you. You come from a bloodline that is prone to selfishness and narcissism, so keep that in mind. Everybody fucks up, but it is probably mostly going to be you."

My cousin Dan and his wife, Sarah, have been married for 13 years. I was interested in their opinions, being from the same generation, with a similar radical lefty feministy artistic bent. Their words echoed those of the previous generations, almost exactly. Communication, always talking about problems before they really become an issue.

"Love is the most misused word in the world."

"Actively pursuing interests together," Dan says. "Show an interest in her interests. If I hadn't started learning about roller derby, we'd be fucked right now. I get her to chase me on my bike on her skates. It's a good time for everyone. Even bystanders."

When pressed, not a single member of my family thought that queer marriage would need a different set of values than their straight ones. "A relationship is a relationship is a relationship," my grandmother informed me. "Whether you've got a piece of paper from the government or not. It is your marriage. You get to make the rules."

I found it interesting that none of my family even brought up things like cohabitation, or enforced monogamy, or rigid gender roles, or "settling down," which were all assumptions made by the predominantly queer friends who expressed their shock over our upcoming wedding.

I do lament that I don't have three generations of queer married couples on hand to look to for marriage advice, as it hasn't been legal for long enough to afford us that. Maybe 30 years from now we'll have a lot more to say to each other about queer marriage than "I never thought it would happen to you."

Image by aly de la Cruz

STAY **SOLID**

JULIE FLETT is a Vancouver-based artist, illustrator, and the author of two children's books. Julie works in collage and mixed media, incorporating elements that are drawn, painted, cut, glued, and stitched, using both traditional and digital mediums. Born in Toronto, Julie has spent much of the last two decades in Western Canada. She worked as a coordinator for a visual communication employment program for First Nations and was involved with a range of advocacy and support work in Vancouver's Downtown East Side. She has received numerous awards for her illustrations and books.

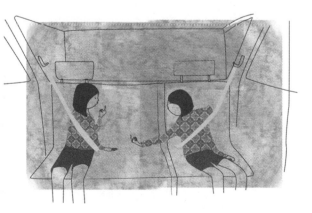

ZORA MONIZ is a senior at Berkeley High School in Berkeley, California, and attends the Arts and Humanities Academy within the larger school. She plays soccer, paints, and creates, writes, and spends time with the community around her for inspiration.

A Letter to Adults

I have some advice for you. I think that what teenagers need the most help with, and certainly me as well, is transitioning into a seriously messed up world. But maybe you shouldn't listen to me, I am just a teenager, I am no great writer, I am not the best in my class, and I have done some scary, stupid, fucked up, but also insanely amazing and inspiring things in my short life. I don't think that people should try and change that, because it is a part of growing up. And I honestly don't really know what I'm doing, but at the same time I do. I am on the fast track to college, where I am supposed to be, and some people believe I started too late, but I also believe I started too early. We are in the most rapidly developing and changing time periods in our lives, from childhood to awkward preteen puberty and serious teenager-hood, and it lasts about twenty years and then we're fucking old. But it's not like we even use those twenty years doing what we want, we follow blindly in the steps of the older generation that we try to emulate until we actually know what we're doing, and if we rebel we are failures in society's eyes. The exploration and curiosity of a developing child is smothered by a sense of guilt and fear when kids begin to understand more things about the society and world we live in. The unwavering bliss and serenity of being carefree ends before a kid reaches the double digits, and I barely remember them.

I want so badly to not be affected by all the pain and complicated elements of this world that I don't understand, I want to return to the sheer joy and tranquility of a 7-year-old's mind. I have begun to realize that the bliss of youth is not totally lost upon us, and it is here that I state my advice to adults. I believe that the ability to rationalize, argue, debate, create, imagine, and mull over controversial things is the power of growing up. But it is finding ways to be able to cope with the chaos through creative energy that return us to the wonder years. The way one returns to sheer bliss is finding the things you truly love. And yes, I do love watching shitty television and movies and being behind the effervescent throb and glow of technology, and I do love bonding cheaply with not-so-close friends on the weekends, but these things just really don't fucking matter in the end.

I find myself in the best mood when playing soccer or sprinting, I am in touch with my breath, my mind, on my feet, pushing myself, I am thinking about absolutely nothing. No teenager bullshit, just letting the instinct take over my actions, as if the way I dribble and pass is nature to me. The best times are when I'm painting and working on art projects, I think about what I want to do but in the end the art takes over, and I just do. I am completely focused on color, texture, and shape, everything kind of snaps into place, and when I take a break, it's as if I woke from a dream.

I am emphasizing the importance of alone time, or sports, or art, or cooking, or writing, or music, whatever it may be, whatever makes you tick, seriously, it makes you tick. So, to my fellow teenagers and my future self, don't forget about the things that return you to a primal and almost subconscious state of mind, do the things you love, because it makes the bitter stuff so much sweeter, and the world slightly more inviting and bearable, I guess that here I am giving my advice to adults and forty-year-olds in general, please don't forget the things you love to do, because that is what creates a life worth living.

TOMAS MONIZ publishes *Rad Dad*, a zine on radical parenting as well as the book *Rad Dad: Dispatches from the Frontiers of Fatherhood*. He also slings a bunch of fiction zines. Look out for his forthcoming book *Without Words & Without Kneeling* as well as a book of poems called *Brazen Like Armpits*. He has three kids, a bunch of chickens, two beehives, and other animals in Berkeley, California.

A Letter to Teenagers

You are totally fucking right.

About so many things you are right.

Most of the shit you have to learn in school is pointless. Anything you really need to know, you can learn when you need it.

Friends are more important than that part-time job, that homework assignment, that family potluck. So be there for them.

Money is too important, and it is wrong for anyone to be hungry or homeless. And it should be uncomfortable if you live in excess while others live day to day. No, it's not your fault, but you're right that it's not fair nor is it just, and you have every right to call your parents out on anything they say that implies otherwise.

And it is so fucking terrifying when, at times, you see the same assumptions about people in your friends and, even worse, in yourself. If you feel something's wrong, something's crossing a line, something's sexist or racist or just fucked up somehow, trust yourself; it probably is.

And your instincts are correct because there is something out there that is against you. There is something trying to hold you down, keep you back, trip you up. Because a young person like you is dangerous to the way society functions. Sometimes it is the cops or teachers or parents or TV sitcoms and all that commercialized desire, but those are just the messengers. It is something much bigger and darker. Some serious Death Star shit.

You are right to want none of it (ok, sometimes you want some of it), but you are right to want to find your own damn path, to believe in yourself despite everything coming your way.

You are totally on point to love hip-hop and punk rock at the same time, to love school at times, and at other times, want to spend three days at the beach because the waves are perfect, you're right to wonder why daily life can't reflect our desires, can't be what we want it to be. You have every right to aspire to be a doctor, a professional surfer, a philosopher, a stoner, a revolutionary, and a poet. And, yes, being all those things at the same damn time is, in fact, possible, is the life you want to lead.

As a 40-year-old man, I realize I really have nothing to offer you, but thinking about you, trying to create a life worth living, you have so much to teach me.

Thank you.

DAVID MADULI is a lifelong writer, veteran public school teacher, active working deejay, and recent father. A San Francisco native based in Oakland, he is the winner of the 2011 Joy Harjo Poetry Prize. His work has also appeared in *Cutthroat, Tayo*, and the anthology *Walang Hiya: Literature Taking Risks toward Liberatory Practice*. He is a proud alum of the VONA and Las Dos Brujas writing communities.

Dear Daughter,

You are almost one year old. If not for poetry, I would not have been here to greet your arrival. It is poetry that grows me to be the person who can be your father.

Poetry learnt me the history and struggle of my family, so I can share with you who your people really are: where we come from, where we've been, who we've been, what our parents and grandparents and ancestors said and want to say. The landscapes of those places we are from: the lands themselves and the spirits that traverse them. The questions we've asked. The more questions they've led to. So you can then find these people, spirits, places and questions for yourself and ask your own.

As a study of myself and a study of the world, poetry teaches me to see magic in the everyday and all around me. Poetry also shows me the magic in me. It is this opening and deepening that permits me to record and share that magic. If not for this I would miss the magic of your coming and the magic that you are and become daily.

The poems themselves are magic. They provide a way to remember and record, but they also are a way to re-imagine: what could have been, what I wish had happened, what I would say that I did not have the words for then. The poems are a mirror to show me the worst I have been, the worst I have the capability to be, the fallout from my mistakes, the chasms in my ability to communicate. By inspecting these parts of myself I begin to see what I need to do to be a better friend, brother, son, husband, father, human.

Poetry has been my path to immerse myself in the all. Through poetry I have felt and will continue to strive to feel how all things are connected, how all creative forms are the same pursuit, how all immersion is into that river of time and continuum of life and death. Through poetry I have listened to and embodied the voices of the past, present and future and witnessed how they all speak to each other. Poetry has generously gifted me brothers and sisters and comrades to share this conversation with.

If I can even teach you one thing it would be this: to find and embrace for yourself the star that will orient your path like poetry has mine. Cultivate that journey and honor it. And as Kahlil Gibran wrote (to bite your ninong's words at your blessing),

Say not, "I have found the truth," but rather, "I have found a truth."
Say not, "I have found the path of the soul."
Say rather, "I have met the soul walking upon my path."
For the soul walks upon all paths.
The soul walks not upon a line, neither does it grow like a reed.
The soul unfolds itself like a lotus of countless petals.

Love, Your Poet Father

2. SCHOOL, EDUCATION, & LEARNING

Aside from family, school is the institution that dominates most kids' lives. It is where most everybody under the age of 18 is compelled to go almost every day, all day, for 12 years or more. School is where we meet most of our friends, get many of our ideas about the world, figure out what kind of person we are, get told what we're good and not good at. It's amazing how much of our lives school constructs, even if you don't go: ways of being that get drilled into our heads every day of our childhood are patterns that can stay with you for life. So it is really critical to find ways to think clearly and honestly about school and our relationships with and to it.

For most of us, school is somewhere between miserable and just something we put up with. Aside from a lucky few, school is something to be endured. Often times school appears to be so all-consuming and so inevitable that it becomes hard to imagine any other reality.

But it doesn't have to be like that! There are lots of other ways to think about this: don't resign yourself to twelve years of killing time, being bored, frustrated, scared, unfulfilled, or depressed. There are plenty of kids doing things differently and you can too, no matter how old you are or where you are living!

Schools are built to standardize everything: kids, knowledge, experience, behaviour, learning styles, culture. But you don't have to accept school logic and one way or another you can resist and build the life you want. Maybe you can drop out or unschool. Maybe there's just no way you can leave school but want to figure out how to make it interesting, useful, and fun. Maybe you can switch schools. Maybe you can start something else….

It's easy to say that school sucks. And very often that's true. But it is a lot harder to say *OK, so what? What then?* And lots of us get dealt shitty school hands—we get stuck in schools that we would prefer to leave, we can't see other options, maybe there just aren't other options, maybe we're too cautious to step out. But moping about it isn't going to change anything.

"Ask for work. If they don't give you work, ask for bread. If they do not give you work or bread, then take bread."

—Emma Goldman

This chapter is a start to answering the question, "*So what?*" There are a totally amazing number of people doing cool stuff out there: so many awesome unschoolers, alternative schools, good people doing crazy stuff in existing schools. This is just the very tip of the iceberg but with any luck it will get you thinking, reading, researching, and talking about how things could be better for you and the rest of us too.

OTHER STUFF TO CHECK OUT:

- **DECOLONIZING METHODOLOGIES**, Linda Tuhiwai Smith

- **SCHOOLING THE WORLD** (film)

- **THE PARROT'S TRAINING**, Rabindranath Tagore

- **EDUCATION REVOLUTION** (organization)

- **BETTER THAN COLLEGE**, Blake Boles

- **DECOLONIZING PHILOSOPHIES OF EDUCATION**, Ali A. Abdi (Ed.)

- **"HOW I QUIT SCHOOL"** (zine)

- **THE WAR ON KIDS** (film)

- **DANCE THE EAGLE TO SLEEP**, Marge Piercy

RENÉ ANTROP-GONZÁLEZ is a teacher at the University of Wisconsin-Milwaukee. He enjoys learning from youth their visions for equitable education. He has been working with and documenting the history and life experiences of students and teachers at the Dr. Pedro Albizu Campos Alternative High School (PACHS) in Chicago since 1999. In 2001, PACHS students named René their student of the year.

When I was 15 years old, I can vividly remember what school was like for me. School was a place that never spoke or listened to me. I only felt the pain of being told about the "glorious accomplishments" and ways of knowing of White males who believed that god had told them that it was their divinely inspired duty to colonize peoples around the world. I was also taught that this colonization was absolutely necessary, because Brown and Black and indigenous peoples were heathen savages who needed to be "saved" from their evil tendencies. School was a place for me to feel ashamed of my language and culture as a Puerto Rican. Therefore, I really only learned from school that I was not worthy of being made to feel fully human and capable of being respected for who I am, for what I thought, or for the language and culture I brought to the learning spaces. This pain of dehumanization would continue throughout my life, as I continued to tolerate schools that only sought to domesticate me.

However, a significant event happened in my life that would forever change the way I thought about the radical possibilities that could take place in places we call schools. I found myself taking courses at Pennsylvania State University for my doctoral degree in 1998. While I was taking these classes, I had teachers who steered me towards the teachings of Gloria Anzaldúa, Paulo Freire, Henry Giroux, bell hooks, Frantz Fanon, Karl Marx, Albert Memmi, and José Solís Jordán, among other radical writers and cultural workers who often spoke of the devastating effects of colonial schooling on the psyche of oppressed peoples. It was Ana Yolanda Ramos-Zayas's work, in particular, that forever changed my life. I came across an article she wrote about the Puerto Rican nationalist community of Chicago called Paseo Boricua. In her article, Ramos-Zayas powerfully described how this community and its community-based organizations facilitated arming its residents with the necessary tools to name their social conditions and transform them. I became really excited when I read this article, because I could see that Paulo Freire's notion of *critical pedagogy* was being put to work in this community. It was also in Ramos-Zayas's article that I learned about a small, but special school called the Dr. Pedro Albizu Campos Alternative High School (PACHS).

I became really excited and interested to learn more about how the PACHS was arming its students with the intellectual tools to make sense of their worlds and transform them, so I contacted Marvin García, who was the director of this school. After some thought, Marvin and other members of the community invited me to Chicago to visit PACHS and learn more about the work they do with high school students of color. As a result, I learned a lot from the students and teachers who learn and work there. I learned that students call the PACHS their sanctuary. Wow! I had never thought of my schools as being sanctuaries, because I never felt psychologically safe in them. I also learned that students and teachers respected each other's cultures and languages and affirmed them in the classes they took together. Additionally, I was able to witness how the language of social critique was woven through all the classes. This language was then used to engage in community projects that worked to improve the lives of community residents and raise radical political consciousness in the spirit of decolonizing transformation.

What I now know is that many youth today go to traditional schools and feel bored, and think that their schools do not address or even mention the relevant challenges that affect our lives. Even though I know that these oppressive schools of great pain still exist, I also now know that there are some radical school sanctuaries like the PACHS that work to decolonize their communities and make education a fully human and liberating experience. Finally, I know that some adults do not think that youth of color are capable of working to transform their communities. I also know that these adults are wrong. I learned much from the work of this amazing school. If I had only known that this school existed when I was 15 years old....

"You never change things by fighting the existing reality. To change something, build a new model that makes the existing model obsolete."

—Richard Buckminster Fuller

DANIEL GREGO is the Executive Director of TransCenter for Youth, Inc. in Milwaukee. He lives with his wife, Debra Loewen, the Artistic Director of Wild Space Dance Company, on a small farm in the Rock River watershed in Dodge County, Wisconsin.

A Primer for Dropouts

Elementary and secondary schooling in the United States is not a *voluntary* institution like a library or a public park, which people can use if and when they want. Schooling is a *coercive* institution. Young people are compelled by law to attend. Dropouts are outlaws. Even so, according to the America's Promise Alliance, every 26 seconds, a teen drops out...a total of 1.2 million a year. That is a lot of outlaws. If you are dissatisfied with school and are considering dropping out, I would suggest the following:

★ Check out any "alternative schools" in your area where you can work with supportive adults in small, personalized learning environments. Make sure they are alternatives to the System, not alternatives for the System to use as dumping grounds. Everyone who attends should be there by choice.

★ Create multiple opportunities to build strong relationships with a variety of adults, not just those who are paid to work with you. The walls of these learning environments, if they have walls, should be permeable membranes, allowing elders from the community to mentor you and help you make sense of things.

★ Tell yourself a different story about yourself. The System often tells dropouts they are "failures," "chronic disruptors," "slackers," etc. Too often, young people accept the System's story about themselves. Don't. Rebel against it.

★ Before dropping out, young people will often adopt behaviors to protect themselves. In being wise guys, trouble-makers, and rebels, you learn how to survive in a System designed to sort people, often in humiliating ways, into prepackaged roles for the dominant culture. In small, personalized learning environments, the defensive behaviors are no longer necessary.

★ Discover your special excellence. Each one of us has unique gifts and talents. Pursue your own interests. Whenever possible, try to discover your vocation. Find your way to a life worth living and work worth doing.

★ Contribute your time and energy to making your community a better place and look forward to gratitude for your contributions. No one likes to do thankless work. Demand "credit" for your work and eventually credentials if you decide you need them.

★ Don't allow yourself or the adults with whom you work to become cartoon characters called "students" and "teachers." Be real. There are enough phonies around. And keep your sense of humor. You'll need it.

ANTHONY MEZA-WILSON is an unschooled teacher, radical educator, and conflicted student. He has organized in free skools and free schools all across this land. When left to his own devices beyond the purview of industrial capitalism he has a tendency to pet cats and eat wild berries.

One of my favorite unschooling texts is "School is Hell" by Matt Groening, creator of *The Simpsons*. He tears apart the school system level by level with some awesome satire ending with *Lesson 19: Grad School—Some People Never Learn*. It's true, some of us don't. Even after one third of a lifetime spent criticizing school, dropping out, and dreaming up alternatives, I still found myself in grad school studying Educational Studies (of course).

I don't mean to be too cynical about the experience. I have learned a ton having had a couple of years to think about, talk about, and read about ideas that are really important to me. Most of my work has revolved around radical educational projects of some sort, and as I've explained what I do to friends and family (and tons of educational colleagues as well) I've learned that there are some ideas that I take for granted now that most people ask for clarity on, mostly definitions of broad swaths of the radical education world. So here's a quick and dirty outline of the world of radical education.

UNSCHOOLING & DESCHOOLING

Unschooling, aka "learning" is the idea that you can and do learn outside of school in the "real world." Unschooling is most often used to refer to a form of homeschooling where students learn without a prescribed curriculum, instead guiding their own education by living everyday life. Deschooling, to contrast quickly, is the act of becoming unschooled once one has been schooled. Folks go through this process when they leave a schooled environment. It's like rewilding your mind.

To learn more: *The Teenage Liberation Handbook* by Grace Llewelyn; *Everywhere All the Time: A Deschooling Reader* by Matt Hern; most texts by John Holt.

FREE SCHOOLS VS. FREE SKOOLS

Free Schools "with a c-h" also known as brick and mortar free schools are places that kids go, mostly meant to replace traditional education. Many free schools came out of the 1960s counterculture as places for children to guide their own education and frequently draw from A.S. Neill's Summerhill as a founding inspiration. Free Skools "with a k" refer to all-ages community education, often run in anarchist activist circles. These skools operate with no credentials, no diplomas, and no official relationship to the state. Basically people get together and teach each other stuff.

To learn more: *Free to Learn: A Radical Experiment in Education* (documentary); *I Want To Do This All Day* (audio documentary); *Free Schools* by Jonathan Kozol; *Making It Up As We Go Along* by Chris Mercogliano.

CRITICAL **PEDAGOGY** & POPULAR EDUCATION

Critical pedagogy is a needlessly jargon-filled way to describe people who study why school sucks. Particularly people who think schools are too focused on teaching kids to be capitalists and patriots. Most folks who write in the tradition of critical pedagogy are coming from some sort of Marxist background. Popular education just means "education by and for the people" and usually refers to a series of ways that people teach by facilitating groups who work together to solve problems within their communities.

To learn more: *The Long Haul* by Myles Horton; *Games For Actors and Non-Actors* by Augusto Boal; *Pedagogy of the Oppressed* by Paulo Freire.* (*This book is famous and I disagree with it, big time! But that's a longer conversation.)

MATHEW DAVIS is a self-determined young man from Indianapolis, Indiana. He is a dedicated member of his community, an artist, farmer, speaker, and whatever else he needs to be to ensure that people in his community continue to survive. (Ed. Note: check Mathew performing this online, totally worth it!

My junior year of high school I wrote a poem called "75108." It was about the madness of my public school experience. It was a way for me to constructively push back against an institution inherently rigged to see me fail. I first wrote it for a youth summit about social justice in education that I helped plan. We brought in speakers from social justice organizations around Indianapolis and a few from out of state. I was the mc for some of the summit. I had just started writing poetry and I was asked to write something for the summit. I had been working on the poem beforehand, and when the opportunity presented itself I finished it and everybody loved the poem. The crowd erupted after I finished. That was the first time I received attention like that from something that was positive and that was real. I have a lot more stories of when I performed the poem and the reactions I have received. Once I even got banned from a school for performing! But I think the point I am trying to make is that there are more proactive ways to critique the system and still be true to yourself and what you aspire to be.

75108

75108 that's my student id number and at times that seems that all they know me by is those five numbers and nothing else

The Indianapolis public school system is like a pipeline to prison

Inmate 75108 I wish they knew me the real me what they don't see is the artist the poet the activist the friend the brother the cousin or in some cases that I am even human

Because see in their eyes kids should be seen and heard and these very social complexities are so complex that they wish not to cope so at the end of their rope with no hope

They throw us in polos and khakis that stifle creativity I act out and protested label delinquent not allowed to express

But don't get me wrong I guess uniforms can form oneness but not when dresscode and school success are used in the same breath cuz that means you don't believe in me but rather your own hype your own greed and not unity

Instead of clothing me in button ups and dickies take my knowledge to higher degrees where I am social and globally aware an inquisitive critical thinker

Show me democracy

Instead of demigods who yell

"OK LET'S GO GET OUT OF MY HALLWAYS"

That's what they say, every day in our hallways

In our passing periods

In our classes in our school

Us as the youth have to navigate the ignorance that adults create but don't have to account for especially if you're black or latino

They make us integrate assimilate then they dominate

The public school system was designed for white males and not for me

Generation after generation of intelligent black males diagnosed stupid with adhd

While white folks just say it's a part of the negroes mentality

So if 75108 graduates I would call that revolutionary

The flawed methodology on hip hop music and philosophy a huge scapegoat for stagnant pedagogy

In this case it doesn't matter your race because nowadays ignorant and oppress don't discriminate

It's a game chess mindful tactical strategic

But they found a way to make us pawns in their master plan and it's not by accident

It's by design

So if all of this truly is a game then watch that pawn make a checkmate and next time my teacher sends me out for failure to comply I hope they see Mathew Davis instead 75108

JAY GILLEN is the Baltimore City Schools Facilitator for the Algebra Project. Jay supports young people in developing an "earned insurgency," using mathematics as an organizing tool in the spirit of Ella Baker and Robert Moses.

Since 2003, the Baltimore Algebra Project has been the leading youth organizer in Baltimore, spearheading campaigns around school funding, youth employment, transportation, food, and ending the school-to-prison pipeline. Over the past eight years, this youth-directed organization has succeeded in paying $2 million in wages directly to high school students and recent high school graduates by securing contracts and grants to conduct math study groups and tutoring. This economic foundation has been used as an organizing base for aggressive campaigns that use the full range of tactics from school-based and community organizing to coalition building, testimony to official bodies, litigation, and direct action. The mission of the Baltimore Algebra Project is to improve the socioeconomic status of youth in poverty by peer-to-peer teaching and organizing, using mathematics education as an organizing tool.

Five Suggestions for Young Activists

1

Be generous towards each other. "We will have to be more generous towards each other than we have ever been before," says Vincent Harding. All young activists find themselves in conflict with authorities. That's fine.

What is not so fine is activists in conflict with each other.

It is good to disagree when you disagree. It is also good to listen, and to try to find each other's strong points, not only weak points, and to do what the other person thinks is best sometimes. This brings power to everyone.

2

Try not to let one person or one small group make all the decisions, or take all the public roles.

People learn by doing, so if you want everyone to learn to lead, let everyone go in front sometimes; but make sure you help them, so they enjoy being in front and will want to do it again!

3

Take time to shape your demands very carefully and make them simple and bold.

In shaping your demands, ask yourself: "If our demand is met, will our power increase?"

Example of a **bad** demand: "No more school uniforms." This demand isn't so good, because the uniforms could be eliminated, but the school might still be stifling and controlling.

Example of a **better** demand: "No more school uniforms, and students must approve all new school policies by majority vote." This lets young people imagine themselves as decision-makers; even if you don't win, picturing yourselves as powerful actually increases your power.

4

Solve problems and keep moving forward. There are a lot of roadblocks, but there are also a lot of ways around them.

When you hit a roadblock, don't wait. Figure out an alternative and keep moving. Maybe the alternative is just gathering people to talk about the roadblock. Maybe the alternative is choosing a different route. Maybe the alternative is making a media show out of the roadblock to embarrass the people getting in your way. Maybe the alternative is finding someone who can help.

Waiting is usually bad. Doing something is usually good.

5

Be yourselves.

Adults often tell young activists to be sweeter and more moderate.

At first, most adults don't understand that young people have their own role, different from adults.

This does not mean they are your enemies, so don't hate. It only means they can do what they want to do, and you can do what you want to do.

Often, they will end up following you, even though at first they told you you were wrong.

CARLA BERGMAN is a community artist and organizer, the co-director of the Purple Thistle Centre, and maker of zines. She lives with her partner and two unschooling kids in East Vancouver, unceded Coast Salish Territories.

MIKE JO collaborates on projects at the Purple Thistle revolving around publishing.

This piece is for those of you out there who are thinking about or have decided to leave school; you're convinced school sucks and that it's not for you, that there's got to be a better way to learn things you care to learn and a much better way to be part of a community. You're right. There are many better ways and engaging in learning where you are not being spoken down to or having to fit into some prefab box that's been designed for all kids is pretty awesome in almost every way! But how do you do this if you've been schooled all of your life? This (challenging) process is known as deschooling.

Deschooling can be tremendously hard and much of the time it can make you feel insecure and very unsure if you've done the right thing by leaving school. If you are like most people you've been fed the line all your life that school is the only way to a better (or awesome) life, and without a good education you are doomed to live a pretty dismal failed life of immense suffering and poverty (if you are a kid from a more affluent home then you've probably been told you won't be as successful or famous).

But hold up, what if you could just learn what you want, when you want; you know that thing you do when time passes so quickly and you are totally immersed and engaged (we've all been there)! But even better, lose the whole idea of separating "learning" from "doing!" For example, say you want to make a zine, you don't need to formally learn how, as in go take an expensive publishing program (to maybe find out that you don't like publishing anyhow!). All you have to do is get busy making one, find friends and mentors who you know like zines, or have made them before and skill share with them, and make it together. Then once you've made one, you're a zinester! As John Holt says:

"There are not two processes, but one. We learn to do something by doing it. There is no other way. When we first do something, we probably will not do it well. But if we keep on doing it, have good models to follow and helpful advice if and when we feel we need it, and always do it as well as we can, we will do it better. In time, we may do it very well. This process never ends."

The real barrier, however, can be resources: both people and things. Of course there are always libraries. Especially if you want to delve into theory, ideas, and so on. They're great, and do go to them! You can get out books, how-to videos, and lots more. The internet, too, has many free resources from which to learn.

CREATING A PROJECT/COUNTER-INSTITUTION:

But we are after something else here; we want to make things, learn real skills that can take us places, and connect to others. We want environments for doing and learning that are not oppressive like school. That's why it's important to have friends—new and old—mentors, and physical spaces to meet and build community. Be full citizens in our community and city. We want to move forward from learning in isolation—whether it be the drop-in-an-ocean isolation of school or the isolation of home learning—and create a collectively powered experience.

So how do you create a radical project or community space that will have yours and your friends thriving at the forefront of whatever it is you create, and that won't mimic school in any way?

Here's a short list to get you thinking:

« Think small. Both with how many people and how big the space is. It can be as little as 5 of you and can be just one room, the basement of a friend's, a garage, the back of a store, etc.... Be creative.

« Find out what you all really want to do, take your time deciding—this process will really make the project/space more solid and truly collectively run.

« Decide about funding! Are you going to apply for grants? Are you going to pool money or welfare checks and collectively pay for it? Can you fundraise every month? Or will you have a money-making aspect of the space like a bookshop or cafe (although these often rely on fundraising and community support anyhow)?

« Reach out to mentors and your community for guidance. People are awesome and love to help.

« Try to make genuine relationships that are based on real solidarity (not tokenistic gestures...that comes off fake) with those who are unlike you and your crew, and also take steps to create a safe space for those who are systematically excluded from the "benefits" of society. Be sure to pay special attention to the voices of queer folx, peeps of colour, those indigenous to your area, or anyone who is denied a voice and representation in mainstream culture. Create something different!

There are a million ways to do this, and you can try more than one. Don't worry if it doesn't last that long, or if it fails, the gauge of a project is not necessarily its length.

Be open, build it based on what folks are wanting, but more than anything have fun! dontgiveupdropout.blogspot.com/

3. COMMUNITY

Not so long ago very few people could survive without the support of their neighbours. You didn't have to be friends with people who lived nearby, but you needed them. Now it is easily possible to live without knowing, let alone being in a relationship with anyone who lives near you. In fact many, perhaps most people do just that: insulate themselves from their neighbours and local community, finding friends and colleagues in other parts of the city, in other towns, and/or online.

The ability to meet, work, and play with people all over the place—all over the world even—is awesome and one of the highlights of modern society and communications. But it should be a complement to, not a replacement for community and neighbourhood. Community has to be a physical, geographical place—a place that includes all the human and non-human inhabitants on a chunk of land. That idea is critical, not just to ecological thinking, but to the idea of a human-scaled, living politics.

It is super-important to find a place to be, to find a neighbourhood to be part of, but there's no hurry, take your time: it might be where you grew up, it might be a place you have to hunt for. Once you find a community that compels you, then figure out how to lay down some roots, get to know your neighbours, and build something in place. You do not have to stay forever, but wherever you are, be part of the local commonwealth: contribute to public space, public life, commonality.

And that's the core story of this chapter: community is not a thing. It's not something you can acquire like a new pair of shoes. You can find and move into a great neighbourhood, but for it to be yours, for the meaning of community to emerge, it has to be a participatory thing. Community cannot be reduced to a consumer item: it is necessarily an activist event. You've got to get out there.

Necessarily then, community means figuring out how to share space with people who are not like you: people who don't think, talk, or look like you do, or believe the same things. That's the essence of a good neighbourhood: appreciating difference and finding ways to live together. It is critical to build solidarity within groups of people, especially those who are typically marginalized, but the goal of community has to be real participation in the commonwealth, in the neighbourhood, for everyone. A community has to take care of all its members, especially young people, and has to develop ways for people to participate: physically, culturally, socially, and politically. But that's a reciprocal thing: people have to be willing to participate, have to be active, have to be willing to be part of the public realm. So that's on you: don't wait for community to come to you, go make it happen.

OTHER STUFF TO CHECK OUT:

- **INCITE!** Women of Color Against Violence (organization)

- **GO TELL IT ON THE MOUNTAIN**, James Baldwin

- **SOLAR STORMS**, Linda Hogan

- **THEATRE OF THE OPPRESSED**, Augusto Boal

- **HIS OWN WHERE**, June Jordan

- **WHAT MATTERS?** Economics for a Renewed Commonwealth, Wendell Berry

- **THE LAST WILD WITCH,** Starhawk

- **CREATIVE INTERVENTIONS TOOLKIT:** A Practical Guide to Stop Interpersonal Violence (online)

- **FIRST AS TRAGEDY, THEN AS FARCE**, Slavoj Žižek

BENITO MILLER DEALE is privileged to build community with the Latina/o Youth Collective. Based in Indianapolis, Indiana, the Latina/o Youth Collective "provides resources and opportunities for youth to engage in personal and community development through critical pedagogy, grassroots organizing, and collective action." Check out: www.latinoyouthcollective.com for more info.

The dark of night engulfs a mass of youth, huddled around the orange and blue hues of a burning fire. Stars above and flickering flames reveal silhouettes and illuminate faces of the beings circled about. One by one, people are given a chance to share traumas from their lived experience. Painful narratives spill forth describing difficult border crossings and transitions into unfamiliar cultures. Participants detail daily brushes with ignorance, discrimination, and hatred. Tears flow as people re-live verbal, physical, and sexual abuses. Respect is offered in the way of deep listening. Often the hurt shared by others elicits a flood of memories for other participants, who connect their own stories to the figurative scar tissue of others present. When one is finished sharing, this new family crowds around to offer consolation in embraces and words of encouragement. Dawn announces the arrival of brother sun, yet this sacred "Soul Wound Healing Ceremony" only culminates when all who care to share have had the chance to do so; some four to six hours after commencing. As we share in one another's suffering, we are more fully human. Community literally emerges from the ashes.

As the Latina/o Youth Collective (LYC), we battle daily to move people from "empathy to solidarity." Our ranks are made up of youth from across the Americas from first and second-generation immigrant families. Victimized by disaster capitalism and divided by powers that fortify false borders, we have arrived at this new home for a spectrum of reasons. Our immigrant identities too often mean we become scapegoats for xenophobia and pawns in political games. Our legal statuses are in constant flux. Daily life is one of struggle.

The "Soul Wound Healing Ceremony" described above is sacred a space for healing that acknowledges our interconnectedness. Deep bonds of friendship emerge and this new affinity to one another allows us to move forward. This form of solidarity directly challenges the dominant culture of individualistic narcissism. Empathy all too often becomes silent apathy and complacency in the face of oppression. We envision a culture of *cariño* (love, caring) and we push for solidarity, where our collective and our allies commit to liberation of our minds and beings, our communities, and all earthlings. For the membership of our growing family, our strength is rooted in each other and our bonds to others across the globe battling all forms of oppression.

STAY **SOLID**

CHRIS MERCOGLIANO taught at and directed the Albany Free School for 35 years. AFS is a unique, inner-city alternative for children ages 2–14 that has become an international model for student-centered, community-based education. He is the author of four books and his essays, commentaries, and reviews have appeared in numerous newspapers, journals, and magazines, as well as in six anthologies.

Darwin and his followers sold us all a bill of goods when they claimed evolution to be a bloody competition for survival. Darwin's wasn't the only theory in his day. For instance, the research of Peter Kropotkin, who was a natural scientist before he became the anarchist philosopher we know him as today, led him to the opposite conclusion: the "fittest" species are those with the highest levels of what he called "mutual aid."

But Darwin was English, ambitious, and politically and socially well-connected, and his take became so dominant that it continues to be the accepted truth today, despite the fact that modern science has gone on to prove Kropotkin almost entirely right. The reason single-celled microorganisms evolved into multi-cellular communities in the first place is because their collective awareness of the environment and their ability to share genes and other resources was highly advantageous. As biologist Bruce Lipton reminds us, it's survival of the fittest groups, not individuals.

And so it is with humans. When we join together into communities in which we care about, support, and share with each other on many levels, we all become "fitter." It's why the 42-year-old Albany Free School, an inner-city alternative that started—and still runs—on a shoestring, is alive and well today. The early teachers and families responded to the financial scarcity and the difficulties of inner-city living by forming a community. We worked together to renovate nine abandoned buildings on the block so that the school could have a source of steady income. Then we helped each other fix up houses for ourselves, with very little cash. Then we helped raise each other's children.

We—about two dozen families in all—did many other things with and for each other. For seven years we even published a national magazine. But at the same time we took care not to isolate ourselves. We got involved in local issues like gentrification and city-wide issues like air pollution and corrupt cops; and in so doing we have infused the entire neighborhood with the spirit of community.

Maintaining a true community requires sustained effort, but the children are proof that it's all worth it. Kids who grew up in the Free School community are adults now with their feet firmly planted in the world. They are resilient and have vision, and they work to create more community wherever they go.

LIZ LICHTMAN helps run RUBARB, an all-volunteer community bike shop in New Orleans (www.rubarbike.org). She started bike clubs in a couple of schools, likes to help things grow, rides her bike everywhere, and can frequently be seen dancing in the streets!

New Orleans has a whole lot of street culture, something we can't deny. We hang out at all hours on our porches. We play music, dance, and parade on asphalt. Footballs get tossed out front of shotgun houses (a very common style of house around New Orleans). Even when someone dies, people celebrate on the streets throughout the neighborhood. Riding along by bicycle, you not only see it all, you smell it, feel it, and sometimes even taste it. You're not locked up and enclosed in a metal machine (i.e. car), but free to say hello to everyone on their porches. Free to toss a ball with the kids. Free to stop and dance as the parade passes. You are closer to those around you. You're creating community **TOGETHER.**

RUBARB (Rusted Up Beyond All Recognition Bikes) is a community bike shop in the 9th ward of New Orleans. People from the neighborhood come in to use tools freely, get advice and assistance about how to fix a bike, search through parts, make art, get a sip of water, or just say hello. The biggest stopper-on-byer is youth. Here is a positive, supportive space for them to not only hang out, but get their hands dirty, become leaders, learn bike fixing skills, be a part of something. The bike shop is a community space—all are welcome, all are encouraged to be self-reliant.

"Can you fix this for me?" are words spoken by both young and old that get quickly shut down with a "No way! I'm gonna teach you how to fix it yourself. I'll show you how to do it, we'll fix it together, but I certainly won't do it for you."

It's really about liberation. Breaking free of our usual ideas. The bike shop creates this because we believe you can do anything. You can't just do it yourself, but **you must**. And when you do, that freedom will take you places. Not like any iPhone, videogame, or internet could, but just you and your 2 wheels. Powered by **YOU.**

Smell that grill burning. Listen to the laughter on the corner. Feel the rain on your face. Fix up your bike yourself and then take it to the streets!

FLY is a Zinester, and a Squatcore Comics & PEOPs artist based in the Lower East Side NYC since the late 80s. Fly is currently working on a book called *Unreal Estate: A Late 20th Century History of Squatting in the Lower East Side* as well as new PEOPs publications & shenanigans. Her band Zero Content continues to regale the Glory of the Gutter & astound new generations of artsy crustcore. Check out: peops.org for more info.

This is page 3 of a comic I did as a fictional representation of my Squat in the Lower East Side NYC—I called the comic "Eyeball House" because we always used to have to "eyeball" when doing construction work.

This page depicts an actual incident that happened in the Spring of 1993—The 80s & 90s were the heyday of the Lower East Side Squat Culture & Activism— we were very organized as an active element within the *Loisaida* Community & there was a sense of unity amongst the Squats—if one Squat was threatened then the Eviction Watch List would go into effect—this was a phone list distributed only to Squatters & trusted Squat Supporters—when threatening shit was going down there would be a phone tree & all the numbers would be called & at the time it was extremely effective—within a half hour there could be a hundred or more people showing up with more on the way.

On this particular occasion the NYC HPD (Dept. of Housing Preservation & Development) had sent a crew to put up a new scaffolding because we had just dismantled the old scaffolding & the City—not wanting any bricks to fall on the general public—decided to put up a new one.

This was a precarious situation. Since we perceived a threat to our building we called the Eviction Watch List & lots of people started showing up—it really freaked out the workers that the City had sent. We had to have many discussions & make the decision to accept the new scaffolding—this was a great example of our community in action—a lot of people responded to our call & we had a sort of "street meeting" & had to make a very quick decision on how to respond. It turned out we did make the right decision—the scaffolding the City put up was not a "demolition" scaffold, so we knew they were not going to demolish our building.

So it was our decision to not force a major confrontation—we decided to allow the City to erect the scaffolding but we took all of the wiring & lighting fixtures down to use in our hallways & I spent a week painting a mural on the front of the scaffold—to claim it as our own. That is a whole other story—a bonding experience between me & the "look-outs" on our street—ai!

MICHAEL HARDT teaches in the Literature Program at Duke University. He is co-author with Antonio Negri of *Empire*, *Multitude*, and *Commonwealth*.

I have often thought of and experienced political activism as a form of love. You might say that in some ways activism is **like** love: it can often give you the same intensities and pleasures and pain and, moreover, romances are often deeply embedded in activist experiences.

But I mean something more than that. I think it is important to discover or invent a political activism that **is** love or, rather, develop a political concept of love that goes beyond the couple, the family, and all the limits in which love is normally confined. By talking about love this way I'm trying to understand the ways in which collective political experiences, which are guided equally by reason and passions, are radically transformative and generate new ways of being together, new ways of feeling, and new ways of seeing the world. That is an experience that seems to me worthy of the name love.

This notion of love and politics (or love **as** politics) raises many issues, which I have been trying to sort through in the last few years. One aspect in particular relates importantly to the question of how we grow older together as activists.

Love, especially the kind of political love we experience in our activist lives, often appears as an event, a kind of break in time that marks a before and after. Love's transformative power, its rupture with the past, and its shattering of the structures of our previous life is one aspect that distinguishes love from other similar political concepts such as friendship and solidarity. In love we lose ourselves and find ourselves anew, remade.

This is beautiful, but on its own this kind of love and this kind of political life is unsustainable. The constant overturning of our lives, the constant transformation, even the thrill is exhausting. If that were the core of our political life, then politics would only be for the young, and then only for a brief time.

Love, though, is more than that. In addition to being an event, love is also a repeated practice of community. We continually return to those we love. Love is the will to repeat eternally the encounter we just had, but different each time. Think of the sex with a familiar lover: I touch you here, then you touch me there, then we do this. If this were just repetition the magic would fail. It has to be understood as something like a ritual encounter.

So as we grow older I propose we think of our political engagements and commitments as a kind of love that is at once both event and ritual. Our collective political lives must be filled with that transformative potential whereby we can become different and see the world anew, while we also return continually to each other again in community.

YOTAM MAROM is a political organizer, educator, writer, and musician based in New York. He has been active in the Occupy Wall Street Movement, and is a member of the Organization for a Free Society. He can be reached at yotam.marom@gmail.com.

We fight because people's needs really aren't being met, because there are simple and systemic reasons for that, because it is unacceptable, and because there is an alternative. We fight because of injustice abstractly, but also for the type of injustice that makes us sick. We fight for other people, but also for ourselves—because none of us get to live out our full human potential in the institutions that dominate our lives today, because another world really is possible, and because we demand it for us and for our kids and grandkids. With all of that, we have a responsibility not only to fight, but to win.

We win when we build diverse movements led by the most oppressed people in society, movements capable of becoming a **dual power**: able to prefigure the values of a free society and lay the seeds for it, while at the same time fighting the institutions that oppress and exploit and toppling them to create space for the new world we are trying to create. We win when we raise social costs so that those hopeless few elites find themselves left with no carrots tempting enough to wave before us and no sticks big enough to do us any harm, when we grow and grow and grow with no end, when we refuse to go home until we've gotten what we came for. We win when do all of this while telling the story of the world we are creating.

We need to tell a story that shatters the myth that there is no alternative, that people don't fight back, that we can be bought off with TVs and iPhones. We need to tell a story that smashes cynicism and identifies it as nothing more than a defense mechanism to protect us from taking risks and dreaming. We need to tell a story of autonomy within solidarity, equity alongside diversity, peace bound with justice, struggle intimately linked with beauty. We must tell the story of the scarring we've gotten from this brutal world and the victories we win as we transform it.

We must tell the story ourselves, tweet and tag it, film and sing it, write it with our arrests and our bruises. We must tell our new story at work and in school, on the picket lines and during demonstrations, at our occupations and sit-ins, in the jail cells where they put us when they are truly afraid of the power we hold. We must tell it by fighting in a way that reflects the values of the world we are dreaming of, and by creating as much of that world as we can while we fight.

We must tell our story in a new language, a language of passion and purpose, vision and creativity, solidarity and direct action. And when we truly find our voice, we should use it to shout, finally and deafeningly: Of course there is an alternative. It is us.

4. MONEY, WORK, & SUCCESS

For so much of our lives the trifecta of Money, Work, and Success are used as bribe, threat, inducement, carrot, stick, and salvific promise. All three are bound up together and are now driven by a capitalist narrative: the general idea is that if you work hard and have something concrete to dream for (be famous, a doctor, dentist, teacher, whatever) then one day you'll have a lifestyle that is rich in material things and you'll be happy: get a job, work hard today for a joyful free retirement (sometime, probably much, much) later.

But why do we have to work so much? Why is it that the more technologically advanced society becomes, the harder people have to work? It is well-documented that happiness is on the decline across the wealthier parts of the world and the gap between rich and poor continues to widen dramatically. Do we really need more stuff? There are many reasons, and most can point to the basic tenets of capitalism: profit for few, bosses make more, workers make less, profit or die, and buy or die. It's apparent, and has been for a long time, that capitalism, and all the promises of the good life that come with it, is not working to bring about happiness or a better life for the majority of people. How about instead we re-imagine a society that is based on ideas of collectivity, equity, community, and mutual respect?

There is nothing wrong with working hard: in fact it is one of the most important virtues in the world. But it is important to distinguish between work and *good work*, and work and employment, and work and toil. Working hard at a project or task is an honourable way to spend time, and it's an important goal for everyone to find something(s) that they can work at with all their heart. But being stuck in a meaningless job that eats up all your hours and energy or weaseling for profit or selling crap that

> "You show me a capitalist, and I'll show you a bloodsucker."
>
> —Malcolm X

no one needs or contributing to an institution you have no love for: that's a lousy way to roll.

No matter where you live though, you'll want and need to make money sometime: it's good to be able to pay the rent and buy food (no shit!), be generous with others, be self-reliant. And it's also an important thing to be able to do a tough job you're not thrilled about for a limited time. There's nothing wrong with doing a job you loathe for a little while, as long you understand why you're making that trade-off—but don't get caught up in that. You don't need nearly as much money as people want you to believe. You don't have to buy much, and most of what you really need you can get for cheap or free.

The key here is to think hard on what "success" means. Your personal success has to be tied to the success of people around you, your community, and your dreams for a better world. Your success is no success at all if it is built on the backs of other people or is degrading the natural world. But have no fears: it is very possible to have a good life if you can learn to live cheaply, be flexible, are willing to work hard and are rigourous in thinking about what real success is. There is an endless supply of good work to be done in the world.

OTHER STUFF TO CHECK OUT:

- **THE DISPOSSESSED**, Ursula K. Le Guin
- **THE TAKE** (film)
- **DEBT**: The First 5,000 Years, David Graeber
- **PEOPLE OF COLOR ORGANIZE!** (online)
- **WOBBLIES**: A Graphic History, Paul Buhle
- **THE VALUE OF NOTHING**, Raj Patel
- **THE CORPORATION** (film)
- **NATIVE SON**, Richard Wright
- **MUTUAL AID**, Peter Kropoktin
- **NICKEL AND DIMED**, Barbara Ehrenreich
- **THE AMERICAN DREAM** (film)

GEOFF MANN works at Simon Fraser University, teaching and writing about labour, political economy, and climate change. He lives in Vancouver with Michelle, Finn, and Seamus.

When anti-capitalists talk about capitalism, it often seems to be code for greed, profit, and exploitation. But the difficulty is that while these problems certainly thrive in capitalism, they don't actually tell us what capitalism is, or how it works. It's not like capitalists invented greed or profit, and exploitation was around long before capitalism, and will probably outlast it. There is nothing especially capitalist about any of this.

If we want to understand capitalism, we need some precision. First, capitalism requires the constant creation of capital. Capital is economic value that grows, and to grow, it has to move. If you have $100 under your mattress, it's not capital. To be capital, it has to be circulating in the economy: invested in stocks, hiring a worker, or buying equipment to produce things. If the money isn't busy, it's not capital; if some ancient king had a room full of gold and jewels, it wasn't capital. When a lot of the value in the system stops moving at once, like in a financial crisis, then in capitalism, you have a problem.

Second, in capitalism most commodities—goods or services produced for sale—are produced by private enterprise; not by the state (as in socialism), and not by households (like peasant communities). These enterprises own the money, technology, and land to produce the commodities, and they hire workers to produce them, and pay them wages for their time. The commodities themselves get distributed by market exchange, not according to need, or best use, or some other criteria.

Third, in capitalism the money that enables all this exchange is mostly produced not by the government, but by banks. Sure, states decide what counts as money, but the money itself is mostly produced by banks, who the state has given permission to lend to people and businesses. In capitalism, when a bank makes a loan, it is not like it has that money in some vault waiting to be lent. When it makes the loan, it *creates* the money that makes it possible for capital to keep growing. This is why in capitalism, banks and the state are inseparable. They can't function without each other.

Finally, because capitalism operates systematically—in other words, it is made up of "parts" that interact according to certain "rules," like property laws, or "reducing costs"—it must allocate people and places to specific structural positions. Among other things, this means that there must be bosses, and there must be workers. In capitalism, we cannot all be bosses, nor can we all be workers. It only works if everyone plays their part. Since, in general, it is more enjoyable to be a boss, one of the most effective ways that capitalism makes sure there are workers is by making it very difficult to get by if you refuse to work for a boss. If markets are the way things get distributed, and you need money to participate in the market, and you have to work to obtain money, then for many people it seems like there are not many options but to shut up and play your part.

Maybe the most important thing to remember about capitalism is that it is one way of arranging our lives—there are others. Although sometimes people talk about capitalism expanding across the globe as if it were natural or inevitable, like we are all just waiting for a chance to unleash our inner capitalist, that's not true.

Capitalism had a beginning, and it will surely have an end, just like every other way of organizing economic life that came before it. We will determine what comes next.

ANITA OLSON wishes she could be a full-time artist and thinker of important thoughts but her full-time student status often gets in the way. She is also a parent, pacifist, psychology pupil, and pirogi lover.

SETH TOBOCMAN is a radical comic book artist and author from the Lower East Side of Manhattan. His books include *War in the Neighborhood*, *Disaster and Resistance*, and *Understanding the Crash*, as well as the graphic magazine World War 3 Illustrated. This is excerpted from *You Don't Have to Fuck People Over to Survive* (AK Press). For more info: www.sethtobocman.com.

HARI ALLURI immigrated to South Vancouver, Coast Salish Territories with his family at the age of 12. His experiences led him to community organizing (No One Is Illegal & more); mentorship led him to facilitation (Asian Arts Freedom School & more); all the above and more led him to writing (thank you VONA). A poet first (*Press Release*, *580 Split*), Hari is also a lyricist (Los migrantes), and filmmaker (*Pasalubong*).

GABRIEL TEODROS is an emcee, teaching artist, and community organizer. He has toured extensively through the United States, Canada, Mexico, and Ethiopia, and has released 3 full-length solo albums to date, as well as group projects with Abyssinian Creole and Air 2 A Bird. Teodros was also a founding member of Hidmo: a community center, cleverly disguised as an Eritrean restaurant in Seattle's Central District. As a teaching artist, Teodros worked with Youth Speaks Seattle and WAPI Community Services, where he developed curriculum and taught regular classes in Language Arts, songwriting, performance, hip hop history, studio recording, and mixing. All of Teodros's future works will be posted on www.gabrielteodros.com.

NADIA CHANEY is a poet and facilitator living in Vancouver on unceded Coast Salish territory. She works as a trainer and lead facilitator with Partnerships for Youth Empowerment (pyeglobal.org) and as a lyricist with local bhangra-glitch-hop trio Banyen Roots (banyenroots.com).

fish hooks (after gwendolyn brooks)

we farmed salmon
fenced in momentum

no refuge up waterfalls
down shoals struggling

dress up in sauce talk
one day i'll make

a good meal we have
our dreams fed to us

sangre nueva

my generation's like a nation / it spans nations nothing you build can / ever contain them / when fighting for liberation / i'm free as my mind can see / think out the box stay alive young g //

to feel like curtis mayfield and heal with words / i was held in this verse it fueled my hurt / wounded now my love does walk the earth / for the young ones searching to build they church inside / away from religious little lies to convert / nah we decolonise realise our true worth / school didn't work for all / we unearth our true stories / freedom fighters and glorious / the system tries to ignore the significance of these brilliant / young minds innovate to survive / make a way inspire / society acts like it wants them to die / twamp 6 nirvana the land is suicide / always was an outsider now i'm still alive / so always have the courage to use your own mind / cuz you do fulfill our dreams and realise / and my love for you is impossible to recite /

sun spots

the vast and rapid day
left us breathless busy

catching buses and soles
smoking in great gulps

crows and pigeons
gulls and shopkeepers

seem still in their knowing
how to measure shadows

> **ANNA HUNTER** is a momma, crafter, activist, and small business owner. She "almost" balances her time between motherhood, running a local yarn store, and organizing around issues of housing and poverty in Vancouver, unceded Coast Salish Territory.

Doing something I love, contributing to my community, making enough money to pay for the necessities for me and my family, providing great work for other women, and not having anyone tell me what to do—those are essentially the reasons that I started my own business.

As an anti-capitalist, the subject of "work" has always been a tough one—I've spent years struggling with how to have enough money to survive/enjoy certain things about life, and also not lose my soul in the process. Opening up my yarn store in the summer of 2009 seems to have answered a lot of those questions for me.

I work for myself, so I am the one who decided what this business looks like. In the beginning I was criticized for not having "financial" goals, but only "social" goals for my business. But I've been successfully open for 2 years and those social goals have totally defined the business. I choose to sell fair trade yarn, products that take into account the environment, and my business practices are challenging the status quo.

I hire people from my community and pay a great living wage. Providing a healthy work environment that values the time and work of the employees is a truly tangible way to make a difference in my community. I hire people who share similar values and passions, and are apart of making the store environment friendly, safe, and fun! I know that my employees also appreciate the living wage that is hard to find in most other workplaces.

I have had the chance to create a community space that many people from a variety of backgrounds can enjoy. It's unfortunate that its often only "political" or "progressive" spaces that are conscious of things like anti-oppression, and so many of the day-to-day places we go to feel unsafe at best and in some cases down-right oppressive. At Baaad Anna's we have created a "community space" that people in the neighborhood utilize and appreciate (even if they aren't knitters). The community and dialogue that happens in this space is outside of that "activist" realm and feels so real, it's created opportunity for change in perhaps the most unassuming place.

Finally, one of the greatest things about starting my own business is that it has allowed me freedom that I never had before—even during the decade that I did NGO work. It's hard work, but it's motivating and rewarding—and did I mention that I don't have a boss anymore?

STARLA BLUE DAVID DISASTER is a nomadic, self-sustaining skid who believes in striking with intent and loving your friends.

When I was really young, I started dreaming of traveling. I grew up with the feeling of wanderlust living inside me. It took quite a few years for me to actualize my desires, but when I did, I had no idea what I was actually in for. Years of friends, hard times, good nights, and beautiful dreams coming true.

Since then I've crossed the country so many times I've lost count. I've lived in a van off and on for three years, and just like before the van I've since spent countless hours on the side of the highway or under overpasses waiting for the rain to pass or for a ride to stop. I've still barely worked a "job" and almost never had to pay rent in the last 5 years. I make things to sell and play music at houses and cafes for whatever donations folks want to throw our way and I take odd jobs when they're offered and don't compromise my self-worth.

I try to live my life in a conscious way that impacts my communities and friends as positively as possible. I seek independence through conscious, considerate interdependence and critical, intentional analysis and by asking for what I need while being honest about the difference between "need" and "want" and how my actions affect those around me.

I'm constantly looking for a solution to the conflict between my values and politics and the learned behavior society enforces on us through institutionalized learning and their ideals of comfort, safety, and stability.

While sharing cans of beans and sandwiches on park benches or at rest stops with friends and strangers, I've discussed community, revolution, poverty (chosen or not), living off the map, and surviving our histories in whatever ways we can while trying to be healthy and happy. It's not an easy choice to make, but to some folks it's our only solution.

I screenprint patches, copy zines, trade for friends' cds, and make other things to sell at shows or on the street to help pay for food or gas or whatever I need. I try not to spend money on junk, which isn't hard now that I've realized I don't need most stuff anyway. I try to eat healthy and get my food from dumpsters or the grocery store, which is surprisingly cheaper and easier than restaurants. When I can I look for resources in cities like soup kitchens, drop-ins, and low income community spaces that have free or really cheap meals. Sometimes I look for work trades with folks at community markets or in small towns for fresh veggies or a meal and a place to stay.

STAY **SOLID**

I share what I can with my friends and folks around me and they do the same. I always try to trust my gut instinct and go with it when I'm traveling and I try to be honest with myself about who I am and what I need. I've realized that there's a difference between need and desire and that sometimes the best choices really are the hardest but that life can be fun and challenging and hard all at the same time if I'm willing to fight for what I want with good intentions and a few friends at my side.

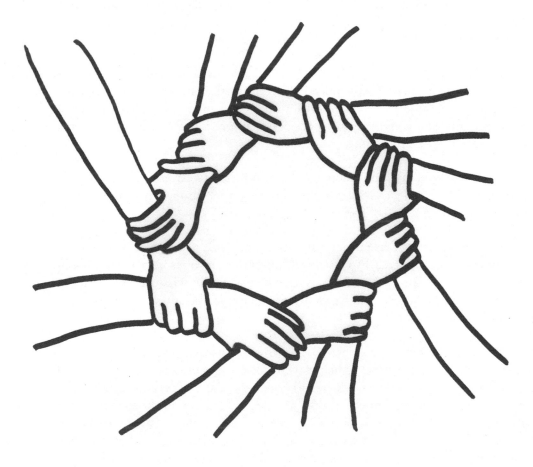

Image by aly de la Cruz

5. SKILLS

This chapter might be called "Get Good at Stuff." If you want to have an impact on the world you need to have skills: you've got to get good at doing and making things, and then go out and do things and make things!

Think broadly about what that might mean. The totalizing logic of school and employment often reduces the idea of "skills" to a very narrow band of activities, but note these synonyms for skill: ability, talent, cleverness, dexterity, expertise, proficiency, handiness, knack, aptitude, competence, flair. There are many skills that are either not respected (because of classism) or invisible (because of misogynist attitudes) or disregarded (because they do not generate money)—but these are critical skills as well.

We conceive of *skill* as something that helps you have a tangible effect on the world. It might be a material skill that you do with your hands such as fixing a bike, sewing, carpentry, cooking; or it can be a less-visible skill such as explaining ideas to others, negotiating between angry parties, connecting people with each other; or maybe it is a creative skill like drawing, writing, performing. Regardless, though, it is essential that you:

★ recognize what skills you already have

★ understand what kinds of skills you tend to be good at, and what kinds you will have to work harder at to develop

★ figure out what kind of skills you want

★ learn how you're going to get them

★ get clear on how they can help you move your own life forward

★ consider how you can use your existing skills, or the ones you will nurture, to have a positive impact on your community

Some of this conversation intersects with paid work, and that's all good. It is really important that you have skills in the short term so you can get jobs. Whether it's babysitting, waitressing, mowing lawns, cooking, treeplanting, fixing computers—whatever—but get some experience and proclivity so you can pick up short-term employment. Having a solid employable skill in your back pocket that you can turn to when necessary is clutch—it will keep you from being broke when you do not want to be.

But also think long-term about what skills you are going to get really good at in the coming years, not so much as a "career" (that's a gross way to think of your life) but as a way to keep you economically and personally self-reliant, and also to contribute to your community.

Maybe more important, however, are unpaid skills. There are so, so many tasks that women have traditionally been responsible for that are not paid. Taking care of the home, child-minding, cooking, cleaning, growing, and preparing food; these are the skills that are most important to our lives and all of us need to get good and proficient at them, men especially. But there is a constellation of other kinds of skills that you can think of that are beneficial to the community and your neighbours.

But no matter what — get good at stuff! Develop some skills. Get proud of your craft. Whatever you might be good at, get better. Whatever you think might be cool to learn, get on it. Getting good at stuff is the way you can have an impact on the world.

OTHER STUFF TO CHECK OUT:

- **THE MONKEY WRENCH GANG**, Edward Abbey

- **SHOP CLASS AS SOUL CRAFT**, Matthew Crawford

- **CREATING A CARING ECONOMY**, Nora Castañeda

- **THE URBAN HOMESTEAD**, Kelly Coyne & Erik Knutzen

- **RADICAL HOMEMAKERS** (online)

- **OCCUPY OUR HOMES** (organization)

- **BEAUTIFUL TROUBLE**: A Toolbox for Revolution, Andrew Boyd

- **FREESKOOLS PROJECT WIKI** (online)

- **THE BEEHIVE COLLECTIVE** (organization)

- **JIRO DREAMS OF SUSHI** (film)

STRANGERS IN A TANGLED WILDERNESS is a small publishing collective that exists to promote anarchist culture and gift economics. Nearly everything it produces, while available in print form, is also available for free download from www.tangledwilderness.org.

STEPHANIE McMILLAN creates the comic strip "Minimum Security," and the award-winning environmental editorial cartoon "Code Green," and works with the anti-capitalist collective One Struggle/South Florida. She has three books including the graphic novel, *As the World Burns: 50 Simple Things You Can Do to Stay in Denial.*

In this time of escalating exploitation, poverty, imperialist wars, torture, and ecocide, we don't need a piece of art that consists of a mattress dripping orange paint, cleverly titled "Tangerine Dream." In this time, as countless multitudes suffer and die for the profits and luxuries of a few, as species go extinct at a rate faster than we can keep track of, we don't need an orchestra composed of iPhones. In this time, when the future of all life on Earth is at stake, spare us the constant barrage of narcissistic tweets juxtaposing celeb gossip with quirky food choices.

If we lived in a time of peace and harmony, then creating pretty, escapist, seratonin-boosting hits of mild amusement wouldn't be a crime (except perhaps against one's Muse). If all was well, such art might enhance our happy existence, like whipped cream on a chocolate latte. There's nothing wrong with pleasure, or decorative art.

But in times like these, for an artist not to devote her/his talents and energies to creating cultural weapons of resistance is a betrayal of the worst magnitude, a gesture of contempt against life itself. It is unforgivable.

The foundation of any culture is its underlying economic system. Today, art is bullied to conform to the demands of industrial capitalism, to reflect and reinforce the interests of those in power. This system-serving art is relentlessly bland. It is viciously soothing, crushingly safe. It seduces us to desire, buy, use, consume. It entertains us and makes us giggle with faux joy as it slowly sucks our brains out through our eye sockets.

The system exerts tremendous pressure to create art that is not only apolitical but anti-political. When the dominant culture spots political art, it sticks its fingers in its ears and sings, "La la la!" It refuses to review it in the *New York Times* or award it an NEA grant. Political art is vigorously snubbed, ignored, condemned to obscurity, erased. If it's too powerful to make disappear, then it is scorned, accused of being depressing, doom-and-gloom, preachy, impolite, and by the way, your drawing style sucks. Also by the way, you can't make a living if your work's not vacuous, cynical, and therefore commercially viable, so go starve under a bridge with your precious principles.

We're taught that it's rude to be judgmental, that to assert a point of view violates the pure, transcendent and neutral spirit of art. This is mind-fucking bullshit designed to weaken and depoliticize us. In these times, there is no such thing as neutrality—not taking a stand means supporting and assisting exploiters and murderers.

Let us not be the system's tools or fools. Artists are not cowards and weaklings—we're tough. We take sides. We fight back.

Artists and writers have a proud tradition of being at the forefront of resistance, of stirring emotions and inspiring action. Today we must create an onslaught of judgmental, opinionated, brash and partisan work in the tradition of anti-Nazi artists John Heartfield and George Grosz, of radical muralist Diego Rivera, filmmaker Ousmane Sembène, feminist artists The Guerrilla Girls, novelists like Maxim Gorky and Taslima Nasrin, poets like Nazim Hikmet and Kazi Nazrul Islam, musicians like The Coup and the Dead Kennedys.

The world cries out for meaningful, combative, political art. It is our duty and responsibility to create a fierce, unyielding, aggressive culture of resistance. We must create art that exposes and denounces evil, that strengthens activists and revolutionaries, celebrates and contributes to the coming liberation of this planet from corporate industrial military omnicidal madness.

Pick up your weapon, artist.

MARISELA B. GOMEZ is a community organizer, social justice activist, physician scientist, mindfulness practitioner, and author of the book *Race, Class, Power, and Organizing: Rebuilding Abandoned Communities in America*. She currently independently consults in organizing mindful action for individual and social change.

The Solidity Toolbox

How are we going to maintain our solidity, our values, our understanding of justice as we walk this path of radical change together? We need tools and skills to help us stay solid as we work on transforming ourselves and society.

What should be in our solidity toolbox?

Stopping and finding space for reflection is a powerful tool for our toolbox. In the midst of hopelessness, fear, anger, depression, sadness, anxieties, and distractions, when we are able to stop and come back to ourselves, we become more stable, more solid. We become the masters of our thoughts, words, and actions. Stopping what we are doing and taking a deep breath in and out three times will help us regain our composure and our solidity. This small act can help to bring balance back into our mind and body when we are faced with difficulties of any kind.

Taking a slow and mindful walk close to nature or in a calm environment is another tool that can help to bring us back to the reality of all the positive things that already exist in our lives. A mindful walk, with awareness of each foot touching the earth, can help bring our mind and body back to stillness and solidity. A mindful walk can remind us of the wonders that already exist, giving us the strength to face the difficulties that we must negotiate. It is not running away from our problems but instead it is transforming ourselves so that we are able to be more solid in the midst of the problem. Addressing any issue, whether it is a joyful or a painful one, from a place of peace and calm will always bring greater benefit.

In the midst of actions that are negative and unjust we must remember that it is the action that is negative and unjust, not the person or people behaving in these ways. This is another important tool for remaining solid and peaceful. This understanding allows us to respond from a place of compassion instead of ignorance. We recognize that their anger comes from their own pain and suffering. When we act with understanding and compassion, we break the cycle of blame, fear, and ignorance. We recognize that we ourselves are much more likely to listen to someone who is calm and understanding than to someone who is blaming and filled with anger.

69

DIANA PEI WU has worked with The Ruckus Society, smartMeme, and many other grassroots people-powered movements demanding change and offering visions to move us towards a solidarity economy, a healthy planet, and a just world free from racism and oppressions for this and future generations.

I grew up in the suburbs of New York City.

One year, I went to an academic camp on scholarship and then got on some youth leadership mailing list. Then it was 1989. I had organized my Chinese School friends to make posters and t-shirts to raise money for Chinese student dissidents after the Tienanmen Square democracy movement and massacre. In the Chinese community we still call it June 4th. It was the first time—and perhaps the last—that my parents would support me to participate in a mass mobilization.

In 1989, this very progressive peace movement summer camp recruited me. I earned enough money to pay my share, working under the table, and got a scholarship to be able to attend the Samantha Smith World Peace Camp in Poland Spring, Maine. My parents were skeptical, but since I had raised the money and the scholarship, they let me go. At camp, I had all these radical camp counselors. I met Russians, Cambodian Americans, Black girls, and progressive white folks. I learned to read Cyrillic, practiced Tai Chi, spent a lot of time walking in tall pine woods and watching stars in the summer night sky, got inspired to learn guitar and more languages. After I came back I started an environmental action club at my high school and I started doing ecological research on fish and pollution in our local waterways.

I didn't know these things: I would participate in mass protests like the WTO in Seattle in 1999 and be radicalized through baptism by tear gas. I'd organize with a people of color anti-war contingent in 2003, a delegation of Chinese Americans to protest the WTO in Hong Kong in 2005, with delegations of youth, people of color, women, and indigenous peoples around the talks of the United Nations Framework Convention on Climate Change in 2009 and 2010, and even for relatively less sexy things like bus-only lanes in Los Angeles and affordable housing for Chinese seniors in Oakland. I didn't know that I would become a professor, a writer, dancer, and musician, or that I would love women as much as I love men for sex and intimacy.

For me, I've learned that I didn't have to choose between being Chinese and being a human rights activist and organizer, being queer, a teacher, artist, dancer, martial artist, being radical and loving my family, and being fully myself. I've also learned that multiracial and international solidarity is central to creating the better world that we want, and that we should do lots of things that don't ask governments to help us or just change policy, but rather, that helps us build the skills and networks to do it ourselves. Participating in collective action and social movements makes you smarter and sharper.

To quote Mao, "If you want to know the taste of a pear, you must change the pear by eating it yourself. If you want to know the theory and methods of revolution, you must take part in revolution. All genuine knowledge originates in direct experience."

Here's a pear.

PETE JORDAN is the author of the books *Dishwasher* and *In the City of Bikes*. He lives in Amsterdam with his son. He is the author of the now-defunct zine "Dishwasher," which chronicled his quest to wash dishes in all fifty American states. For over ten years, Pete moved from state to state washing dishes in restaurants, resorts, canneries, and communes—anywhere, basically, that dishes were dirty. This piece is an excerpt from *Dishwasher* (New York: HarperCollins, 2007). Reprinted here with the permission of the author.

If indeed, I was born to wash dishes, no one had ever bothered to tell me that it was my calling. I didn't grow up dreaming about becoming a dishwasher. I never yearned for the prestige of being an unskilled laborer: I never craved the glory of scrubbing the crap off America's pots and pans. If I had, though, having such fantasies could've saved me a lot of time trying to figure out what I was going to do with my life.

That night I wrote a couple of letters to pals who, coincidentally, had also fallen into dishwashing. Tony—my buddy from the paint crew—was dishing with his friends on a five-man crew at a large college cafeteria up in Davis, California. He'd written me a letter about his stubborn refusal to wear the requisite plastic apron because of his aversion to plastic clothing. My pal Dave was working two different jobs in Olympia, Washington. He wrote to me about his struggles with the alcoholic owners at one of the restaurants.

Reading and writing these letters about dish work gave me an idea: collect these tales and print them up in some sort of pamphlet. The other guys liked the idea too. But the problem with starting a publication devoted to the work of laggards was that Tony and Dave were too damn lazy to send me their promised contributions. Then again, when it came to lethargy, I had them both beat.

...

Life as Mr. Reliable was good for a couple of months, until I started to notice the blue-rimmed plate. The deli used only plain white plates, so the sudden appearance of the oddball blue-rimmed plate was a mystery. Had a coworker brought in a plate of homemade cookies and forgotten to take the plate home again? Had a customer somehow slipped it in? I asked my coworkers, but no one knew where it'd come from.

Each time I washed him, Blue-Rimmed caught my attention. As soon as he was returned to the clean stacks, up he'd pop again in my sinks. It seemed like I was washing him constantly. Then on a busy Saturday in the deli, I counted how many times Blue-Rimmed passed through my hands. Twenty-seven times! I couldn't believe it.

Up until then, I'd always considered dishwashing a progressive pursuit: I'd start a shift with dirty dishes, finish it with clean ones, then move on to the next town, the next job, always moving forward. But as Blue-Rimmed went round and round, he pointed out that I had it all wrong. Really I was just moving in circles: washing things that only got dirty again within minutes. The next town, the next job, the story would always be the same: the dishes would never remain clean.

Over and over, Blue-Rimmed seemed to ridicule me, saying, "Dishwashing is pointless."

I tried to silence Blue-Rimmed by hiding him on the bottom of the clean stacks or leaving him on the bottom of the sink while I washed the anonymous white dishes in his place. But no matter what I did, Blue-Rimmed always worked his way back into my hands, where I was subjected to his taunts yet again.

Finally I had enough of him. And with great satisfaction I threw him at the floor and watched him smash into blue-rimmed shards.

But the satisfaction was short-lived. Though the messenger was dead, his message lived on. Despite the shattered corpse on the floor, dishwashing still remained pointless. Even worse my nemesis had the last laugh. Instead of kicking the shards under the counter as the Dishwasher Pete of old would've done, Mr. Reliable dutifully swept up the remains and deposited them in the trash.

A couple of nights later, I took a tumble of my own. While exploring a new route home from work, my bike hit a speed bump in the dark. I flew over the handlebars and landed on my face.

...

As the doctor stood over me and tweezed the gravel out of my head and sewed up the gash, I lay there in a daze. With the lamp shining in my face, I admired his work. It must be nice to be skilled, I thought. If someone had come to me with a nasty head wound and asked me to help him, I'd be confounded. If he'd bloodied his dishes in the process, then I could wash those. Otherwise, he'd be shit out of luck.

During the hours in the emergency room, I admired the work of all the nurses and doctors that treated me. Maybe it was the concussion, maybe it was the Percocet, but I couldn't stop thinking about how these people were using their skills to do valuable work. They were actually making a difference in the world. Meanwhile, what was I doing with my life? Over and over, I was just washing the same dishes (blue-rimmed or not) that only ended up dirty again within minutes.

...

(Ed note: The irony of all this is, of course, that Dishwasher Pete wasn't just washing dishes for all of those years. He was gaining experience and knowledge about the world through travel and work. He made enough money to sustain himself and he wrote. He published his zine, which reached many people, and now works as a writer.)

73

MARK DOUGLAS gave up his car to the crusher more than a year ago. He has no regrets about the decision and gets where he needs to by walking, jogging, biking, or taking the train. He has lost some apparently unneeded weight. Mark works as a music educator in Burnaby, BC and has been growing food in the city for the past 25 years.

SO **YOU WANT TO LEARN HOW TO PLAY MUSIC WELL**? HERE'S MY **ADVICE**:

PRACTICE: Mastery of your instrument(s) is important; put in 60 hours of practice on fundamental technique for one 3-week period and just see what happens. Be able to read more than one type of notation (Standard, Charts, Tab, graphic, etc.). Learn solos off recordings note for note. Get yourself good enough to work with established musicians that are a few steps better than you. It's hard to make contacts, find gigs, get paid, so learn how to do it by finding work with an established working group. Ready-made rep.

BE OPEN TO EXPERIENCE: Don't pre-judge stuff that's unfamiliar to you; try and see/hear it all, give it a reasonable shot. Remember John Cage's dictum: If after one minute something is not interesting, try it for 2 minutes more; if after 2 minutes it's still not interesting, try it for 4, then 8, 16 and so on… eventually you'll find it is really very interesting after all. And if you don't, then chuck it.

CULTIVATE A RELATIONSHIP with those who inspire you: You will go through doubts and tough times, and so it is helpful to have mentors who can give you the benefit of their experience of going through doubts and tough times. Mentors can be real people you know, people who are occasionally willing to talk/write to you (it is a great and under-used piece of info that many people that you admire are incredibly generous, approachable, and willing to give you a little time of their day). If that is too daunting mentors also exist in books and films as biographies and autobiographies. These can be great because you can find whatever strikes you as the wisdom you need and refer to it frequently.

FOCUS ON ONE THING: This seems at odds with the "be open" idea, but really they go back and forth. Don't be afraid to focus on just one thing. Staying with one thing still leads to a multitude of opportunities. How many great instrumentalists/musicians do you think feel dissatisfied because they stuck to one instrument? Clapton? Cassals? Marsalis? "Focus on just one thing" can lead you everywhere you want to go.

Discover what interests you most, master an instrument or technology that will take you there, fearlessly stick to what interests you the most, and find support to provide you with backbone when yours fails you.

Whatever you decide, the world of music is HUGE and there is plenty of room for your ideas out there.

JOHN HOLT (1923–1985) was one of the grandparents of the homeschooling and unschooling movements. He championed the idea of children's rights and challenged compulsory schooling in all his guises. He founded Holt Associates and *Growing Without Schooling* magazine and published ten books including *Freedom and Beyond* (1972), *Escape from Childhood* (1974), and *Instead of Education* (1976). This is an excerpt from *Never Too Late* (1979).

I have long had two favorite proverbs: one is Shaw's "Be sure to get what you like, or else you will have to like what you get," the other a translation from an old Spanish proverb, "'Take what you want,' says God, 'and pay for it.'" To find out what one really wants, and what it costs, and how to pay what it costs, is an important part of everyone's life work. But it is not easy to find out what we like or want, when all our lives other people have been hard at work trying not just to make us do what they want, but to make us think that we *want* to do it. How then *do* we find out what we want? What sort of clues, experiences, inner messages, may tell us? What do we do about such messages when we get them? [...]

Another reason I am writing this book is to question the widely held idea that what happens to us in the first few years of our lives determines everything that will happen later, what we can be, what we can do. Musical people are particularly prone to talk this way... Most of all, I want to combat the idea that any disciplined and demanding activity, above all music, can never grow out of love, joy, and free choice, but must be rooted in forced exposure, coercion, and threat. Most of what I have read about music education says this one way or another. The idea is not only mistaken, but dangerous; nothing is more certain to make most people ignore or even hate great music than trying to ram more and more of it down the throats of more and more children in compulsory classes and lessons. The idea is wrong in a larger sense; in the long run, love and joy are more enduring source of discipline and commitment than any amount of bribe and threat, and it is only what C. Wright Mills called the "crackpot realism" of our times that keeps us from seeing, or even being willing to see, that this is so. [...]

If I could learn to play the cello well, as I thought I could, I could show by my own example that we all have greater powers than we think; that whatever we want to learn or learn to do, we probably can learn; that our lives and our possibilities are not determined and fixed by what happened to us when we were little, or by what experts say we can or cannot do. [...]

Oddly enough, I am much less threatened by the enormous skill of the players in the Boston Symphony than I am by the lesser skill (but still much greater than mine) of the cellists in my own little orchestra, or the players in some of our local amateur or youth orchestras... I sometimes feel discouraged when I think how much I will have to improve just to be as good as the other players in my orchestra. To have to work so hard to get not into the major leagues, but just the lowest of the minors! But then I realize this business of comparing myself with others, or berating myself because (so far!) I can't do what they can do so easily is silly. The baby learning to walk does not reproach himself every time he falls down. If he did, he would never learn to walk. When he falls down he gets right up and starts to walk again. Just the other day I saw a little girl at this stage; she was walking like someone on a ship in a very rough sea. In the hour or so I was near her she must have sat or fallen down thirty or forty times. Up she rose each time and went on her way. Not being able to do what she was trying to do may have been a nuisance, but not *failure*, nothing of which to feel guilty and ashamed.

What I am slowly learning to do in my work with music is revive some of the resilient spirit of the exploring and learning baby. I have to accept at each moment, as a fact of life, my present skill or lack of skill, and do the best I can, without blaming myself for not being able to do better. I have to be aware of my mistakes and shortcomings without being ashamed of them. I have to keep in view the distant goal, without worrying about how far away it is or reproaching myself for not being already there. This is very hard for most adults. It is that main reason why we old dogs so often do find it so hard to learn new tricks, whether sports or languages or crafts or music. But if as we work on our skills we work on this weakness in ourselves, we can slowly get better at both.

Image courtesy of 10incheslab/FreeDigitalPhotos.net

SHAWNA MURRAY is a twenty-four-year-old social worker, community advocate, poet, and jewelry artisan in Baltimore City. She is the Vice President of Outreach for Leaders of a Beautiful Struggle.

LEADERS OF A BEAUTIFUL STRUGGLE is a youth-run, community-based, traveling think tank that is dedicated to advocacy for Baltimore City. LBS analyzes and highlights the ways that external forces have contributed to the overall decline of our city while providing tangible, concrete solutions to Baltimore's problems. The Executive Board is comprised of Baltimore City residents; all are younger than twenty-five years of age. LBS seeks to change the city by utilizing governmental policy action through policy debate, research, community outreach, organizing, and collaboration.

At 15…

 I was asleep on a bench with my momma…
 Asleep in the back… in the bottom…
 I was asleep in the home of a friend of a friend of my momma.
 I was discreet in my sorrow…
 I wanted to sleep through tomorrow…
 I used to dream I could borrow the life of one without sorrow.
 I was convinced I was blue…
 That beauty and love wasn't true…
 And that sleep would become the end of my fight.

At 15…

 it would have been nice to know…
 that hardships come and they will go,
 that the strength in one's heart is cavalier.

At 15…

 someone should have told me…
 to translate fury into movements for justice,
 to find love from fear,
 to turn doubt into promise.

At 15 someone should tell you…

 One within many can change the world as small as it may be…
 As far as your heart and your eyes can believe
 …Only those willing to dream the dreams almost shattered…
 …to envision and extend beyond those that don't matter,
 will move the world at valued speed.

 So embrace the love that's received and forgotten…
 Reach out to the hands of the downtrodden.
 Be an example of the change you wish to see.

As young leaders struggling to bloom, you must be able to vehemently envision your idea of a just society. You must do this so much that even when elders or those who are comfortable with the status quo tell you otherwise, you have the courage and drive to move forward. We, Leaders of a Beautiful Struggle, did just that, we attempted to translate what was happening around us, consulted our mentors, and looked at models that were successful and those that were not. All the pain and anger within… we translate to practice, recognizing our belief that no one else should experience what we have. So, put your ideas on paper… map them out into reality and create a plan for execution. All of us are unique with different gifts… look for that gift in yourself and spend time to develop it. Poetry, beat-boxing, drawing, writing, making jewelry, research, or building structures; perfect your craft like no other… your way. When mapping your plan, create a space for yourself—to uniquely impact community where your gift will grow. With mentorship, loud music, good times, love, and positivity never stop. It's worth it.

"If you give me a fish you have fed me for a day.

If you teach me to fish then you have fed me until the river is contaminated or the shoreline seized for development. But if you teach me to organize then whatever the challenge I can join together with my peers and we will fashion our own solution."

—Ricardo Levins Morales

SEVÉ TORRES received his BA in Sociology from the University of California, Berkeley. He is a former teacher for June Jordan's Poetry for the People and three-time Voices of Our Arts Foundation (VONA) alum and will be published in the upcoming VONA Anthology from Thread Makes Blanket Press. Sevé has been a fixture in the San Francisco Bay Area poetry scene.

Samuel Hazo argues in an essay on poetics that it is the poet's job to "…create silence. Not mere quietude. Not solitude. Rather it is a silence spawned within and by the experience of the poem itself." He then reminds us, "within this silence the imagination and the feelings are renewed, and because of that renewal they live momentarily with a will and momentum of their own."

…the poem must be alive…

I want to write poems that spring from a deep feeling, a feeling that the reader/poet cannot escape no matter how hard we try. I strive to create a poetry that contains magic in its very DNA, poetry that moves toward the myth and truth we need at a given moment to survive, and whether that truth be dim, beautiful, eloquent, light, fantastic, it must produce a sense of wonderment and exert a magical force on the poet/reader. Why does this poem need to exist? How best can I write this poem to capture the magic, the beauty, the music, and the truth that changes me as a poet? These are my guiding questions.

…you can hear truth as the hair rises on your arm in spontaneous static…

I would argue that at the core of our projects poets have a series of questions that we are asking. They may be particular to the poet, like the one that I am addressing at the moment, why do I keep running and how does running save my life? Or they may be based in craft.

…the form a poem takes can control the silences…

As a poet I am aware that there is an enduring and profound relationship between the way we live and the way we write our poetry. If there is a failing on the page it is likely to have its origins in the series of problematic engagements the poet has with the world around them.

…repeatedly, my mentors identified my voice as an area that needed development…

I meet at a cross-roads of many cultures and voices: If I am an MC in the hip-hop tradition, a poet exploring the prophetic voice of Philip Levine and Khalil Gibran, a man who is driven by faith and a belief in God, a male poet of color in an all-white MFA program in South Jersey, thousands of miles away from the people I love most, and if I am someone in becoming how then can I speak in one unified voice, where does the nomad find continuity between the many codes they switch between on a daily basis? Within the process of writing, I have (re) discovered a music that I was avoiding, that music is the unifying thread through which my mythopoetic voice must find itself in each telling.

…urgent, important, and beautiful…

A poem should change the poet, should provide new insight and never allow the poet to hide behind things known or mastered. Without a journey into the unknown, in between the edges of a blank page, a poet will remain stagnant.

…one day, one word, and one syllable at a time weighed against the backdrop of music…

To move through language is to survive, it is an incredibly social act, which allows the bearer of language to articulate at the level of the necessary. Poetry for me is an essential act; it is as crucial as breathing, through poetry I have acquired the tools to communicate love. Because I believe that life is to be lived through love, and the act of faith, traveling in the music of poetry is the highest form to which I dedicate my life.

6. SEX

SEX! is an ultimately powerful (maybe *the* ultimately powerful) word. You can feel flushes of heat, awkwardness, excitement, fear, shame, curiosity, empowerment, desperation, rejection, and desire run through your body just reading the word. Or maybe you feel disinterest and your hands get clammy.

We want this chapter to provide a sex positive, inclusive, and liberatory platform to help you in your thinking about the real essentials of sex. There is a boatload of information out there, lots of it really good, but it is typically overwhelmed by a hyper-sexualized media culture, religious and cultural weirdness, guilt, shame, disinformation, misinformation, lies, peer pressure, and confusion (among other things).

Every young person, no matter your gender, sexual orientation, religious or cultural background, has a ton of questions—and frankly, they are never all going to get answered. All through your life sex is going to be on your mind in good and unsettling ways. But don't be afraid of that—sex is one of the core parts of our experience, it is worth plenty of consideration, and your thinking will constantly be evolving and developing. And so it should, and the less weird the conversations are (with yourself and/or others), the more likely they are to be fruitful. This chapter is not going to answer all your questions (not even close), but it is going to make a simple point then suggest a bunch of resources for further reading and investigation.

This is our pretty simple argument: thinking about sex, and your pleasure in particular, is not that much different than thinking about politics, or community, or work, or most anything else and should be subject to the same basic sets of criteria. Our sexual politics should support equity and fairness, self-determination and self-reliance, cre-

> "Our visions begin with our desires."
>
> —Audre Lorde

ativity and mutual aid. We want a world where people feel good about themselves and their desires, work toward others feeling the same, actively fight oppression and violence, and can talk openly and honestly in private and public about what that means. How's that work for you?

In the mayhem of sexual shame, manipulation, repression, oppression, and power, people get weird, and sometimes ugly. But fight through that—for you and everyone around you. Our hope is to encourage people to care about themselves, their pleasure, their health, and that of their partner(s), with communication, self-empowerment and self-care as the building blocks of self-determination in one's choices about sex.

OTHER STUFF TO CHECK OUT:

- **MIDWEST TEEN SEX SHOW** (online)

- **THE FIRST TIME: TRUE STORIES**, Charles Montpetit (Ed.)

- **NOT VANISHING**, Chrystos

- **KINSEY**: Let's Talk About Sex (movie)

- **LEARNING GOOD CONSENT** (zine)

- **SEX AT DAWN**: The Prehistoric Origins of Modern Sexuality, Christopher Ryan and Cacilda Jethá

- **THE ETHICAL SLUT**: A Guide to Infinite Sexual Possibilities, Dossie Easton and Janet W. Hardy

- **SCARLETEEN**: Sex Ed for the Real World (online)

LEE NAUGHT is a radical, genderqueer, chican@ organizer and sex educator who has participated in a variety of collective, feminist, and sexuality-based projects. Currently the most prominent of those endeavors are positions as a co-founder of the sex positivity collective Fuckin' (A) and as a collective member at Bluestockings Bookstore in NYC. Lee plays in the riot grrrl band Titfit and the screamo duo The Facts We Hate, and enjoys bikes, politically rowdy queers, and anything that involves lots of glitter.

What would you say if I told you that awesome sex is a *crucial* element in our work to change this world for the better? I'm totally serious, too. Okay, well, maybe not just sex alone, but how we *do* sex, how we think and talk about sex, and how we engage sex and sexuality in our everyday lives. These things are helluv important. These things contain power, and the ability to shift how the world works. They're deeply connected to radical social politics.

Let's back up a sec, though. Hi! My name's Lee. I'm kind of an anarchist. I'm definitely a queer feminist, and I work a lot around an intersectional (meaning cross-issue) political perspective that me, my friends, and my companer@s call Radical Sex Positivity. Folks often want to know what sex positivity means… like, does that mean you're into sex? Well, yes, I think sex positivity often means liking sex, but it means a whole lot more, too. At its core, sex positivity is about breaking down shame and taboos around sex and bodies. It's about each person having access to the type of pleasure they want to find. But what does this have to do with changing the world? Hmmm… let's add a hint of anarchism to sex, and we'll discover some explosive elements, like respect, autonomy, and consent!

BAM! **RESPECT!**

We break taboos around sexuality by building respect and appreciation for all bodies—inclusive of all sizes, shapes, colors, and genders—and by respecting the diverse kinds of sex different people want to have. Most of us live in this fucked-up world where shame is used to keep people in line and to keep people silenced. Shaming people into remaining unaware of the power contained in their bodies (and in sex) helps maintain power as it is—in the hands of very few. We can break sex-negative cycles of rejection and shame by respecting people (and their desires) as unique and awesome and even beautiful! Respecting folks' diversity is also about recognizing your responsibility to participate in other folks' battles—because if other people aren't able to happily live out their desires, how can you expect to? Fighting for respect means fighting to create space for everyone *and* their desires (as long as they're consensual! Read on!).

KABOOM! **AUTONOMY!**

One thing many feminists and anarchists have in common is that they strongly believe that each person should get to choose for herself what ze wants and does.

No one else should get to choose for us. If we think about sex in this context, it becomes very clear that each person should have control over hir own body, in addition to hir energy and hir work. Most of us live in this fucked-up society where we're expected to make decisions that will mold us to social stereotypes, which, again, help maintain power as it is. There are a lot of structures and social punishments already in place (from shaming to grades to cops) to coerce us to make the "right" choices, or at least the acceptable ones. We need to help each other learn that there is no "right" choice when it comes to how we each have sex, or how we each want to live our lives. Let's empower and support each other in making decisions based on our desires, on what we want for ourselves, instead of with the coercive cultural grain.

KABLOOEE! **CONSENT!**

Consent is the way we communicate what we choose and what we want. It's how we create a situation of supportive mutual choosing. When it comes to sex, a lot of this is done through talking—you say (honestly, gently, and with transparent intentions) what you want, what you like, and anything else that you think is important, and other folks communicate the same things to you. Then, together, you get to decide what you'll do together! If something isn't feeling right as you're going at it, you get to pause and renegotiate. AND this can be super fun and sexy! (Try whispering words in between kisses!) Consent is a great way to organize lots of things: work, activist groups, houses… even neighborhoods, cities, and whole continents of people! Pretty much, consent is rad.

So, here's the super-political-question-of-the-day: What would your world look like if it were organized around the principles of respect, autonomy, and consent for you and everyone you know? What would the world look like if these principles shaped *life on this planet*? Would capitalism's inhumane practices be crushed? Would racism, patriarchy, queerphobia, classism, ableism, and other fucked-up systems of oppression be dismantled? I think so. And I think sex is a great place to practice breaking all this fucked-up oppression. So, let's practice, practice, practice! (Haaayyyy.) And let's spread the word, too, because we're all responsible for teaching each other how to better be consensual, caring co-inhabitants of this world.

LEAH LAKSHMI PIEPZNA-SAMARASINHA is a queer mixed Sri Lankan femme writer, performer, and cultural worker with a fabulous chronic illness. The author of *Love Cake* and *Consensual Genocide* and the co-editor of *The Revolution Starts At Home: Confronting Intimate Violence in Activist Communities*, she also co-founded Mangos With Chili, a performance incubator and North America-wide tour of queer and trans of color and Two Spirit artists. Her life's work is at the intersections of teaching for liberation, queer of color art and politics, disability justice. and community accountability strategies for ending violence and abuse. See: www.brownstargirl.org.

1 There is no excuse for bad sex. Don't put up with sex that is unpleasurable or hurts in a crappy way. Get lube (good lube, not K-Y!). Check out feminist sex toy stores like goodforher.com, Babeland.com, goodvibes.org, for lots of info, fun toys, and mail order.) Also, if you have a clitoris and labia and are having a hard time achieving orgasm, buy a vibrator—the Hitachi magic wand is amazing, but even a little silver bullet (which is under $20) is great—and believe me, you will not have a problem anymore.

2 If you don't know, ask. Or go to the library or good sources on the internet and find out. Some places I like: www.ourbodiesourselves.org/; ywepchicago.wordpress.com/media/ (esp. "Girls Do What They Have to to Survive" and their "Harm Reduction Guide"—these are badass resources created by youth of color in the sex trade and street economics which has info about sex, how to give yourself a self exam, how to be your own social worker, how to give yourself a tattoo safely, and tons more); queerfatfemme.org (esp. the "How To Have More Queer Sex" and "Breakup Survival Guide" posts, but this is an awesome queer body positive resource); Fucking Trans Women (www.fuckingtranswomen.com/); and the Brown Boi Project's *Freeing Ourselves: A Guide to Health and Self Love for Brown Bois*, which is a health guide for bois, studs, and masculine of center people of color, to name just a few.

3 If you numb out or can't feel things during sex (dissociate)—or in general—you're not weird or broken. This is something that is super common with people who have lived through trauma, violence, or abuse—which is a hell of a lot of people. It's a tool that keeps us alive, and it is also something you can totally work with so that you will be able to feel great shit when you are having sex. Check out the book *The Survivor's Guide to Sex* by Staci Haines for lots of really good info about how to take your body back, heal and have mind blowingly good sex after abuse and trauma. There's also a DVD, *Healing Sex*. You could also check out this blog: www.vanissar.com/blog/emotional-first-aid-for-the-holidays-or-anytime, which talks about

our bodies' automatic fight, flight, freeze, appease, and dissociate responses, and stuff you can practice doing instead.

4 It's okay to be awkward.

5 Don't date people who make you feel like shit.

5a Don't date people who don't consistently make you feel great.

6 Trust your instincts. If you think someone is bullshitting you, they probably are.

7 Sometimes we make trade offs and date people who are mixed bags of wonderful and awful because they are taking us on adventures or giving us something really crucial we're not getting elsewhere. That doesn't make us stupid, that makes things complicated and that's life. However, don't be afraid to bounce when the shit outweighs the gold.

8 Your sparkly gold dust heart is beautiful and awesome. Don't let anyone make you feel like you're weak or stupid for being vulnerable and risking falling in love.

9 It's okay to just want to do it for doing its sake, but find people who know how to have hook up sex that's still respectful. It is also badass to masturbate like crazy. And jerking off = "real sex."

10 Think about what emotional consent means. Basically, think about how you fall in love.. Do you bounce when things get emo? Do you fall fast and hard? Are you able to keep things emotionally chill if your date doesn't sleep over? Even though you may not know the answers to all these questions, spend time figuring it out. And even though it can be nerve wracking and awkward, try and tell your lovers these things.

11 You get to create the exact kinds of relationships that work for you. They can be anything from monogamous life partnership to hella polyamorous. Check out the book *Opening Up* by Tristan Taormino for more ideas and info about how people do nonmonogamy without it being a giant hot mess disaster. But basically, you get to write your own script of what kinds of love, sex, and desire your head, heart, and junk want and need. And you get to define sex any way you want to, too. Spend some time thinking about what kinds of love and sex you want. I recently had a date write me this letter entitled "If We Are Going to Fuck, Here's What You Should Know," when we had the "so, I'm still really attracted to you" conversation, which had stuff about their gender, abuse history, and how it had affected them, and also all this amazing stuff they desired. I wrote my own back to them, and I was like, "how hot is this?" I recommend this.

12 If you are a baby queer femme, know that your gender and sexuality is a badass revolutionary force of nature that has been present in queer communities since the dawn of time. Be nice to other femmes. Work on creating communities of solidarity, support and love. If you are butch/genderqueer/transmasculine, know that, and work on undoing internalized misogyny and femmephobia. These are good resources: brownboiproject.org & zinelibrary.info/1-2-3-punch-how-misogyny-hurts-queer-communities.

13 "So here's the deal. About family, you have to make it up… People who don't have partners create families in everyone they touch. I know women and men from a multitude of sexual orientations without any children just doing their lives who create families that kick the can down the street. The heterosexual trinity is just one of many stories… I'm saying I think you have to break into the words 'relationship' or 'marriage' or 'family' and bring the walls down… Make up stories until you can find one to live with. Make up stories as if life depended on it."—Lidia Yuknavitch, *The Chronology of Water*

14 "Shit will not always be easy, but it will be god-damn beautiful."—My friend Ami Patel

DAN SAVAGE writes an internationally syndicated sex column "Savage Love." He is the co-founder of the "It Gets Better Project" and author of five books. He is all over the American media landscape from *This American Life* to *Real Time* with Bill Maher to MTV among many other places. He is also the bane of Rick Santorum's life.

ADVICE FOR THE **HARD-UP TEENAGE BOY**

Here, at your request, is my advice for the hard-up teenage boy:

You're having a hard time getting girls. That sucks. I remember what it was like when I was a young teenager and wanted boys and couldn't get any. It sucked. But the sad fact is that most young teenage boys are repulsive—that is, they are half-formed works in progress. Girls mature physically more quickly than boys, which means most girls your age already look like young women and they're generally attracted to (slightly) older boys—and there you are, aching for your first girlfriend, but still looking like a short, hairless chimp.

But don't despair, HUTB. Your awkward/repulsive stage will pass. In the meantime, here's what you need to do: Worry less about getting your young teenage self laid and start thinking about getting your 18- or 20-year-old self laid. Join a gym and get yourself a body that girls will find irresistible, read—*read books*—so that you'll have something to say to girls (the best way to make girls think you're interesting is to *actually be interesting*), and get out of the house and do shit—political shit, sporty shit, arty shit—so that you'll meet different kinds of girls in different kinds of settings and become comfortable talking with them.

Some more orders: Get a decent haircut and use deodorant and floss your teeth and take regular showers and wear clean clothes. Go online and read about birth control and STIs, and learn enough about female anatomy that you'll be able to find a clitoris in the dark. Masturbate in moderation—no more than 10 times a day—and vary your masturbatory routine. I can't emphasize this last point enough. A vagina does not feel like a clenched fist, HUTB, nor does a mouth, an anus, titty fucking, dry humping, or e-stim. If you don't want to be sending me another pathetic letter in five years complaining about your inability to come unless you're beating your own meat, HUTB, you will vary your routine *now* so that you'll be able to respond to different kinds of sexual stimulation once you do start getting the girls.

Good luck, kiddo.

(The above advice was for a straight teenage boy. Gay teenage boys should read "boys" where I said "girls," "anus" where I said "vagina," "prostate" where I said "clitoris," and "fist" where I said "fist.")

RJ MACCANI is a co-founder and organizer of the Challenging Male Supremacy Project, and a member of the leadership team for generationFIVE. His work focuses on building transformative justice responses to violence against women, queer and trans people, and children. How RJ actually pays the rent living in New York City is another story…

"'You know, you could make a woman feel real good with this thing. Maybe better than she ever felt in her life.' She stopped stroking the dildo. 'Or you could really hurt her, remind her of all the ways she's ever been hurt in her life. You got to think about that every time you strap this on. Then you'll be a good lover.'"

—From the novel *Stone Butch Blues* by Leslie Feinberg

Although often approached with so much silence, sex is rarely a private matter. Sex is online, on billboards, on TV, and (in one way or another, at some time or another) on our minds every day. Sex is used worldwide as a weapon of colonialism, enslavement, and exploitation. The sexual abuse of children, "1 in 3 girls and 1 in 6 boys" say the statisticians, is an early lesson in domination for much of humanity.

I'm a 32-year-old cisgender man. I experienced sexual abuse as a child and teenager. I also grew up in a male supremacist society. I lived with a great fear of sex well into my mid-twenties. I feared that I would find myself having sex that I didn't want, or that the often reckless ways I was sexual with friends and acquaintances would destroy the deep relationships and community-building we needed in the struggle for a better world.

Thanks to the work of organizations such as generationFIVE, generative somatics, and INCITE! Women of Color Against Violence, and the work of individuals like Silvia Federici, Leslie Feinberg, Staci Haines, and Andrea Smith, that fear is transforming.

I'm learning and re-learning how I want to live with sex. The biggest pieces of that are:

★ Building EMOTIONAL INTELLIGENCE AND RANGE (Aren't I feeling a lot *more* than "Good," "Fine," and "OK"?)

★ Gaining the skills and analysis to PREVENT, INTERVENE in, and support HEALING around sexual violence (cuz a lot of us are going through it!)

★ Getting good at CONSENT: Whether it's at home, school, work, or out in the city, for most of us our boundaries are getting crossed without our consent *every day* without so much as a "Do you mind if I…" This really hurts our ability to understand and assert what we want and don't want, and to explore and respect what others want and don't want ("Oh, you want to do that totally kinky thing too? Awesome!")

★ Making decisions around sex based on my highest VALUES ("Having sex with you right now would be fun, and I like to have fun, but I also get the sense that it's gonna totally fuck up our friendship... and I value that more. Wanna go bowling?!")

Sex can be an amazing force for good in our lives. Sure, liberation will not be won solely through having incredible or transgressive sex; but if we pay attention, get engaged, and learn our way around, we might just find in sex a taste of that better world.

LEROY WAN is a 20-year-old performance artist & musician of East Vancouver. One day, Leroy was born. He's been alive ever since.

Dear Leroy,

How are you? I know I haven't gotten in touch with you for a while so I'd thought I'd write you one of those corny cheesy shitty Hallmark letters to tingle your taste buds, just so you know how I'm doing.

Well, to start off, life is a party. I'm still married to music, and I know, by now, I've only had my first sip of a Cosmo and my heels could be bit higher, but my ass looks great. And I've been very good this week, so I am having dessert! But for the longest time, old friend, I haven't been doing so well. For the longest time, my life has been very sheltered.

I went to the party all the other kids went to. I wore what they wore, ate what they ate, drank what they drank from the same cup everyday. I drank the water, a la fountain of ignorance. It didn't hurt me, but I didn't get anything out of it either. And these daily drinks just doped me up and got everyone drunk off these ideas that fitting in was the crème de la crème and everything else was crème de la crap. So since a part of me always knew and always will know I am "different," I felt like crap. (This is where the shitty part of the letter comes in.) And when shit hits the fan, so did I, and I had to deal with all this shit: outside of the club, inside the soiree, and most importantly, inside of me. It was hard, L, let me tell you, but remember Lily's 17th birthday bash when we all wore lingerie instead of bikinis in Robyn's hot tub because his brother's just that right amount of attractiveness that we would still try to impress him? That night we practically bathed in "Baby Duck"? Well, I was pretty smashed, but I totally vowed never to be a party-pooper, right? So I thought, nobody puts baby in the corner! I'm just going to continue to do my own thing, and know in my heart of hearts you will always appreciate my pearl g-string. Eventually, life was a lot like getting over a hangover. There was a lot of greasy food, walks of shame, and coming going on. There was my coming to terms with my identity along with my coming to terms with my sexuality. Then, there was my coming of age, and then, there was my cumming of age.

I was blessed with a wonderful high-school, and my GSA (Gay Straight Alliance) was my AA. They taught me to always have respect for yourself and others; no matter what we are, what we might have or where we come from. They taught me the beauty of friendship, and though sometimes you forsake them as buoys in the sea of love for you to hang onto, when a man swims by, you don't want to let them go. And most appreciably, they taught me not to have any hate or shame for what I believe in.

I used to believe finding your passion and making that your party of life was the key to happiness. But now I know the key to a great time on this journey of ours is not finding one passion but all of them and keeping them around: like my passion for music and performance, my passion to create a positive change in the world by the end of my lifetime and to never shut up, my passion for sex and hopes you inspire someone someday, that though passions can change as time goes on, even when people grow up, grow apart or go up to that great party in the sky; even when nothing ever stays the same; love is eternal.

SHIRA TARRANT is an unconventional feminist redefining gender justice. She is the author of several books and articles, and a professor of Women's, Gender, and Sexuality Studies at California State University, Long Beach. Read more at: shiratarrant.com.

I wish someone had told me a thing or two about sexuality. Not some bullshit kind of message, but the real deal. I wish someone had asked me fair questions and cared about my answers. I wish they hadn't planned to judge me before I even replied.

When I was fourteen, my boyfriend and I started having sex. We ditched school to hang at my friend's house while her parents were at work. On her bed—exactly when we did it for the first time—Dave said that he loved me. I remember thinking, "No you don't. You think you're supposed to say that, but I don't really care if you love me or not. I'm still going for it."

But I digress.

Dave and I drank a lot, especially for fourteen-year-olds. Or maybe *because* were fourteen. Then we turned fifteen. We got wasted. Had sex. Some people called me a slut. Sometimes I wasn't sure I wanted to be having sex but I definitely didn't want to have a reputation. So I felt confused and got wasted some more.

Plenty of adults knew I was sexually active, but nobody asked me the question screaming inside my head. My dad asked if I needed condoms (helpful). My mom asked why I had to be that way, like it was a personal affront to her (not helpful at all). My school guidance counselor asked me details about what my boyfriend and I did together.

With a chronic threat of suspension hanging over my head for ditching class, giving up this info about what Dave and I did naked and letting Mr. Guidance Counselor "help" me seemed like a streetwise trade. But his questions were lecherous. Ten years later, I realized that Mr. Guidance Counselor was a voyeuristic perv. I wish somebody had told me that I had the right to remain silent in the face of abusive grown folk.

All I really needed was for one adult to ask me this simple question: Do you *want* to be having sex?

The answer would have been yes. And no. A jumbled I-don't-know. I needed help figuring out my personal line between pleasure and coercion. I needed to know how to say yes *and* no to sex. I needed unconditional support. I wish someone had asked, "Do you wanna talk about it?" And I wish they'd followed that question with the promise: "I won't judge you."

7. DRUGS

People use drugs for all kinds of reasons, with all kinds of intentions and all kinds of results. Sometimes it is to relieve pain or mitigate disease, sometimes to have fun, sometimes to enhance experience, sometimes for spiritual clarity, sometimes just to relieve pressure. Regardless of what kinds of drugs we're talking about, conversations tend to be fraught with all kinds of judgment and weirdness. But it's totally possible to have straightforward and thoughtful conversations with yourself and others.

Figuring out your relationships with drugs is a key part of being a teenager. The goal should be to get to a place where you know what you will take and why, and to able to make good, solid choices. Self-determination is the key: think through what you want, know why you are doing or not doing drugs (whether it's ibuprofen or something stronger), be realistic and honest about the impacts, and be able to follow through.

A drug is any substance that changes your normal bodily functions when ingested or otherwise introduced into the body. There are many kinds of drugs and they have always been part of life and society, and they will continue to be so whether we want them around or not. Some drugs are used medicinally to improve, heal, or diminish symptoms of physical discomfort or malfunctioning in the body (like antibiotics to get rid of bacterial infections). In this chapter though, we're talking specifically about the use of drugs for their narcotic or stimulant effect in order to enhance sensations, relieve pressures, socialize with peers, explore new forms of consciousness or spirituality, party hard, find a measure of control, relax, or escape from life.

Worldwide, the most common forms of drugs used to alter consciousness are smoking tobacco and drinking alcohol. Smoking cannabis (marijuana) has also become widely popular in the past couple of decades, especially in the global north. There is also the use of natural hallucinogenic (or entheogenic) drugs, such as mushrooms, or synthetic ones such as LSD. Others include the use of stimulants such as cocaine (snorting cocaine or smoking crack), ingesting amphetamines (speed, meth), using opiate derivatives (injecting heroin, smoking opium, drinking cough syrup), among others.

Regardless of the legality or illegality of drugs, what makes drug use difficult is the toll they take on our body and lives. Most drugs, including the legal ones, such as alcohol and cigarettes, may be harmful to our body and our mind if they are used regularly or heavily. The epidemics of tobacco smoke-related cancers and liver disease due to alcohol abuse in North America alone reveal the impact of these substances. With varying degrees of severity, all drugs have impacts on the body, and can alter moods over time, which can bring the drug user to struggle with the management of their life. For some people, this means having difficulty cutting back or stopping, which are signs of drug addiction or dependence. For others, it can mean making risky decisions while under the influence.

Everyone, teens and young adults certainly included, has to deal with drugs on an almost daily basis, whether it's you, family members, friends, or partners using drugs. These drugs might be medicinal or recreational; legal or illegal; the occasional cigarette or the pack a day; the recreational joint or the morning doobie; the after-work drink, the Friday night binge, or the next morning start-up; the after party pill or the weekend acid trip.

Regardless of your relationship with drugs it is critical to be, well, critical: really assess how you interact with drugs, what they are for, and what the results really are. And very fundamentally, regardless of your own decisions around drugs, never, ever force or coerce drugs into other people's lives and bodies!

Most young people struggle sometimes—being a teenager or young adult can be tough—and for many people drugs present themselves as a particular kind of answer to that struggle. As Peter a 21-year-old poet, actor, and stone carver put it:

> Being a Teenager is not easy, being a human being is not easy and when you realize your space in this world… when you are in your teenage years, you are coming to terms with who you are, and what the world around looks like, what it really looks like, and it is not easy at all, your mind is changing, your ideas are changing, your concepts of the world are changing, and not to mention with all the physical and hormonal changes within you… it is a tough time of your life. But it doesn't have to be that hard… I think it is a lot harder now, than say when we had the support of the community, the support of our families, of our grandparents, of our siblings, of our older siblings, and we had guidance… but… you know, the reality is, that does not nec-

essarily exist in every home… and… drugs become a kind of way… in some way of escapism, in other ways… it is just a way, you may think, to help you understand yourself… I left my house when I was 15 years old and because of the circumstances I came into close contact with all kinds of drugs. Whether it was me doing drugs or everyone around me doing drugs, it was always present.

Sometimes drugs appear to be simply a recreational game. There is truth there, but it is important to challenge this view in order to contextualize drugs within frameworks of oppression and understand the larger roles drugs play in our culture.

Jim is a 21-year-old native youth with Fetal Alcohol Syndrome whose family survived residential schools and is now heavily affected by the use of alcohol. Jim has been dwelling in foster homes, the streets, and drugs as long as he can remember. He has a daughter who has been taken away by the Ministry of Children and Family Services, and he is a heavy drug user today:

> I know that I should not be afraid of this turn in my life and should be willing to face the challenge as a person willing to kick it. I know I can do it. I know that not everyone will support me and that is my challenge. I lost my world, I want it back. I know that I can deal with the pain in a healthier and better way. I can't be expecting to get all I've lost back in my life by quitting using, but I will stick with it because that is what I really want and that is important for me and for the people who care for me…

> I know that the feeling I feel as I am writing this isn't how I want to feel. I am looking for the happy things that are real, not somebody's creation. I know what made me happy when everyone said different: it was my girl, but the drugs got in the way. Happiness is like a bonfire, and without her that's nothing more than a spark, and I am done. That is not who I really am and I am sorry to anyone who has to see this or deal with it. I'll show you who I can be, who I was before, who I really was, because I haven't forgotten yet and I don't ever want to.

According to Dr. Gabor Maté, who is a physician heavily involved in working with street addiction: "Instead of asking why the drugs? We should first ask why the pain?" This will refocus our attention from judging a dependent drug user into wondering about each personal history causing the pain leading to their addiction.

That's the question we need to be asking about addiction and drug use in general: what are the root and contextual stories that cause people to use, misuse, and abuse drugs of all kinds? That leads to us think about historical and systemic oppressions, racism, colonialism, disempowerment, familial abuses, and a whole range of interconnected issues—and to understand that problematic drug use is a complex set of issues. Blaming users, criminalizing their behaviour, or attributing drug use (whether it is alcohol or crack) to moral failing is hardly useful. If someone is using aspirin don't judge them for using pain pills, instead, try to understand why they have a headache.

As a young person you are going to be constantly confronted with drugs, as psychoactive substances have been around since pre-historic times and are unlikely to disappear any time soon. Solidarity with those who use drugs (including yourself, your family and friends), and compassion for people with drug problems, should be your basic stand.

Other stuff to check out:

- **RITALIN NATION**, Richard DeGrandpre

- **FAST FOOD NATION** (movie)

- **HOOKED**: A Thriller About Love and Other Addictions, Matt Richtel

- **IN THE REALM OF HUNGRY GHOSTS**: Close Encounters with Addiction, Gabor Maté

- **OVER THE INFLUENCE**: The Harm Reduction Guide for Managing Drugs and Alcohol, Patt Denning, Jeannie Little, Adina Glickman

- **FOOD OF THE GODS**: The Search for the Original Tree of Knowledge A Radical History of Plants, Drugs, and Human Evolution, Terence McKenna

- **GENERATION RX** (film)

KENNETH W. TUPPER holds a Ph.D. and is an Adjunct Professor in the School of Population and Public Health at the University of British Columbia. He researches and writes about drug policy and drug education. See www. kentupper.com for more information about Ken and his work.

Almost all human cultures have a history of using psychoactive substances for medical, spiritual, and social purposes (the Inuit are a notable exception, as before European colonizers brought drugs like alcohol and tobacco, there were no plants or substances in the Arctic that could get them high). There is evidence that humans were using drugs long before we learned to read and write, raise crops and animals on farms, and build cities. The kinds of drugs that early cultures used were primarily plants or simple products made from them, like beer and wine. We had not yet learned to distill alcohol into potent forms like whiskey and rum, or to refine white powders like morphine from opium poppy or cocaine from coca leaf.

Traditional ways of using plant-based drugs were often socially positive. They helped families, friends, and communities bond, or allowed shamans access to visionary realms for healing or spiritual insights. There were often strict rules, taught and modeled by community elders, about when and how to use substances helpfully and safely.

In modern times, drug use has become a much more complex issue. Traditional social or cultural bonds in many places are not as strong as they once were. As a result, people may feel disconnected and seek ways to distract themselves (with not only drugs, but also television, video games, gambling, and other consumerist activities).

Unfortunately, information about the risks of drugs is sometimes exaggerated by police, teachers, parents, and other authorities, in the hope that this will frighten young people into lifetime abstinence. Similarly, information about how to reduce risks or minimize harms is often withheld, because of fears that such knowledge may encourage drug use. So for those who choose other than to "just say no," it is important they learn how to minimize the negative impacts drugs can have on themselves and others.

In 1998, the world's leaders met at the United Nations to discuss how to solve the global drug problem. At the meeting, they made a goal to achieve a "drug-free" world within a decade. When they met again ten years later to reflect on progress towards this goal, they downplayed the fact that drugs are cheaper, more various, and more easily available than ever before.

Instead, they congratulated themselves on their hard work and committed to continue a global war on (some) drugs.

They did not discuss why people who manufacture or use alcohol and tobacco are not considered criminals, but those who simply possess other kinds drugs are often sent to prison. They did not seriously address the fact that many countries where drugs come from, such as Mexico and Afghanistan, as well as places where they end up for sale, such as the United States and Canada, are suffering terrible but preventable drug trade violence. And they did not seem to consider whether trying to achieve a "drug-free" world might be an unrealistic goal.

Young people today need to be aware of the risks of drug use, but equally importantly they need to think about how they can thrive in a world where drugs aren't going away, and be leaders in envisioning sensible laws and policies to reduce their harms.

"Imperialism leaves behind germs of rot which we must clinically detect and remove from our land but from our minds as well."
—Frantz Fanon

CHRYSTAL SMITH is a young aboriginal woman, a proud mother, a loving sister, and a poet.

They Stand (Excerpt)

They Stand there
There; being one busy place
The place; Broadway station

So they stand
"Hang out"
Sometimes they stagger

They drink
They fight
They drink some more

They embody my opposite
They drink
They fall into drugs

They fight one another
They look stupid
They are aboriginal

Ages; young to old
All drinking
All high

I am young
I am aboriginal
I am NOT like them

No
They stand for what I hate
The stereotypical Native
They cry brutality
They cry racism
They are angry with the "white man"

However, I
Who is young
And aboriginal

I, who had a hard life as well,
And had no father
But an alcoholic mother

I, who moved many times,
And witnessed. And felt
Racism
I Am not there

And I am not there
Because I CHOOSE not to be
I choose to be Strong

So those who stand
Stand for what I hate
Realize you don't have to stand
there

Realize what you stand for
Realize what we have to fight
for
And not stand in the way

CHOOSE to be strong
Don't stand for what I hate
Stand strong for our future

PEGGY MILLSON is a Professor Emeritus in the Dalla Lana School of Public Health at the University of Toronto, and is a physician with a specialty in Public Health and Preventive Medicine. She has evaluated harm reduction programs including conducting the first evaluation of Toronto Public Health's needle exchange program in 1990, and an evaluation of Toronto Public Health's Methadone Works program and the Streethealth methadone program in Kingston, Ontario. She is also a member of the team who wrote the "Best Practices for Needle Exchanges in Ontario" document which won the Kaiser award for national leadership in harm reduction in 2006.

What Is Harm Reduction?

People use a variety of drugs for a variety of reasons, with many different results. Two of the primary reasons are to reduce pain, and to create pleasure, or even spiritual experiences. At a relatively recent point in our history, decisions were made that some of these drugs would be illegal and tightly controlled. As a result, a massive illegal market has developed for particular drugs, which are not being successfully prohibited despite huge public spending on law enforcement and imprisonment of users. For drugs like heroin and cocaine, the fact that they are illegal and can only be obtained on the black market means that they are highly expensive. For this and other reasons, users often turn to injecting as the best way to get the maximum effect from these drugs. The stigmatization and discrimination that they experience as people who inject illegal drugs means that they try to hide their drug use. Until the development of needle distribution programs they often had poor access to sterile injection equipment, and a sizable percentage (but by no means all) of them shared equipment.

Then it was realized that hepatitis B, HIV, and hepatitis C are all easily transmitted from one person to another by the tiny amounts of blood that remain in a previously used needle, or in shared injection items like water, filters, cookers, etc. The origin of harm reduction programs was this public health concern about spread of blood-borne diseases among drug injectors, and from them to their sexual partners. The goal of harm reduction programs initially was to make sure that people who inject drugs understood the dangers of sharing equipment, and had sterile equipment readily available when they needed it to prevent sharing. In some places there was concern about used needles being discarded in public, so programs made particular efforts to collect used needles and to encourage program users to return used equipment or dispose of it safely, including giving out personal sharps containers to service users.

Over time, harm reduction programs have moved towards greater advocacy for their clients for things like more reasonable drug laws, better access to housing and to drug treatment, etc. They have helped people reduce their risks for death and serious disease when they continue to use illegal drugs, and as they have developed trust with users, they have also helped people to modify their drug use, and to find treatment when they want to do so. Harm reduction at its best is health promotion for drug users—focused not on drug use alone, but on all the needs and concerns, like history of violence and abuse, poverty, homelessness, mental health problems, that are part of the lives of many people who use illegal drugs.

As more people who use drugs have become engaged in users' groups and in doing paid and unpaid harm reduction work themselves, the understanding of these issues has expanded. The principles of advocacy and empowerment, with a focus on risk environments—not just individual behaviours, but how behaviour change can be supported and made possible—make harm reduction a powerful approach to addressing the needs of the most marginalized people who use illegal drugs, who are in turn among the most vulnerable groups in our society.

On an international level, harm reduction workers and associations have advocated for the human rights of people who use drugs in countries where they can be subject to extremely harsh punishments or even killed for their involvement in drug use. Worldwide, including Canada, imprisonment of illegal drug users is being practiced and expanded in many places despite the evidence that it does not reduce drug use overall, and causes serious harm to the users who are jailed, including risks of becoming infected with HIV and hepatitis C while in prison, as well as further reducing their opportunities to find employment, safe housing, and the like once they are released. Only drug law reform and a commitment to take a more reasonable, evidence-informed approach to drugs and drug use can hope to address many of these harms which are related not to the drugs themselves, but to how society treats users.

To learn more about harm reduction and the many issues involved, check out these websites:

CANADIAN HARM REDUCTION NETWORK:

canadianharmreduction.com

INTERNATIONAL HARM REDUCTION ASSOCIATION:

www.ihra.net

MARK HADEN has been working in the addictions field and providing public education on drugs and addictions for over 25 years. He lectures and publishes widely, has two children, and lives in Vancouver, BC. See www.markhaden.com for more.

AN **APOLOGY** FROM A **DRUG EDUCATOR**

OK, so I lied. I lied about drugs. In my defence I did this with the best of intentions. I really believed that if we could make youth scared of drugs, this fear would result in teens staying safe. As I am now coming clean about my dishonest past I will admit that I told three lies; I exaggerated the harms of drugs, I never acknowledged the benefits of drugs, and I completely avoided any discussion about the harms of drug prohibition. I guess I owe my past students an apology.

This apology is important because we now know that the fear-based approach to prevention actually backfires and contributes to the health and social problems that we are trying to help. As our new goal is "honest drug education/prevention," we need to tell the truth and the best way to start to do this is to confess and discuss our past dishonesty.

When you work for a health service organization you have to learn many "buzz words." The term "evidence-based" is used a lot. By "evidence-based" we mean that we do what actually works and that just feeling good about what we are doing is not enough to justify a program. While it feels good to tell youth that "all drugs are bad" and "bad people do bad drugs," this approach has failed to keep the youth of our society safe. Our new prevention model involves looking at actual evidence for preventing harm from drugs.

So we are working hard at rethinking how to talk with youth about drugs. Notice that I said "talk with" not "talk to" youth. In the old model of drug education I was the ultimate authority who would tell youth how to think about drugs. In the new model we actually ask youth for their own experiences and do not make teens feel bad for telling us what they experience.

The most unfortunate outcome of the old model of prevention was the targeting and marginalizing of the youth who most need our support. In many classrooms there are the youth who sit at the back and never participate if they can avoid it. These teenagers often feel very different and disconnected from the other students and traditional drug education increased their sense of disconnection with the "bad kids use bad drugs message." "Yes," these youth use more drugs and are more likely to develop a drug addiction but the reasons for this are complex. There are many reasons why teens develop health and social problems and we call these "risk factors." On the list of "risk factors" are physical, sexual, and emotional abuse. Other things, like coming hungry to school, and not having a loving parent at home and available to you when you need it are also really important. The new model of drug education actually talks about the real reasons kids develop problems and explicitly states that one of the goals is to help youth to support each other and to reach out to (and not shun) the teens who appear to be disconnected from most school activities.

The first lie I told was to exaggerate the harms of drugs. The old message that "all illegal drugs are bad" has to go if we are going to tell the truth about drugs. "No," drugs don't make holes in your brain and most drugs don't kill brain cells. In fact the drug which does the most damage to people's brain cells is alcohol which is not even considered to be a drug. The new message is a little more complex, as we now say "any drug can be used and any drug can be abused." Any drug has potential benefits and harms depending on the context of use of the drug. For example cocaine, when purified, concentrated, and smoked or injected, tends to be associated with many health and social problems for example, cocaine psychosis. This is drug abuse, but in a different cultural context, cocaine can be used without problems. In South America chewing coca leaf or drinking coca tea is perceived as being beneficial by the huge number of people who use it. Heroin can also be used or abused. Overdosing with an injection of heroin is an abuse but when heroin is given to opiate drug addicts in a supervised health setting their behaviour and health improves. This is a beneficial use of heroin. Psychedelics (e.g. mushrooms) can also be used or abused. A teenager who takes an unknown dosage of an unknown mushroom in an unsafe setting and has a bad trip has abused this drug. Psychedelics can also be used in a beneficial way. Psychedelics have been used for centuries by various aboriginal groups in accordance with ancient spiritual belief systems. Individuals who use in this context are guided by an experienced elder in the process, and the positive outcomes range from increased connections to community to strengthening positive spiritual belief systems. Cannabis can also be used or abused. If an underweight AIDS patient smokes cannabis and gains weight this is a good thing. If a teenager smokes cannabis before a class and is distracted from the learning process, this is a problem and therefore an abuse of the drug. The conclusion from the above examples is that if we are going to have an honest discussion about drugs then we can often start with the observation that the difference between drug use and drug abuse is often about the context of the use of the drugs. Honest prevention programs support an open discussion about all of these issues.

The third lie which has been told by traditional drug educators like myself is "drug prohibition is needed to protect our youth." We said that jail is a useful deterrent to crime. Neither of these is true as sending youth to jail is actually sending them to crime school and drug prohibition paradoxically maximizes involvement of youth in drug use. One of the unintended consequences of drug prohibition is that now high schools are primary distribution points for drugs in our society. Illegal drug dealers never ask youth for age ID. The old drug education model said that drugs caused violence. The new model is willing to acknowledge that drug prohibition is the main reason that drugs and violence are connected. The same violence happened with alcohol prohibition when murderous gangsters ruled the alcohol trade. An honest approach to drug education acknowledges the failures of drug prohibition and openly explores other non-criminalizing ways of controlling drugs in our society. When we discuss non-prohibitionist ways of controlling currently illegal drugs we need to be guided by evidence and not by fear.

If youth and adult prevention workers walk the path of honesty together we will go to some very interesting new places. We will discuss the fact that drug use has been around throughout human history and usually without health or social problems. For example we can discuss the question, "is entheogenic education helpful?" Entheogen is a term used to describe psychedelic drugs when used in traditional aboriginal spiritual contexts, often in family groups.

I am going to end by making two suggestions for those youth who want to be powerfully radical. If you want to change the world and get adults to stop giving you the old messages and lying to youth about drugs you will need to be a person with credibility and clout. In order to do this, my first suggestion is: behave as though you have power in the classroom. Show up to class on time with your homework done and ask very pointed questions about the failures of drug prohibition. Second, work hard to support prevention workers who are trying to tell the truth. Specifically if drug educators are willing to acknowledge that not all drug use is bad, teens need to acknowledge that "not all drug use is good." A good way to start this is to acknowledge that many teens have died from combining intoxication with driving. In order to have an open discussion everyone needs to be willing to explore new ideas.

So I lied about drugs and now I have confessed, which is a good start, but if others continue to lie about drugs the problems will persist. Youth will not trust adults to give them good information about drugs and other important issues. I have done my part in the process of change. If you want to be a powerful radical, go for it. Now it is up to you.

DAWN PALEY is a freelance journalist who splits her time between Vancouver and Mexico. She's also a founding member of the Vancouver Media Co-op.

Maybe you've heard of something called the war on drugs. Maybe not. Either way, here's a sketch: the words "war on drugs" were first uttered by disgraced US President Richard Nixon in 1969. The logic of the war on drugs is based around the idea of prohibition, or that making certain narcotics illegal protects the population. Prohibition is based on moral and social panics, and not based on science or medical research, which has generally pointed to the fact that drug addiction is a medical issue and not a criminal issue.

What large scale prohibition effectively does is create exaggerated markets for substances deemed illegal, boosting the power of the mafia, while also increasing the power of police, jailers, and repressive state forces, who criminalize individuals, communities, and neighborhoods because they allegedly produce, carry, or use drugs.

The war on drugs means different things in different places. The primary consequence lived by people on the ground is increased social control.

In Colombia, the US carried out a major anti-drugs program known as Plan Colombia between 2000–2006. Since Plan Colombia was launched, the US government has spent over $3.6 billion on narcotics and law enforcement initiatives. Yet the US government itself reports "Colombia remains one of the world's largest producers and exporters of cocaine, as well as a source country for heroin and marijuana."

Much of the know-how for supposed anti-drugs initiatives in Colombia and Mexico flowed from US experiments in other countries, including Afghanistan and Burma. US diplomats, police, and otherwise shuffle around to and fro, bringing different forms of the drug war with them wherever they go.

The drug war as it has been unfolding in Mexico since December 2006, is far more than a drug prevention initiative. Instead, it appears poised to re-open Mexico's economy to foreign direct investment, in part through legal changes connected to the supposed fight against drugs, and in part through the militarization of the country.

What we learn about the so-called drug war on TV and in the newspaper rarely connects this style of war with the expansion of corporate control over new territories and markets. But this is just what happened in Colombia, and it is what appears to be happening in Mexico.

When you read about the drug war, remember, wars aren't fought against terror or drugs. They're fought against people, often in territories rich in resources.

ISAAC K. OOMMEN is Communications Coordinator for the BC Compassion Club Society, the oldest and largest medical cannabis dispensary and wellness center in Canada. He has provided cannabis education and harm reduction workshops for service providers and contributed to media on drug policy. Syrian Nasrani by birth, he grew up in the Gulf Middle East and traveled the peninsula as well as south Asia before coming to Sto:lo and then the unceded Coast Salish Territories.

"Drugs are bad. You shouldn't do them; because if you do them, you're bad, m'kay?" says Mr. Mackey, the school counselor on an episode of South Park. This bit of satire sheds light on the sordid state of drug education in Turtle Island.

An early piece of wisdom given to me when I got to Vancouver was, "Only take what you can handle, and always know your dealer."

But what about the idea that weed bought on the street can be laced with other drugs?

In this sense I would approach cannabis (and any other drug) as a relationship not just with yourself but also your personal and social history. In these unceded Coast Salish Territories or elsewhere on Turtle Island, the process of colonization brings inter-generational trauma to everything. Plants that have been removed from their spiritual traditions and harvested in mass for profit using chemical fertilizer and pesticides are far less healing for the body, with or without being laced with other drugs.

During my first year working at the BC Compassion Club Society (BCCCS), I met TJ: a local hip-hop aficionado who started smoking cannabis at 18 to deal with inflammation brought on by fibromyalgia. I also got to see an eight-year-old boy come in with his parents to access medicine. He had facial tumours from cancer that left him in pain, which could be relieved by eating cannabis-infused baked goods and tinctures.

The reality for those accessing cannabis is very different than the images shown on television and film. The majority of BCCCS's new members are 55+, often people who have never tried cannabis before. At the same time, there are also members who have tried pot in their youth and are confronting the stigma associated with the medicine.

To the person picking up a joint for the first time I'd ask—what are you trying to treat? What is it that is making you take comfort in the cannabis?

There are a myriad of folks out there who are "recreationally" using cannabis, but in actuality need it to control their anxiety, depression, pain, or inflammation. Realizing what you are treating is key to actual healing.

The BCCCS advocates for clean, safe cannabis grown in small quantities without the use of chemical pesticides or fertilizer. We also provide a number of other services on-site, from counseling to reiki and massage. Balanced with alternative modalities, cannabis can be the gateway to holistic healing.

Any herbalist will tell you that healing, with cannabis or any other herb, requires understanding the relationship between you, the medicine, and your personal/ intergenerational trauma.

Image by aly de la Cruz

8. MEDIA

Media dominates our lives, and no one more so than youth. Most of us spend more time consuming media than doing anything else, including sleeping or going to school or work. By some estimates the average kid multitasks enough to pack 31 hours' worth of media activity into every 24 hours. What is youth culture today if not Facebook, cell phones, and texting? How weird would that have sounded twenty years ago? How weird will it sound in twenty years?

What are we even talking about when we talk about media? Not that long ago it was pretty clear what "mediated communication" meant: it was TV, magazines, radio. Now what the hell isn't mediated? And what were once distinct technologies have merged so that your phone, television, net access, music and movie source, advertising exposure, communication network, information source, and primary entertainment are all conflated and merged into one seamless flow. And by all indications that trajectory we are on towards digital communication and information dispersal is only going to intensify.

There is plenty to feel nervous or cynical about in a world made of screens, but that's only a starting point: the idea is to critically engage with this ocean of mass media, pop culture, and technology and learn how to swim. What parts of media culture are worth incorporating into your life, which are worth rejecting? Which new technologies are possibly making the world a better place, which are degrading it? Do new forms of social media deepen democratic possibilities, or cheapen it? What kind of media generate radical social change, and what happens then?

Beware of clichés (always, but when thinking about media for sure). Sometimes people will claim that the internet makes everything more open, makes governments accountable. Sure, in some ways, but it also makes authority that much more powerful, corporations that much more capable of dominating our lives, and government that much more invasive. Cell phones with video capacity are very useful for activists in demonstrations, but maybe more useful for cops. It is often said that the internet saves trees, lets people talk without ever having to drive to meet, and is thus essentially "green." Think again: the internet is gobbling ever-more-massive chunks of (often dirty) power and will soon pass transportation as the worst climate-change culprit.

But also recognize and appreciate that we all get a lot of pleasure and inspiration from pop-culture and technology: some of it is from brilliant, thoughtful pieces of art, but some of it is from cheesy, ironic, sleazy, dumb, and ignorant stuff too. No one should "feel bad" for liking *Jersey Shore*, *Americans Idol*, Ke$ha, WWE wrestling, "Grand Theft Auto" or whatever—but be really alert to what they are saying, how they affect your body and mind, and what kind of world they are suggesting. We all have critical faculties, we can appreciate irony, we can laugh at inappropriate comedy—but make sure you stay critical and articulate about what is going on. In a world made of media we are neither totally helpless nor totally free.

And that's what we hope for all of us: to stay critical. The goal of being "media literate" is a solid one: learn how to "read" the media (use your analytical faculties always and be alert and thoughtful) but also be able to "write" (participate: write, make zines, movies, music, websites, etc.). That will give you a chance to talk back and fight back.

OTHER STUFF TO CHECK OUT:

- **MANUFACTURING CONSENT** (movie)

- **OUT OF YOUR BACKPACK MEDIA** (online)

- **RACEBENDING** (online)

- **PROMETHEUS RADIO PROJECT** (organization)

- **BORN IN FLAMES** (movie)

- **EXIT THROUGH THE GIFT SHOP** (movie)

- **BOMB IT**: The Global Graffiti Documentary (movie)

- **BARAKA** (movie)

- **PRAXIS PROJECT** (organization)

ANDREA SCHMIDT is a journalist, producer, and border-crosser who grew up in the anti-globalization movement and spent her twenties organizing with social justice movements in Montréal and Toronto. Currently Washington DC-based, she works for an international news network. Tweets: @whatescapes.

Dear comrades,

I'm writing you with the urgency to communicate that great beauty and tremendous horror inspire. This letter begins in Northern Kenya's arid lands. With my team, I'm working on a TV documentary about drought, climate change, and hunger.

A journalist by trade, my interpretation of the news these days is that we're heading into difficult times, in which the disparities that divide us will grow greater, more unjust, and more deadly unless we manage almost unthinkably massive global transformations. Working in the shadow of what now exists, we need to build economics, energy systems, and governance structures that let us honour our shared life together on this planet.

We're in this struggle together. And "media" are simply tools, if and as we strip away corporate and state ownership of "the media" and the interests they represent.

So this is an invitation to become the media—as activists in the Indymedia movement have exhorted—and to use the tools.

An incomplete list of what the tools can do:

* amplify voices that are stifled by prison walls, or ignored by politicians and corporations

* hold mirrors up to our societies to show us what we look like in our pettiness and despair, in our propensity for cruelty and destruction, and also in our moments of compassion, steadfastness and brilliance

* build bridges for our communities (of the criminalized, dehumanized, vilified, occupied, colonized, dispossessed, pushed-out-of-sight and their allies) to walk across in order to meet

Also, bridges of the moat-spanning kind that allow us to storm the fortresses of power. Tell stories.

And stories are powerful things—whether they're told in a photograph or in 24 frames per second, in feature-length articles or 140 characters. They can teach the histories of resistance that are the foundation of struggle, and inspiration to change. They can call the powerful to account, cast new political horizons, provoke us to recognize each other and foster solidarity in isolating times. Good stories are a matter of life or death.

The tools aren't perfect, and neither are we. As we use them and innovate new ones, we also learn, sometimes painfully, what knowledge, experiences, and privileges we lack—or what knowledge, experiences, and privileges we have—that make some things invisible, unrecognizable, or unspeakable to us. That's ok. If we're honest, using the tools forces us to develop a practice of attending to what escapes the frame, and a healthy respect for all that exists beyond the stories we're able to tell on our own.

That's how the re-building of a just and sustainable world together begins. At least, that's how it looks when I picture it in my heart, and when I've caught glimpses of it in our shared history. And I wanted you to see it too.

Love,

a

CHRIS CARLSSON is a long-time agitator, writer, satirist, publisher, and historian in San Francisco, where he co-edited the notorious underground magazine *Processed World* for over a decade, helped launch the monthly Critical Mass bike rides that have spread across the world, and co-directs Shaping San Francisco, a living archive of San Francisco's real history. He has edited five anthologies, written a futurist science fiction novel, *After the Deluge*, and a nonfiction look at a new politics of work called *Nowtopia*.

ZINES

"Let's start a zine!" Excellent idea! These days, starting a publication is probably easier than it has ever been, but that doesn't mean it's easy. There are many pitfalls and frustrations that go with the territory, so here's some food for thought.

There are a number of technical considerations to take into account when planning a zine, especially if you are doing it for the first time. What size? How many pages? What binding? Where to make the copies? How much hand-made art do you want to put into the project? There will be people you know who can give you good advice on these issues, from choosing an easily reproduced format, to finding free copying and free paper.

Think carefully about how many to make. The distribution side of zines is not a small problem. If you want to make it free, then distribution will be entirely your own problem, and it can be surprisingly difficult to put dozens or hundreds or thousands of copies into the world in a way that doesn't lead directly to a dumpster. If you want to charge enough to pay for printing the next issue, look into the distributors who will take a first-time effort, how many they usually accept, what kind of financial deal they'll make with you.

More important than the technical side is the purpose of your zine. What do you have to say? Who cares? I ask this last question not because I think you should direct your energies to writing for a perceived audience, but because I want you to answer emphatically, "I CARE!" If you aren't producing this zine first and foremost for yourself, your project will not be very interesting to anyone else either. So what's interesting to you? What matters? A zine depends on your literary or journalistic voice. Pay attention to and trust your own experience, interview friends and family. Real life, real history is in the air you breathe—stop and notice it, write about it!

Having established that you're in it for yourself, MAKE IT READABLE! If you hand scrawl the whole thing with illegible penmanship, it might be interesting as abstract art, but it's not communicating with anyone. Think about the art of the publication. Make it beautiful! Most importantly, enjoy the process! It's really fun!

ANDALUSIA KNOLL is a Brooklyn-based multimedia journalist, popular educator, and organizer. She has facilitated workshops around community media as an organizing tool with groups across the US and Latin America working on prison issues, immigrant rights, & land struggles. (Big Ups to all my fellow media educators who taught me the logo/plant exercise and inspired me to adapt it for the 2011 internet era.)

Let's say you're in NYC walking to the subway to go school. You see the green subway entry posts sandwiching an advertisement of some sexy lady selling you the latest fashionable headphones, you enter the station and wait on the subway platform among walls plastered with movie ads, the train arrives, you get on, sit down, look up and there it is again, more advertising! Mind you, this bombardment of images and propaganda was all in the course of five minutes. I know what you're thinking, "I don't pay attention to that crap and it doesn't really affect me," but is that really true? Let's do this exercise as a case in point:

Look at this alphabet:

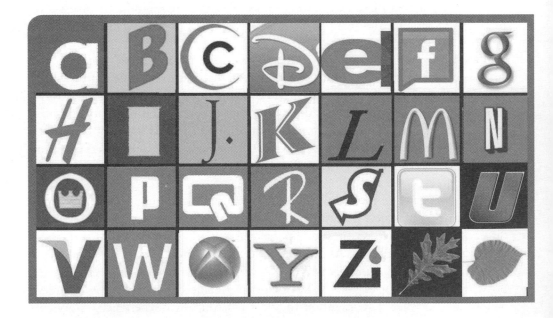

How many of these letters come from corporate logos that you can recognize? Look at the plant pictures next to the logos? How many of the plants can you recognize? Do they grow in your area? What are their names?

What does it mean that we can recognize all these corporate logos but not our natural surroundings? What does it mean when we can't pass five minutes without being bombarded with tons of advertising created by people who spent millions of dollars scheming how they could get us to buy certain things?

As women and especially teenage girls, how are these advertisements portraying us and what are the magazines that we read (or at least other teens, if you have already rejected them) saying to us? If we look at any teen magazine be it *Seventeen* or *Essence*, we will see incredibly sexualized images of girls our age. Then we can take quizzes to find out which celebrity we should be, which makeup will suit us best, or which expensive jeans would look just right on our legs.

How do we reclaim our lives from this negative advertising? We can make our own media, Damnit!!! Get together with your friends and think about the issues that you actually care about—is it the fact that your school lacks funding and supplies, or that your area is too rural to get internet? Research the back story, why is it that way? Then decide what medium you wanna go for—you can rock it old school... write your thoughts and research down, lay them out zine style with some drawings and photos on paper, take to the nearest copy shop then distribute to your friends, fellow students. Or you can make a video using your cell phone, iPod, or with a Flip camera (between $50 and $100). Go up to random people on the street or in your school and ask them what they think of teen curfews or immigrant rights or whatever. Make sure you ask open ended questions instead of "yes" and "no" ones. For example "What kind of impact do you think curfews will have on teenagers?" instead of "Do you think curfews are bad?" Edit a variety of responses using quick free editing software like Windows Media Editor, iMovie, or an open source one you find online, and then upload to YouTube or Vimeo. Share links and also hold an in-person screening. And *Boo-Yeah* you're making your own media.

Don't just hate the media.
Be the media.

CORIN BROWNE is a media maker, community artist, parent, and prairie transplant laying down roots in East Vancouver. Her current projects include: planning a large scale media institute exploring creative solutions to the housing crisis, a documentary about the Purple Thistle as a counter institution, and a digital storytelling project with seniors.

For two years, I worked with a group of young folks in my neighborhood to create a pirate television station. We hoped to re-embrace a dying technology in our digital age—the analogue TV broadcast. In the process, we learned an enormous amount about each other and our neighbors. We soldered circuit boards, shot video, and met for countless hours to write our manifesto. Although we gathered to build a pirate TV station, you could follow our steps for any creative, radical, community building process—zines, radio broadcasts, community theatre!

1. BECOME CRITICALLY MEDIA LITERATE

★ Hone your skills as both a media consumer and producer. Learn to be a critical, not passive viewer and seek out opportunities to create challenging, meaningful videos

2. GET TO KNOW YOUR COMMUNITY

★ Your community will be defined by your broadcast range. Deepen your understanding of your neighbourhood, its inhabitants and their support for community produced TV. Do cultural and social research by meeting with local historians, activists, and artists.

3. KNOW WHERE OTHERS HAVE BEEN BEFORE

★ Investigate the history of community video to avoid a stereotypical ahistorical point of view. Ask questions about cable access community video and other media education experiments. Look at other work to develop a "community video" barometer. What makes a good piece? What can you learn other groups?

★ Let theory help. Become or seek out someone who will explore academic knowledge to enhance your community-based research. If you are in high school or university, get credit, dammit! The learning you instigate and take responsibility for is usually the most meaningful and relevant.

4. WRITE A MANIFESTO

★ Individually and collectively, you need to get very clear on why you are doing this, how you will make decisions (cooperatively, consensus, or participatory democracy, for a few examples), what limitations you will place on content (if any), who can broadcast, and how you are going to work with your community. You also need to decide who takes responsibility if you get caught, and how that will play out. Your manifesto should balance the interests of the smash-Starbucks-direct-action-oriented activists with the more academic-leaning-let's-use-video-as-a-capacity-building-tool artists.

5. BEG, BORROW, OR UMM, LIBERATE EQUIPMENT

★ Get a decent, working videocamera. For your work to be more than just watchable, you'll need a good microphone, headphones, a tripod, a bounce-board for basic lighting, and a computer to edit on.

6. CREATE THE CONTENT

★ Aspire to both a technical proficiency and specific communication goals. Don't re-broadcast cringe-worthy YouTube cat-movies. What do you want to say to your neighborhood? Don't shy away from artistic or challenging content—stick with your collaborative goals, but push your storytelling boundaries. There are no 22 min. "half hour" time slots in pirate TV land.

★ Find local filmmakers and writers to act as mentors—but on your own terms!

7. BUILD A TRANSMITTER, AMPLIFIER, AND ANTENNA (AND PUT IT SOME-WHERE SAFE)

★ The easiest, but also the non-law abiding part. The internet has info on how to build your own transmitter. Whoever "owns" the tower, "owns" the danger of discovery, fines, and potential criminal charges.

★ Be prepared to help people track down old-school TV sets with antennas. These are the huge cathode-ray tube monsters filling up landfills everywhere.

8. GUERRILLA MARKET YOUR STATION

★ Let people know what you are up to, and when you plan to broadcast. Spray-paint sidewalk stencils, t-shirts, or your bodies with a logo, channel, and time.

9. FLIP THE SWITCH

★ Combine pirate broadcast with guerrilla screenings to raise awareness about your station and the issues in your videos.

★ Construct neighborhood screening stations so folks can gather, watch, and talk.

10. REFLECT (CONTINUOUSLY) AND KEEP A RECORD

★ Share your successes and failures, so that others may do the same. How does this project fit into your larger idea of social change? How effective is this medium as a vehicle for community engagement? How can you balance the historical tension between process and product? Will you commit to both engaged storytelling and a high technical standard? Will you rebroadcast digitally on YouTube or stick to old-school tech?

THE GUERRILLA GIRLS are feminist masked avengers in the tradition of anonymous do-gooders like Robin Hood, Wonder Woman, and Batman. They use facts, humor, and outrageous visuals to expose discrimination and corruption in politics, art, film, and pop culture. They undermine the idea of a mainstream narrative by revealing the understory, the subtext, the overlooked, and the downright unfair. They've unveiled anti-film industry billboards in Hollywood just in time for the Oscars, dissed the Museum of Modern Art, New York, at its own Feminist Futures Symposium, and created large scale projects for the Venice Biennale and the Centre Pompidou, Paris, and have executed projects in Istanbul; Mexico City; Athens; Rotterdam; Bilbao; Sarajevo; Shanghai; Ireland; and Montréal. They are authors of stickers, billboards, posters, street projects, and several books including *The Guerrilla Girls' Bedside Companion to the History of Western Art*; *Bitches, Bimbos and Ballbreakers: The Guerrilla Girls' Guide to Female Stereotypes*; *The Guerrilla Girls' Art Museum Activity Book*; and *The Guerrilla Girls' Hysterical Herstory of Hysteria and How it Was Cured, from Ancient Times Until Now.*

The Guerrilla Girls' Guide to Behaving Badly (Which You Have to Do Most of the Time in the World as We Know It)

Be crazy. Political art that points to something and says, "This is bad" is preaching to the choir. Instead, try to change people's minds in some unforgettable way. Here's a trick we learned: use humor. If you can get people who disagree with you to laugh at an issue, you have a much better chance to convert them.

Be an outsider. Even if you are working inside the system, we say act like an outsider. Seek out the understory, the subtext, the overlooked, and the downright unfair. Then expose it.

Just do one thing. If it works, do another. If it doesn't, do another anyway. Don't be paralyzed if you don't get it right every time. Just keep chipping away. We promise that, bit by bit, your efforts will add up to something effective.

Complain, complain, complain. But be a creative complainer. And don't assume people already know the facts about an issue: tell them. When we put up banners and billboards about the pathetically low number of women and people of color in art collections—or working in the film industry—people tell us how shocked they are that they didn't know this stuff before.

Use the F word—Feminism. We think it's crazy that so many people who believe in the tenets of feminism—equal access to education, equal opportunity for women, reproductive rights, freedom from sexual abuse and exploitation—still stop short of calling themselves feminists. Women's rights, civil rights, lesbian, gay, and trans rights are the great human rights movements of our time. Feminism doesn't get the respect it deserves. It changed the world, revolutionized human thought, and gave many women lives their great grandmothers could never have imagined.

Last, but not least, be a great ape. In 1917, Franz Kafka wrote a short story called "A Report to an Academy," where an ape talks about what it's like to be held captive by a bunch of stultified academicians. The story Kafka published ends with the ape tamed and broken. But in an earlier draft, Kafka told a different story. In that draft, the ape instructs his fellow prisoners to "break the bars of your cages, bite a hole through them, squeeze through an opening."

Let's all make that our ending, not the tamed and broken one. Rattle your cages, everyone!

And don't forget to have fun along the way!

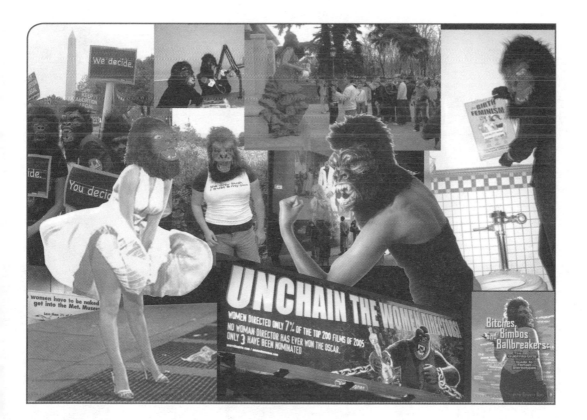

9. RELATIONSHIPS

Relationships are the stuff of life. You can try to stay in bed all day with the covers over your head and not come out of your room, but at some point you have to get out there. Whether we like it or not, we're all social beings who live in this world, meet all kinds of people, fall in love, have friendships, make enemies, hang out with randoms, talk to people in stores, say hey to the neighbours, stay close to people for decades. It's all part of living an interesting life, and in lots of ways the quality of life is governed by the quality of your relationships.

In this chapter we're talking about all kinds of relationships: sexual, romantic, friendly, familial, occasional, fraught, tendentious, and everything in-between. But we're contending that there is a thread that runs through all good relationships, elements that we can look for, recognize, learn from, and create. We're not suggesting that you treat everybody the same, nor should you expect that everyone will treat you in the exact same way. Like Gloria Steinem once said, "Equality means treating people differently," and we can treat everyone with respect, love, dignity, and humour, and lots else.

That's not to claim that there's an easy formula for navigating relationships, but how do we build a world of relationships around us that are meaningful and give us the support, love, humour, and critique that we need? How come we always end up too high, too drunk, and/or in jail every time we hang out with certain friends? How do we have empathy for others and how do we build trust, fun, and creativity into our relationships? How do we make up when we fuck up? How do we build real, long-lasting relationships that are good for us? How do we communicate when relationships are hurtful and painful? How might we end relationships in a responsible way? What does consent mean? What is respect, really?

These and a host of similar questions are the most compelling questions of everyday life and really are the building blocks for an ethical life. But we're arguing here that there is something so important about the idea of *friendship*. Whether it's our relationships with pals, lovers, family members, or with people on the street, *friendship* is the not the fruit of good relationships, but the root. Treating people right and getting treated right is more than just a nice, pleasant thing, it is the radical presumption of possibility.

"Either you respect people's capacities to think for themselves, to govern themselves, to creatively devise their own best ways to make decisions, to be accountable, to relate, problem-solve, break-down isolation and commune in a thousand different ways… OR: you dis-respect them. You dis-respect ALL of us."

—Ashanti Alston

OTHER STUFF TO CHECK OUT:

- **THEIR EYES WERE WATCHING GOD**, Zora Neale Hurston

- **THE GOD OF SMALL THINGS**, Arundhati Roy

- **ALL ABOUT LOVE**, bell hooks

- **INVISIBLE MAN**, Ralph Ellison

- **RED EMMA SPEAKS**, Emma Goldman

- **DANGEROUS ANGELS**: The Weetzie Bat Books, Francesca Lia Block

- **BLANKETS**, Craig Thompson

- "**DORIS**" (zine)

- **DERAILING FOR DUMMIES** (online)

SASSAFRAS LOWREY is an award-winning author, artist, and educator who believes that storytelling is a tool of social change. To learn more about Sassafras visit www.PoMoFreakshow.com and www.KickedOutAnthology.com.

As a teenage activist I made a promise that when I grew up I wouldn't be like the adults I saw, by that I mean I swore that I wouldn't tell youth what to do. I'm not going to tell you what to do, but I will share with you what has worked for me.

Family, the one that I built once I escaped the one I was born into, is what saved me. I believe that as queer folks there is nothing more radical we can do than to build the kind of family we've never even dared dream of.

I left home as a teenager, stumbling out of my county and into the closest city, hungry for connection, for community. I built family with the other queer kids I found who were as crusty, dirty, and lonely as I was. In the years before I escaped my parents I would dream about finding groups of kids like me. Even as a small child I would fantasize about running away and finding kids that understood what it felt like to hurt, who grew up scared and skittish. More nights than I can count I rocked myself to sleep with that dream never knowing if it was something I could really find. When I did, it was like coming home.

I built family in the back of queer youth centers. We claimed each other, becoming brothers, sisters, parents in ways that would never fit onto the family trees we all drew in elementary school. We created something more real than the families we ran away from, escaped from, were thrown away by. Created family is the one who loves you when no one else will. They are the ones who understand your pronouns, who value what's important to you, and who do not shy away from your scars and stories.

> "I believe that as queer folks there is nothing more radical we can do than to build the kind of family we've never even dared dream of."

IVAN ILLICH was an uncategorizable writer, scholar, historian, anarchist, Catholic priest, polymath, social critic, and founder of the Centre for Intercultural Documentation (CIDOC) in Cuernavaca, Mexico. His books include *Deschooling Society, Tools for Conviviality, Medical Nemesis,* and *Energy and Equity.* This piece is excerpted from a 1996 interview by Jerry Brown of KPFA's "We the People" radio show.

Friendship, in the old tradition, was always viewed as the highest point which virtue can reach. Virtue, meaning here, "the habitual facility of doing the good thing," which is fostered by what the Greeks called *politaea*, political life, community life. I know it was a political life in which I wouldn't have liked to participate, with the slaves around and with the women excluded, but I still have to go to Plato or Cicero. They conceived of friendship as a supreme flowering, of the interaction which happens in a good political society.

I do not believe that friendship today can flower out —can come out—of political life. I do believe that if there is something like a political life to be—to remain for us, in this world of technology—then it begins with friendship.

Therefore my task is to cultivate disciplined, self-denying, careful, tasteful friendships. Mutual friendships always. I-and-you and, I hope, a third one, out of which perhaps community can grow. Because perhaps here we can find what the good is.

While once friendship in our western tradition was the supreme flower of politics, I think that if community life exists at all today, it is in some way the consequence of friendship cultivated by each one who initiates it. This goes beyond anything which people usually talk about, saying each one of you is responsible for the friendships he/she can develop, because society will only be as good as the political result of these friendships.

Here is the right word. Hospitality was a condition consequent on a good society in politics, *politaea*, and by now might be the starting point of *politaea*, of politics. But this is difficult because hospitality requires a threshold over which I can lead you—and TV, internet, newspaper, the idea of communication, abolished the walls and therefore also the friendship, the possibility of leading somebody over the door. Hospitality requires a table around which you can sit and if people get tired they can sleep. You have to belong to a subculture to say, we have a few mattresses here. It's still considered highly improper to conceive of this as the ideal moments in a day or a year. Hospitality is deeply threatened by the idea of personality, of scholastic status.

I do think that if I had to choose one word to which hope can be tied it is hospitality. A practice of hospitality—recovering threshold, table, patience, listening, and from there generating seedbeds for virtue and friendship on the one hand—on the other hand radiating out for possible community, for rebirth of community.

Image by aly de la Cruz

How to Heal a Broken Heart in 10 Steps
— Tasnim Nathoo (see p. 306 for bio) —

Romantic love isn't the only cause of a broken heart. These steps work equally well for a heart filled with sadness for any reason. Even the best of us get wounded, there's no shame in taking some time out to heal and re-invent yourself. Proceed gently and with compassion.

It's a truth universally acknowledged that hearts do break. However, it is often forgotten that they do heal. Quite speedily in some cases and quite slowly in others. You never really know which category your heart is going to fall in, but the important thing to remember is that hearts do heal.

1. Repeat silently or aloud and frequently: "My heart knows how to heal even if I don't."

    Broken hearts result from a range of events: failed loves, strained families, intergenerational hurts, oppressive societies, lack of empathy, an inability to trust, and overwhelming fear are just a few I can mention.

2. Write down what you think caused your heart to break. Other people might have different explanations, but for today, this is your personal truth. Remind yourself: "This is what happened to me. But it's not who I am."

    Pick up the pieces. Broken hearts can leave a mess behind them.

3. Apologize to the people you need to, wash your face, go for a walk, clean up the house, and take a break from feeling sorry for yourself.

    Some people think that if your heart is broken that you can't love anyone or anything until it's healed. This is not true.

4. Find another thread of love in your life and hold onto it. Love your friend, your mother, your dog, your little sister, a social movement, surfing, god, Mother Earth, an afternoon free for napping.

    The past does not determine the future. Broken hearts can be a little stupid sometimes and can sneakily convince your brain that this is true.

5. Identify broken heart-induced faulty thinking and banish these thoughts from your vicinity. You know the ones I'm talking about. "I'm cursed in love." "People like me only get one chance." "I will never love again." "I'm just like _____." "The world is too hard. Why bother trying anymore?"

Have you ever tried to draw a heart? It's pretty hard to make them even and perfect. But you still know it's a heart, don't you? And they still make you smile, right?

6. Remind yourself that lopsided, shattered and re-glued, and misshapen hearts are still hearts and can do exactly what perfect, untouched hearts do—love.

    Broken hearts can unearth lots of big questions. That's okay. You don't have to find the answers to them all. Some of the questions might not even have answers. Some might take a lifetime to answer.

7. Take a look at yourself and your life. Ask yourself "What's one thing I can learn from all of this? What do I know now that will help me move forward?"

    Laugh at yourself. Joy and sadness are closely intertwined. We don't always have to do things the hard way, right?

8. Ask yourself "What strangeness, quirk or absurdity has my broken heart revealed?"

    Broken hearts rarely result from one clean blow. Whatever the circumstances and events that led up to your broken heart, remind yourself that you survived. Use this same strength to help you heal.

9. Catalogue your strengths and ways of coping and surviving. Repeat "I am strong and I will get through this, no doubt about it."

    Just like we trust that a seed will sprout and a flower will bloom, trust that your heart will heal.

10. Plant a seed, metaphorically or literally, and wait.

Repeat these steps as often as needed.

CHING-IN CHEN is the author of *The Heart's Traffic* (Arktoi Books/Red Hen Press) and co-editor of *The Revolution Starts at Home: Confronting Intimate Violence Within Activist Communities* (South End Press). She is a Kundiman and Lambda Fellow, part of the Macondo and Voices of Our Nations Arts Foundation writing communities, and has worked in the San Francisco, Oakland, Riverside, and Boston Asian American communities. She can be found at www.chinginchen.com.

The longest relationship you'll have with anyone in your lifetime is with yourself.

I'm still figuring out how to make this relationship work well and ask for what I need from my often-harshest critic. It's a daily practice for me to practice compassion for myself in the ways that I would for a partner. It also helps me to remember that my current partner doesn't have to be the last person in the world that will ever love me or have sex with me or kiss me.

It's okay not to know.

Relationships are hard and confusing. It usually takes me awhile to figure out what works and what's not okay for me. Also, what may have worked for me a year ago may not work for me now because my needs have changed. What works for others may not work for me. Take time to figure out what you, your body, your heart needs and ask for it from your partner(s).

Talk to others about what's going on in your relationship(s).

When I was in difficult relationships, I isolated myself because I didn't want to hear what friends had to say. But I learned that I often didn't want to hear things that I already felt insecure about. Keep up your support system and keep tabs on what they may say about your relationship that make you uncomfortable or push a button.

You are the person who knows best what you need in your life.

Spend some time thinking about what kind of relationship and relationship partner you want in your life, which includes thinking about what your boundaries are, what makes you feel safe, what makes you feel sexy, what makes you feel loved, what makes you feel hurt, etc. If you're in a relationship with someone who makes you feel like shit, isn't willing to meet your needs or makes you feel bad about what you need, there are most likely other people out there who would be excited to meet those needs. You really are the person in control of your body and heart and who has access to it. It's often times easier for me to look elsewhere for validation, but I am the one that I keep coming back to.

TIERANEY CARTER is a Queer, Black, highly-sensitive aspiring healer, baby witch, and musician. She/They currently lives in Oakland, Ca.

Have you ever met someone, felt like you'd finally found something special, and made hot passionate spiritual love only to have them disappear and never contact you again? Or maybe you thought ya'll were just kicking it and now you have 15 texts by a heartbroken lover, all caps, cussing yo ass out?

So there's a lot of talk in Bay Area queer communities about consent. We ask each other questions like: "Do you have a preferred gender pronoun?" "Can I kiss you?" "Can I put this in your ass?"

Well, I say we start expanding that practice. I'm talking about EMOTIONAL CONSENT.

WHAT IS EMOTIONAL CONSENT?

It's basically us checking in with each other about the ways we connect romantically and sexually.

Questions one might ask yourself or a crush while practicing emotional consent:

- « What kind of relationship are you looking for? Platonic friendship? Something casual/friends with benefits? A monogamous partner? A poly primary?

- « If you're unsure what you're looking for at the moment, what has been your experience with sexual/romantic connections? How do you historically respond to these types of relationships?

- « What is your attachment style? Do you tend to get attached quickly? In ways that are long-lasting or temporary?

- « What are your boundaries around intimate activities? What is the point at which things go from casual fun to emotional investment? For example, are you cool having sex with friends as long as there's no cuddling after?

- « How do you tend to communicate your changes in intimacy needs? Do you tend to be clear and direct? Do you tend to drop off?

WHEN TO HAVE AN EMOTIONAL CONSENT TALK?

Tricky. But my friend Nube suggests that talks happen once the desire or intent to be physically or romantically intimate is expressed. That could be after the first time holding hands, making out, getting it on, looking deeply into each other's eyes or leaving each other dopey/flirty Facebook comments. For me, who falls hard and fast, earlier is better. If you're a person who takes a while to feel attached, or even someone who doesn't tend to, having the conversation early is still probably pretty wise just in case your friend is a fast-falling type.

It also seems really important to check in regularly to see if needs, desires, and feelings have changed. And to check in to see that you both still have the capacity to accommodate each other.

CONCLUSION

Sex/Romance is pretty serious stuff. It can range from being fun to magically euphoric to soul rejuvenating to boring to exhausting to nightmarishly painful. It's super important that we're sensitive and communicative with it, cuz as beautiful as this shit can be it also has the power to disrupt our sense of community and safety.

I know emotional honesty is totally hard. That's why this is a call to practice these types of dialogues with each other. Becuz I'm pretty sure most of us care about each other's hearts, we just don't always know how to.

Image by aly de la Cruz

ROMI CHANDRA-HERBERT immigrated from the island of Fiji as a child and is in great company amongst the diverse South Asian diaspora in Canada. He spends much of his time in the not-for-profit sector building capacity within local and international communities to increase inclusive practices. He is a facilitator, educator, community developer, and a lifelong learner on social justice issues.

"If you can't love yourself, how in the hell are you going to love anybody else?"—RuPaul

"Your task is not to seek for love, but merely to seek and find all the barriers within yourself that you have built against it."—Rumi

I wish someone had given me those quotes when I was in high school. A couple of years before I started high school, I had just left my home country of Fiji, settling into a very white community in the suburbs of Vancouver. I felt pretty alone especially when people called me names because of the colour of my skin or purposefully mis-pronounced my name or didn't invite me to things, sometimes even people with the same colour of skin as me. I pretended I didn't care. My family didn't have a lot of money so we lived in a basement suite and slept on carpets that smelled of dog urine because we couldn't afford a bed. I didn't see my parents much because they worked so hard to make sure that we eventually had a bed to sleep on (literally).

During my high school life, I came to the painful realization that I was even further from being "normal." Being queer was not something everyone was accepting of, including myself so I never told anyone. That didn't stop people from shoving me into lockers, spitting on me, threatening me with violence. I was called disgusting names in the hallways, in classrooms, on my way to the bus, on the bus, and as I walked home. It followed me everywhere. At home, I shut everyone out, including my family. I stopped talking to my parents and my brother because I was hiding who I was. I hated who I was so much so that it was easier to change myself and to present myself as someone else. However, it wasn't as easy to live with these horrible thoughts running through my mind.

Lunchtime at school was the hardest: not knowing where to sit and definitely knowing which areas to avoid. It would have been easier to feel sorry for myself for the victimization I faced, but I chose not to. I started to talk to other students who liked similar things as me; and they talked back to me! While their stories were different from mine, we also had a lot of shared experiences! We found a safe place to sit, by the art wing of our school, but not too close to the woodworking/mechanic area, though we were often curious. This is when I started to love myself. My friends invited me to their homes, I invited them to my place, though sometimes fearing that they might not like the smell of my Fijian-Indian food, a smell that brought me comfort. But they liked our food, and even better, they liked me and my family!

133

At 15, one of my friends decided to volunteer at the rec centre with youth programs so I joined her. Helping others and meeting new people made me feel good about who I was and it made me feel like I belonged. I got to hear other people's stories and it made me realize that my experience wasn't so bad. I was humbled by their experiences. I started to build confidence in myself, so I decided to come out to my friends and family. Some had great reactions, others not so much. I started to learn what real relationships were all about by seeing how people supported me when I was going through rough times. They talked to me when something was up, they stood up for me when I was getting beaten down. They took me to my first gay youth group where I met others who were going through similar things. My life changed because I learned to love and accept myself and that opened up my world to those who were different from me. I learned that everyone has a story and I wanted to hear their story, even my family's story. Building good relationships is hard. It takes time to learn a person's story. The moment we choose to invest our time in learning about a person, we start the process of building those lasting relationships, which everyone needs in their lives.

"When I dare to be powerful—
to use my strength in the service
of my vision, then it becomes
less and less important whether I
am afraid."

—Audre Lorde

CINDY CRABB is the author of the long running, autobiographical feminist zine Doris, and the editor of the zines "Support," "Learning Good Consent," and "Filling the Void: interviews about quitting drinking and using." Cindy lives in SE Ohio with her sister, mini-horses, sheep, dogs, and a cat. Among other things, she is a sexual assault survivor advocate.

People tell us we should be in healthy relationships, we deserve to be treated well, but when we come from families that have neglected or abused us, ignored us or suffocated us, or refused to see us, then it can be hard to even begin to create something healthy around us. When our homes—our places of origin—were not safe, safety feels wrong, and nice people often feel much too simpleminded to ever understand what we're going though. It's important for you to know that what you did to survive has saved you—whether it was running or fighting or freezing or going along with it all, or dissociating—you are alive.

Our bodies have an instinctual desire to heal. You will heal from it all one day. So, even if you can't be in healthy relationships now, it's good to try and identify abusive ones and get the hell out of those. Does the person you're with tell you you're crazy, make you feel crazy, hurt you physically or sexually, take your words and twist them, use your words against you, tell you you're stupid, keep you isolated from your friends? If so, I am serious, get the hell out. Even if you love them. Even if they are hurting too. Even if they threaten to kill themselves if you leave, get out, no matter how hard it is and no matter how long it takes, try.

See if you can grasp for a minute something that feels ok inside of you. May be there is a place, real or imagined where it feels calm or real. See if there's anywhere in your body that notices that feeling, even if you can only stay with it for a short time. People will say that you can only be loved if you love yourself first, which is not true. We are social creatures, we learn about ourselves from the people around us. We love ourselves when we are around people who love us. See if you can find any friends who you feel ok around whenever you are around them, not just some of the time. Try to build on this. Try and find relationships where you can talk at least a little bit about consent. Ask for consent. Know that you can heal. Know you can be part of someone else's healing. Embrace this whenever you can.

MELIA DICKER is a co-founder and the Communications Director of IDEA, a national nonprofit organization that advances democratic education. Prior to her work with IDEA, Melia co-founded Spark, an organization that empowers youth through leadership development and apprenticeships in their dream jobs. Melia is a San Francisco Bay Area native who now lives in Jackson, Mississippi, with her husband and three irresistible cats.

Like many kids, I dreamed big. Even before I could hold a pencil, I loved to make up stories, so I decided that I wanted to be a writer.

My dreams began to seem less realistic as I got older. The messages I heard around me were that artistic pursuits are hobbies, not career goals. By the time I finished high school, I wasn't writing stories anymore because I had to produce term papers instead.

By the end of college, school had slowly sucked the creativity out of me. After 17 years as a student, I excelled at learning the rules of achievement and following them exactly, but I had forgotten how to make up my own rules, and how to envision the kind of life I wanted to live.

I decided that other kids deserved a more fulfilling educational experience than I'd had myself. With my friend Chris Balme, I started a youth program called Spark. We matched 12- and 13-year-olds with an apprenticeship in their dream job, to give them hands-on experience and a caring mentor in that field.

In Spark, students rode in patrol cars with police officers, decorated cakes, and learned how the human heart works. Our students and their mentors both found themselves transformed by the one-on-one relationships they developed. The youth realized that with the help of an ally, their dreams were in reach. Their mentors, in sharing their passion with an eager apprentice, remembered why they loved it.

One student, Brianna, apprenticed with a writing professor/novelist. Even though Brianna would probably hear, as I did, that writing isn't a practical career, she saw with her own eyes that it can be. She knew a professional writer who showed her how to make her dreams real.

As for me, I eventually found my way back to writing, freelancing for magazines and starting a creative agency with my husband. But I wouldn't have stopped writing for ten years if I'd had a mentor to guide me.

My advice to you is this: Surround yourself with people who have their own big dreams, and support each other in going after them. Ask your friends if they know a professional in your dream job, and if they'll introduce you. Do an interview or apprenticeship; ask for mentoring. And if anyone suggests that your dream job isn't realistic, name-check your mentor and say, "It works for her!"

WENDY-O MATIK is a Bay area based freelance writer and author of *Redefining Our Relationships: Guidelines for Responsible Open Relationships.* As an educator and spokesperson for the polyamory community, Wendy has become a revolutionary activist of the heart. Since the release of her book, she has taught over a hundred Radical Love & Relationship Workshops globally, excavating important social trends and reshaping the future of alternative relationship models for the 21st century.

When I was 15, I knew that I never wanted to get married. I also knew with absolute certainty that I was attracted to men and women equally, so there was no way that I was going to get cornered into a strict, monogamous relationship by having to choose between two genders when I loved both. Not only that but I felt an uncontrollable desire to love lots of people, lots of different kind of people, and I didn't want to be limited romantically and sexually by only being with one person. I wanted to love whoever I wanted and as many as I wanted.

You can probably imagine how hard this was. I pushed against firmly rooted beliefs that you're supposed to only be in love with one person forever and then this will lead to marriage. If someone could have told me one thing about relationships when I was in my teens, I wish someone had said that there isn't just one kind of relationship called monogamy.

There's thousands of ways to love people and there isn't just one formula for everyone. I've been a radical love warrior for over 25 years, practicing open relationships and fearlessly loving as many people as my heart desires. I can't imagine one person being able to fulfill all my needs—that's why you have friends, lovers, family, partnerships, allies, community, and everything you can dream of in between. I call this kind of liberated philosophy "Radical Love"—this is the freedom to love who you want, the way you want, and as many as you want, so long as honesty, respect, integrity, and consent are at the core of every relationship.

That means your lovers know about your other lovers, and everybody agrees on the openness of loving other people. These kind of open relationships take a lot of work, that's for sure, but at least you're free to make a choice and to live your life based on your own ideals and values, not based on what society, peer pressure, Hollywood, your parents, or your cultural background imposes on you.

I want to love my friends in limitless ways. I want to love the planet the way I love people. I truly believe that we can change the world, possibly save the planet, if we just put less restrictions on who we love and how we love, and invent new ways of connecting.

10. TRAVEL

There's nothing quite like getting out of town: getting on a bike or a bus or a plane, hitch-hiking, going camping, catching or hopping a train, going on a road trip, taking a boat. Traveling is a fantastic, important, enriching, and exciting thing for most everyone, and young people maybe especially. There's a freedom, an independence, a getting out of your comfort zone, an unsettling of your rhythms and patterns that's hard to duplicate in any other way.

There's every reason for you to consider traveling, for a day trip or a whole lot longer. To the next town over, up the nearest mountain or a few other continents. You'll get new perspectives on the world, get out of your bubble, encounter all kinds of difference, be challenged and challenge yourself, meet new people, wonder why you live the way you do, and for a ton of other reasons.

But traveling can't be done thoughtlessly, or else it becomes just another consumptive product—one more thing for privileged folks to tick off on their self-absorbed "bucket-lists." Certain kinds of travelers have and continue to do enormous damage the world over by bringing corrosive Western values and money that very often degrade local culture, turn local economies dependent and wreck ecosystems. And that's not even to speak of the huge climate-change and ecological issues around planes, trains, ships, and automobiles constantly sloshing round the globe burning vast amounts of fossil fuels.

We all have to think really carefully and consciously of where we are traveling (even if it is very close), why we are going there, and what impacts our travel will have. It's important to think creatively and critically about travel, in all its senses, and to be able to ask yourself hard questions about your trips. All trips have to be done really mindfully. There are an endless number of clichés about travel, but you don't have to fall into them.

And you know what? If you never travel, if you never feel like leaving (for whatever reasons), that is just fine. You should consider at least a small trip, but if it just ain't for you, no fears. But there are probably an equal number of awesome reasons to want to get out of town.

It's really common to resist the pull of the road, or to find reasons not to travel (we all do it): you don't have enough time or money, you're scared, you don't like change, you don't like feeling lonely, you're tired, it'll be weird, your friends won't be there—whatever. And they're probably good reasons too, but if you want to get past them, there's really nothing like traveling.

You can travel really cheap, there are lots of ways to meet people and find free places to crash, and sure it'll be weird but that's what you're traveling for: to run into people who don't look, act, talk, behave or believe like you do. It's the best if you can go stay with friends but you don't have to—it's gold to meet new people in new places, or just be by yourself. You can work or volunteer or intern all over the world, you don't have to be an ugly tourist. You can do a lot better than that and have a whole lot more fun while you're doing it!

OTHER STUFF TO CHECK OUT:

- **GRAPES OF WRATH**, John Steinbeck

- **BLACK LAMB AND GREY FALCON**, Rebecca West

- **CHEAP MOTELS AND A HOT PLATE**: An Economist's Travelogue, Michael D. Yates

- **CRITICAL MASS** (organization)

- **HITCHHIKING VIETNAM**, Karin Muller

- **HOMAGE TO CATALONIA,** George Orwell

- **COMETBUS**, Aaron Cometbus (zine)

- **ON THE ROAD**, Jack Kerouac

- **MOTORCYCLE DIARIES** (movie)

- **HOW TO HOP A FREIGHT TRAIN** (online)

WWOOF stands for WILLING WORKERS ON ORGANIC FARMS.
This overview was compiled by Becky Young who is the Coordinator of
WWOOF Canada.

WWOOF started nearly 40 years ago with the intent to expose city dwellers to the understanding of where our food comes from, to share knowledge of organic growing, and provide needed help to farmers for this labour intensive method of growing food. Forty years ago there was a comparably small faction in our developed societies who appreciated the importance of organic and sustainable farming. WWOOF has grown from that 1st movement in the UK in 1971 to formal organizations in over 100 countries around the world. Today there are more than 6,000 WWOOF Hosts around the world who receive tens of thousands of WWOOFers each year. WWOOF Hosts now include homesteaders and urban and rural organic gardens grown for family or community sustenance, as well as traditional organic farmers. Today, the understanding and importance of organic and sustainable living has finally reached mainstream populations. WWOOF continues to contribute significantly, one WWOOFer at a time, to that increased knowledge and concern of where our food comes from and the protection of our environment to ensure continued supply of safe and healthy food. WWOOF is now a common word found in many on-line dictionaries.

WWOOF is a worldwide network of organizations. We link volunteers with organic farmers and small holdings, and help people share more sustainable ways of living. WWOOF is a volunteer work exchange: in return for volunteer work, WWOOF hosts offer food, accommodation, and opportunities to learn about organic lifestyles.

WWOOF organizations link people who want to volunteer on organic farms or smallholdings, with people who are looking for volunteer help. We publish lists of organic farms, smallholdings and gardeners that welcome volunteer help at certain times. The diversity of hosts available offers a large variety of tasks and experiences.

WWOOF HOSTS:

★ grow organically, are in conversion, or use ecologically-sound methods on their land.

★ provide hands-on experience of organic growing and other learning opportunities where possible.

★ provide clean dry accommodation and adequate food for their volunteers.

WWOOFERS (VOLUNTEERS):

★ choose the hosts that most interest them and make direct contact to arrange a stay. Volunteers (WWOOFers) usually live as part of the family.

★ WWOOFers need a genuine interest in learning about organic growing, country living or ecologically sound lifestyles.

★ WWOOFers help their hosts with daily tasks for an agreed number of hours (typically 20 to 33 hours per week).

WWOOF is structured on a national level. While there are many WWOOF organizations around the world there is no central list or organization. We are in fact a loose network of over 100 national organizations. There is no international WWOOF membership.

You need to contact the WWOOF organization that you are interested in. Hosts contact the WWOOF organization that looks after hosts in your country. WWOOFers contact the WWOOF organization where you would like to go WWOOFing (volunteering).

"If you eat, you are involved in agriculture."

Being "green" seems to be in vogue. More and more people are becoming aware of environmental issues and seeking to reduce their negative impacts on the earth. Nevertheless, the question remains as to how we move beyond the rhetoric, paying more than just lip-service to the concept of sustainability. I believe that the WWOOF program has an important role to play in turning environmental awareness into action, by allowing travellers to explore new ways of living and new ways of thinking about how they inhabit this world. WWOOFers are often young people at critical junctions of their lives: our future leaders at a time when they are most open to new ideas and change. For those already interested in sustainable lifestyles, WWOOFing is often used as a way to gain the necessary skills, knowledge, and self-confidence. The opportunity for the greatest impact, however, lies with those who are not already committed to the environment. For these travellers, the WWOOF experience can truly be life-changing. As was incisively summed-up by one former WWOOFer: "I have become a better person, to myself, to others, and to the planet in general" (Margo Lipman, PhD Candidate at James Cook University Queensland, Australia).

I believe WWOOF has contributed greatly to radical change in regards to the understanding and importance of organic and ecologically sound growing methods, and what and how we feed ourselves. And the knowledge that there are alternatives to the destructive, and wasteful modern methods in practice.

"WWOOF instills the values of appreciation and respect for other cultures and lifestyles in each of its participants. But unlike technology, it brings people together in an honest, symbiotic and healthy way." —WWOOF Switzerland

COLE ROBERTSON is a writer and freelance journalist based in Vancouver, British Columbia. His poetry, fiction, and journalism has appeared in *The Nation*, *The Incongruous Quarterly*, *The Tyee*, *Adbusters*, and *Artist Bloc*.

I remember my trip to Spain in two very different ways. First, holistically, as a general feeling: the hazy fugue of hot sun, language barriers, and long days (sore feet). This memory comes all together, an undifferentiated blur, arising from the kernel at the heart of any trip: the persistent act of moving your body through a transient environment. A still point in the passing world. Rather than a transient person passing through a static environment, I seem static while Spain all swirls around me.

The second type of memory is a collection of images: a woman in Bilbao glaring at passers-by while her toddler son pees on the portico of a street-level door, the stick-insect-yellow-brown of the walls in a basement hotel room, small round steel tables and straight-backed chairs stretching out from a café (any café, all the cafés) into a square, teetering on the cobblestones in the wind. The images flip though my mind like a Rolodex of postcards—distant, flattened, soundless.

Not all my memories are like this and these two types make sense when I think about what I was *doing* in Spain. Traveling is a sensorial activity, as opposed to, say, intellectual or creative. In Spain, I was mostly just *moving my body looking at stuff*. These are shallow things to do. The reason my memories of the trip are as they are is because of this. The images are flat and the general feeling is one of a hazy and undifferentiated swirl of tired knees, travelers' stale sweat, and hot buses.

In the end, I found myself listless and bored. I remember passing through Spain, Portugal, and Morocco and switching from Spanish to Portuguese to French in a couple of weeks. The only words I learned in the different languages were how to order a coffee—testament to what I spent most of my time doing.

Since then, I've instead tried to find deeper ways of being in other countries and places. An internship at a newspaper in Buenos Aires, the same at a New York magazine, moving to Montréal for school. These are ways I've tried to get past the postcard flatness of "traveling." And the memories from these places are different. There are more people in them, feelings, stories, even languages (you learn pretty fast transcribing interviews in fast, Buenos Aires Spanish). These are memories I'm glad I carry with me. They've made me who I am in a much deeper way than "traveling" around Spain.

While completing her graduate studies at the University for Peace in Costa Rica, **BIANCA BOCKMAN**'s passion for food became concrete and she now works with the Brooklyn Food Coalition on creating a just, sustainable, local food system. Being an organizer and systems thinker, she also helps coordinate an office for Occupy Wall Street.

City cops, then chiefs, then armed units. Finally, over a dozen soldiers marched toward us to stop this "threat to national security." We were five international citizens who had flown to Beijing to scale an Olympics billboard surrounding the Central China Television (CCTV) headquarters. The billboard's Olympic slogan "One World, One Dream" underscored the government's One China policy of rampant colonialism. Our 350 sq. ft.-banner completed their otherwise paradoxical slogan, now reading, "Beijing 2008: One World One Dream… Free Tibet!"

Just five months earlier, Tibetans nonviolently rose up in unprecedented numbers. They and the exiled Tibetan youth activists I had been working with for over a decade wanted the same thing: to self-govern, to practice their religion, and celebrate their culture. The uprising was summarily suppressed as occupying Chinese forces locked down areas to tourists, imposed travel restrictions on Tibetans, and jailed over 500 people. There was no way Tibetans could travel to Beijing to spread their message. So, as part of a series of coordinated actions, I was one of about fifty activists sent to Beijing to lend a voice to millions of Tibetans, who wanted their country back.

Behind its ritzy veneer, China thirsted for freedom. Walking near the Chaoyang district, I passed one of the many giant street-level Olympic billboards that barely hid abandoned neighborhoods. I remembered reading articles about the government forcing evictions of nearly 2 million of its citizens, creating these ghost-towns to make way for their Olympic spectacle. While I was in Beijing, a group of elderly women were sentenced to hard labor for simply petitioning to protest these actions.

When I was in police custody and interrogated, I was in a privileged position. My US passport would force them to deport me. They couldn't risk tarnishing the image the government was paying so much to their public relations firms to maintain. I thought of the Tibetans' unrelenting courage during the uprisings. They didn't have my privileges. They risked their lives for freedom.

Before climbing that billboard, I posed as an archetypal tourist. I walked on the Great Wall, ate dozens of dumplings, and stared at the gargantuan image of Mao Zedong in Tienanmen Square. However, my Beijing trip meant so much more... It was a growing experience tied to the great strides the movement was taking. In the following months, Tibetans reported that our actions made a real difference in increasing morale despite extreme repression. Our actions simply demanded attention for the Tibetan struggle. With their own actions coupled with those of the exile community and supporters, Tibetans felt united. Tibetans believed the world was ready to stand with them.

> **ELISE BOEUR** is a musician loosely based out of Vancouver, BC. Having satisfied herself that you're never too young to travel, she hopes to spend the rest of her life proving that you're never too old.

Trust nobody, that's what everyone told me. My family, our friends, the neighbour down the street who had no business telling me anything. I was fourteen, going to Ireland alone for a month. I had busked for a year, argued my way into a Gaelic language workshop that didn't take teens and bought my very first plane ticket. I had been playing the fiddle since I was small, learning Gaelic for a few years, and Irish music was my passion. In my mind it only made sense to go to the source. I was not the most worldly person, but all of a sudden I was getting off a plane with wide eyes.

Everything was a first. Reading maps, navigating bus terminals. Seeing dawn from the far side walking home after a session, and then over and over again. The incredible overarching freedom of nobody knowing where I was. I met my favourite band in a tiny pub, and stayed up until the morning playing tunes and listening to ghost stories about the 800-year-old building we were sitting in. My fiddle was a great travel companion. It gave me a reason to be where I was, and it made introductions for me when I was too shy.

Trust was a shifty thing. It wasn't until years later that I realized I could stay with people when I was invited. On that trip I stayed in hostels and B&Bs, kept my fists up. I shared hostel bunks and airport benches with my violin, the case strap wound around my wrist. But in the small towns of County Donegal, I took the rides that were offered.

Trust nobody. That piece of advice is worth as much to a 14-year-old as to a 24-year-old: only what you make of it. You don't need to qualify for anything to travel. You don't cross some threshold at 16, or 18, or 20 and find the world is magically yours. Now I'm a musician and I travel for a living... every second night I sleep in a stranger's house. I'm still learning to keep my fists by my side when I'm on the road, but at this point I've built my life around the kindness of strangers.

S. BRIAN WILLSON is a trained lawyer, long time anti-war activist, and a member of Transition Town Initiative Portland who dabbles in permaculture. He is a double BK amputee who walks on prostheses and a handcylist who enjoys regular travel at 12 mph while refusing to fly in airplanes. He is the author of a psychohistorical memoir, *Blood On The Tracks: The Life and Times of S. Brian Willson*.

Modern human travel assumes faster is better, signaling "progress." This assumption is result of the one century blip of the fossil fuel revolution burning stored sunlight (carbon) that took millions of years to form in the ground. The blip will NOT repeat.

This assumption is riddled with delusions: (1) that these energy "resources" are infinite. Of course, the Planet is finite and many will be depleted in our lifetime; (2) that extracting and burning these resources are necessary and benign. Extraction is extremely energy/capital intensive preempting biocracy as it severely damages the ecosystem (i.e., us). Burning these resources creates fatal consequences for all life, threatening climate instability equaling nuclear winter ["*Biocracy*" incorporates nature into all cultural policies. Democracy is a conspiracy of humans against nature as if humans are not intrinsically nature]; (3) that moving faster is desired. In fact, traveling faster impairs individual and community awareness of egregious consequences of fast movement while preventing important experiential inputs on one's journey; (4) that the energy *embedded* in complex transportation and communication technologies can be ignored. When incorporating embedded energy into the equation, most renewables are not sustainable.

When calculating energy consumed and pollution emitted for every passenger mile of airline travel, I chose to stop flying. Though not as onerous, car travel nonetheless is nearly as polluting and energy devouring. Being addicted to moving our 150 to 200 pound weight in 4,000 pound vehicles spewing carbon molecules equivalent to particles of mass destruction threatening all Planetary life is just plain absurd, and ecocidal.

Extracting, manufacturing, and burning finite raw materials to provide our monstrous air and land "tanks" is producing massive *negative* energy sinkholes.

Humans have evolved for hundreds of thousands of years in small, locally-cooperative food and simple tool sufficient communities, that is, until the advent of hierarchical, patriarchal power complexes called "civilization" some 6,000 years ago. We are now staring at a huge "correction" from having dangerously exceeded the restrictions of finite systems, and destroying the diverse, sacred interconnected natural world. Our survival begs re-discovery of our ancient eco-consciousness where life is experienced in smaller, slower, and simpler rhythms, living locally and cooperatively with less.

Cultural historian Ivan Illich concludes that "high speed is the critical factor which makes transportation socially destructive" ("Energy and Equity," 1973). He suggests that social health is maintained when moving weight at efficient bicycle speed, or about 15 mph. Moving faster hinders social and economic equity as it increases scarcity of both time and space. It saves time for some as it forces others to lose it, increasing class-based inequities.

My primary bioregional transportation is my arm-powered handcycle—traveling nearly 60,000 miles over 14 years, riding at 10 to 12 mph. Moving slowly without a surrounding cage is a dramatically different experience than moving faster in an airplane or car. It not only aids in promoting physical and mental health, it facilitates community conversations while expanding sensitivities to our larger nature as we journey without burning fossil fuels.

High tech, high speed modern lifestyles have dramatically shaped our thought patterns, language, values, and living habits around unsustainable bigger and faster addictive practices. Human powered movement represents a dramatic metamorphosis from a noisy, fumy car society to a more quiet, sustainable bicycle one. This is as radical as the metamorphosis that occurs in the chrysalis cocoon woven by the devouring caterpillar that fiercely resists its transformation into a nearly weightless, cross-pollinating butterfly. It is up to us to re-discover that we are part of nature, living lightly and responsibly.

STAY **SOLID**

EYLEM KORKMAZ is one of the founding members of Alternative Education Association and Another School is Possible Association. She is currently studying for her PhD and conducting dissertation research on democratic education. She has published a book on the Montessori method and articles on alternative education in various journals. Translation: Emrah Özcan

As a woman, and as a friend from Istanbul where the east meets the west, I write to you to share my experiences as a traveler.

For me, travelling to different countries means more than adding some pictures of historical places to my photo album or tasting local food. Travelling makes the world smaller, melts down borders, shows how united we are as human beings, and demonstrates how we can open the door to accepting our differences—as long as our hearts are open for this.

I remember talking with two German women in Damascus, Syria. They were criticizing Syrian men and talking about issues around women's rights in Syria, comparing the lives of women in Damascus to those of women in Europe. I asked them what it was like 50 or 60 years ago in Europe. They resented that a bit, but I think that when you decide to hit the road, you should take your "me" and "my beautiful country" hats off, get rid off your bag full of prejudices and the information you learned from your history classes, and then put on your "I want to understand" hat. If you're wearing that hat now, let's hit the road!

In April of 2010, I had an opportunity to go to Israel, but airfare was incredibly expensive. I chose to go by bus instead, which meant spending less money and seeing more countries. I am so glad that I made that choice, because now the Middle East is less stable, and it's become impossible to go there by bus. When you have a chance like that, embrace it, otherwise you may never get it again. You can create those chances by yourself if necessary. When you have the energy and time, who needs large amounts of money? All you need is couchsurfing, a hospitality club, your tent, your sleeping bag, cheap hostels, friends' houses, local restaurants, cheap or street food, and hitchhiking…

I remember my first day in Nepal… Alone… No one accompanying me… While I was walking around the Hippi Temple, a smiling Nepali approached me and we started to chat. He ended up becoming my tour guide for the day, and I had the opportunity to learn so much more about Nepali culture that day. After I said goodbye to my new friend Hari, I started to look in the windows of a shop. The owner of the shop invited me inside, then he showed me his late son's pictures, and we started to cry together… That same night, I bumped into someone that I barely know from Turkey. My trip started alone but every day I was able to make a different friend. Don't wait for someone to travel with. The road itself will provide you with many friends and stories if you ask for it.

I went hitchhiking with a friend in the Czech Republic once. At some point, we asked two ladies for directions. They gave their advice, and added that we might need to wait for a long time. Then they asked whether we had money and food... We thanked them for being polite and they left us. My friend and I wondered why the women had asked us about food and money, making up stories about their intentions as they walked away. A short time later, we saw the two women coming back, and were frightened by our own stories! The women tried to give us something ... what was it? Surprise! They had brought us food and some drinks. My traveling companion got shy and did not eat, but I took these new friends up on their generosity.

It is important to understand that we cannot trust everyone we come into contact with while traveling. But instead of seeing everyone as a threat, perhaps it is better to take a leap of faith. These days, the media tells us to be afraid of anything and everything. We build houses more securely, and approach foreigners with more trepidation. Even guidebooks tell us about the dangers of our destination. To help people without something in return is largely seen as being foolish... but we are foolish if we are unable to forget our learned behaviors and if we are not open to the beautiful things that travelling will teach us.

Before I went to Nepal, I read about the culture of clothes there, and learned that women wear clothes that cover their legs. There was no reason to bring shorts and mini skirts in my bag then. Choosing to conform to the traditions of attire allowed me to travel without getting too much attention as a woman, and demonstrated my respect for the Nepalese who were hosting me in their country. For me, the choice to parallel the typical clothing choices of the women in the countries I visit has been a positive one: I have never experienced anything that I could call harassment, including the time I hitchhiked. I have always thought wearing moderate clothes lessens the attention you get as a foreigner. I think, you should keep in mind that you are not going there to make some kind of a revolution of your own. The country you are visiting may be too conservative for your liking, and their rituals may be different than yours, but if you are going there to learn more about daily life in these countries, it is important to show respect for their life, including clothing and culture. Never forget that you are a guest.

I love to look back at the pictures of my trips; they increase my desire to see new places. But then again, I wish I had taken less pictures. It is a bad habit for tourists to take pictures of everything that interests them like I used to do. It may be a beautiful panorama, but the camera creates a wall between you and the residents. If you do not want to be treated like a tourist, then don't act like one...

In a nutshell, my dear friends, every road creates its own story and memories. The ones I've shared here are my own little stories. If you want to create *your* own stories, melt down the boundaries, make the world smaller, and experience how beautiful human beings can be, just hit the road... and go wherever the road takes you.

11. CLASS & CLASS STRUGGLE

A class is a group of people whose relationships are defined based on economic and social terms. An individual person alone is not a class.

For Karl Marx, the most famous critic of the modern economic system, there are two important classes within capitalism: the bourgeoisie and the proletariat. And, as he says in the *Communist Manifesto*: "the history of all hitherto existing society is the history of class struggles." Marx defined class as our human relationship to property and the means of production. If you are a boss—a capitalist who owns the means of production—then you are part of the bourgeoisie class, and if you are a renter and a worker for wages, then you are part of the proletarian class. Of course, class is much more nuanced than this...

Class is not just an economic relationship that is based on what you can buy or what you earn, it's also socially defined, and for Marx and others a class is also determined by its acts in opposition to other classes. Therefore, both competition and unity can characterize a class. For example, take the military. If you are in the military (or in a military family) you will be defined as being part of the military class. It's not separated out from other classes based on a wage and economics alone, but rather on where you are positioned in society compared to another class.

You probably won't be defined by just one class; you can fit into different classes at the same time, ie. someone in the military class can also be working class and so on. The more marginalized your class is in society, like working or poverty class, the more barriers you'll be faced with: your class can get you places, or it can lock you out. Many people will try to overcome these barriers by hiding their class and that's all good, but being able to do this can come down to how you look or where you live. Folks usually hide their class by simply dressing up (or down), hanging out in certain parts of a city, with the "right" people, etc. This isn't as easy as you might think, especially if you are a marginalized race, or in some cases a woman.

All societies are classist, some are more rigid than others, so how easy it is to "pass" will be determined on many other socio-political factors such as race and gender. But in capitalist democracies like the US and Canada, if you are white, then it's easier to pass, to hide what class you are in order to break down some of the barriers.

And, as an activist, you may decide to reject your class lot in life—especially if you are middle/upper class—and choose to live your life in a radical, anti-capitalist, ecological way. That's great, but just note that there are some things to think about along the way because in doing so many of you will embody a type of lifestyle radicalism that'll have you becoming a bit purist. Which is super normal, how else can you shed off all the crap!?

OTHER STUFF TO CHECK OUT:

- **READING MARX'S CAPITAL** with David Harvey (online)

- **STUDENT/FARMWORKER ALLIANCE IMMOKALEE** (organization)

- **EVERYDAY REVOLUTIONS**: Horizontalism and Autonomy in Argentina, Marina Sitrin

- **THE FEVER**, Wallace Shawn

- **EL TEATRO CAMPESINO** (organization)

- **THE BATTLE OF ALGIERS** (film)

- **WORKING**, Studs Terkel

- **MODERN TIMES** (film)

- **EYES WIDE OPEN** (film)

- **POETRY AS INSURGENT ART**, Lawrence Ferlinghetti

- **ON THE POVERTY OF STUDENT LIFE**, The Situationist International

Most people will be super impressed, while others will be calling you out for being "holier-than-thou." And to top that, those who can't choose this radical lifestyle are feeling disrespected and maybe even oppressed by your attitude and preaching—and you probably won't be able to fully figure out why. But no worries: below is a starting point, a check-list, for you to read over. The key word in all this is that you *choose* a lot of these "radical" ways of living; for many people it is not as easy to shed off their class. But you know you're middle class when:

★ you think dumpster diving is cool.

★ for you, squatting is fun, easy and safe to do.

★ you talk about being broke all the time even though you have a large savings (or a large family to fall back on at any time).

★ you can decide not to work and are down on folks who have a job and a boss.

★ you judge everyone for not being radical enough about things like food choices, medical treatments, and so on.

Don't worry if you answer yes to many of these! It doesn't mean you should just give up on the radical route, just watch how you speak about your lifestyle choices and how you make others feel about their choices. Many folks don't have the freedom to make these choices due to chronic poverty, racialized policies, health, being parents, and so on.

It is really critical, though, to emphasize that. What "class" you are born/raised in does not have to define your life or your future or limit what you can and want to do.

"After all, if you do not resist the apparently inevitable, you will never know how inevitable the inevitable was."

—Terry Eagleton

> **BEAST HERO** is a twenty-something mixed-heritage male born in Toronto. He moved to unceded Indigenous territory on the west coast a few years ago, where he first started questioning the ongoing colonization of "Canada." Until then, he believed the dominant culture when it told him he's "white."

My first acts of resistance to the dominant culture came early when, at the age of 7, I got in the habit of pretending to blow up cars on my walk home from school. It was the '90s and I already knew shit was fucked up because *National Geographic* said so: logging in the Amazon; holes in the Ozone layer; mass species extinction; and the list goes on.

But the cars I was pretending to torch were those parked in the driveways of upper middle-class homes in the upper middle-class, big-city suburb where I grew up. My dad was (and still is) a brown man, but nobody minded because he's a doctor. The only time anyone ever talked about sexuality was when the young boys called each other "fags." Nobody talked about class or gender, resisted capitalism, challenged ongoing colonialism at home and abroad, or hated the government. Instead, in school we sang the national anthem and smiled under the flag, regardless of where our parents came from, because this nation privileged us.

None of those things even occurred to me, though. I'm a straight, able-bodied male who passes as "white." I always had enough to eat, was liked by my teachers, never had trouble with the cops, and almost never experienced crime. There was no struggle in my childhood: just family, school, books baseball, skateboarding—a quiet life. And my parents always told me that "after school, you go to university." They started saving up for my education the day I was born.

In high school, it was the '00s and shit was fucked up because "anti-globalization" and climate change said so. So I went to university and studied Environmental Science so that I could learn how to save the world.

Now it's the '10s. I'm 25 and shit is fucked up in too many ways to count, many of them benefiting and privileging me. Nonetheless, I often turn to activism, seeking change that my own physical well-being does not presently depend on and never has depended on. It is in these moments that the paradox catches comfortable, straight, "white," male me.

Without personal struggle, each flirtatious burst of activism becomes a struggle with my own privilege, forcing me to ask: What am I acting for? Who is silenced each time I speak? If I disagree with a marginalized perspective, am I an elitist? If I try to change someone's mind, am I colonial?

The paradox then compounds itself when I recall the voice of a friend reminding me that "It takes a lot of privilege to ask so many questions. A lot of people have to act."

I am not such a person, leaving me to wonder, "Should I be following them?"

TINY aka LISA GRAY-GARCIA is a poverty scholar, revolutionary journalist, lecturer, Indigenous Taino, Roma mama of Tiburcio, daughter of Dee, and the co-founder of *POOR Magazine* and author of *Criminal of Poverty: Growing Up Homeless in America.* Her newest book to be released in 2013 is entitled: *Poverty Scholarship: a PeopleSText–The Population Brings the Popular Education.*

Poverty Skolar-Ship

Anthropology,
Ethnography
Psychology

The study About us
Without us

Our spirit,
Our cultures
Our language
Our traditions

Through your lens,
Your frame
Your perspective

Fetishized
Researched
Deconstructing our struggle
Figuring us out while our communities are dismantled and left in rubble

Funded by fellowships
Acquired with academic privilege.
Linguistic domination gifts
Long ago parsed out to the sorted and separated
Who Excelled in amerikkka school systems, formal institutions of learning, the myth of inclusion and independence

How you gonna take photographic essays of gente pobre in Nicaragua, Arkansas and Bangladesh
But not give them so much as a slice of your
Privilege,
equity
and access

How you gonna fly
Back to your lands,
Your publishers
Your nests

With warm feelings
of 21st century colonizers,
our stories
and a good grade on your thesis and final tests
Sooooo I have a new plan
Its called sharing the wealth
Accreditation and linguistic domination
Mess
Flipping the hierarchy
Of who is an expert, scholar
Who does the picture-taking, story-making
And who gives the tests

Mamalaure, jewnbug, Gloria, teresa, queenandi, marlon, tony, bruce, jasmine,
tibu vivien, me, and gente pobre the world over hold the knowledge, of survival,
struggle, thrival to create a new kind of sister-ship, brother-ship and mama-ship,
that is rooted in all of our gifts
It's a new non-colonizing, non-hierarchal, equity sharing tip—
We call it poverty scholarship.

"It is not our differences that divide us. It is our inability to recognize, accept, and celebrate those differences."
—Audre Lorde

DAVE MARKLAND is a writer and long-time participant in movements of labour, environmentalism, and peace. He lives in Vancouver with his partner, Marla.

To talk about a person's class means to talk about their status in the economy. The economy is everything that people do when they hope to buy or sell or get paid, and you can tell someone's status in the economy by asking socially inappropriate questions like: how much money do you make? Or, do you give orders or take orders at work? Or, how many people have you fired from their jobs? Or, what sort of education do you have?

CLASS:

A section of society whose economic situations are similar enough that they have common policy goals and can possibly work for those goals as a unified group. This unified action requires the members of the group to recognize their membership in the group. That is, such action requires CLASS CONSCIOUSNESS.

The Big Three:

In the western world, it is useful to focus on three classes:

Capitalist class: Members of the capitalist class own the workplaces where the middle class and working class work. Owners make their money selling the products of others' labour.

Middle class: Members of the middle class give orders, have control over their work and the work of others, and yet they also sell their labour to make a living. Examples include managers, engineers, doctors, and lawyers. They are represented by professional associations such as the College of Physicians rather than labour unions and they usually have a university education and make more money than the working class. In the old Soviet Union, this class rose to take over the society when the owning classes (landowners and capitalists) were abolished.

Working class: Workers take orders and have little control over their work conditions, and sell their labour to make a living. In general, they attend trade schools and are represented by labour unions. While the working class usually despise managers and others of the middle class, they also usually want to see their children go to university and join the middle class. Working class values place a particular importance upon personal loyalty.

We also might want to think about these classes:

Underclass: Formed of people who don't have enough work. They may work part-time or in low-wage informal jobs; can include migrant and immigrant labourers as well as the disabled and long-term unemployed. In some very poor countries, the underclass is a majority of people.

Peasants and landowners: In some farming economies, such as Europe many years ago or Latin America today, the class system is based on large landowners and small farmers called peasants who usually work some land of their own and some belonging to the landowner.

CLASS STRUGGLE:

Class struggle is a very big part of what decides wages, working conditions, salaries, and profit rates. Traditionally we think of class struggle as strikes and other job actions by workers, along with capitalist class tactics like lock-outs, strike-breaking, and capital flight. But such enormous efforts in society go towards the class struggle that it spills into other domains of life, for example in the domination of politics by business. Those other realms also project power into the economy and the class struggle, as when very powerful political or cultural groups, like military officers or clergy, are part of the capitalist or landowning classes.

CLASSISM:

Classism is the cultural expression of class hierarchy, including discrimination against members of the lower classes and hostile attitudes toward them. That is, classism is a form of oppression, much like sexism and racism. And like those other two oppressions, classism excuses and perpetuates a power system, in this case the hierarchy of classes. One sees a lot of classism in popular culture. For example, TV shows and movies tend to have characters who live more like judges than like janitors. On those occasions that working class characters appear, they are seldom dignified. Classism even effects popular movements: the environmental and anti-nuclear power movements have long had problems attracting working people, largely because those movements are seen to reflect middle class values. For the upper classes, classism is a weapon in the class struggle.

DANA PUTNAM is a library worker, a button-maker, a lover of the arts, a lapsed cyclist, and a recalcitrant writer.

4 THINGS I KNOW ABOUT **CLASS:**

1. CLASS IS **BIGGER THAN YOU** AND IT PERSISTS; **THEREFORE, IT'S NOT YOUR FAULT**.

I grew up on welfare in a single-parent household. For much of my childhood I lived with shame, bewilderment, and hunger. Existing in survival mode meant I couldn't participate in most of what was going on outside of school or with my friends. I learned quickly to not even want to do stuff because it just wasn't possible. We didn't have vacations, I didn't go on trips or to summer camp, and I didn't do much or receive many presents at Christmas. We moved a lot because we were always looking for cheaper housing. I didn't get piano lessons, or play organized sports, or belong to any clubs or extra curricular activities. All of that requires money and adults who can chauffeur you around, or at least make arrangements for you. I missed out on a lot of social learning. This helped maintain my social class.

Because mainstream rhetoric tells us that we all have equal access to wealth and opportunity, the expectation is that when we don't have what others have, we just have to pull ourselves up by our bootstraps and make it happen. So, I believed that I couldn't do or have the same stuff that my peers did or had because I wasn't smart enough, motivated enough, organized enough. Of course, none of this was my fault. I didn't understand that it was bigger than me. In order to adapt, I just told myself that I didn't want to do all of those things, I didn't want to belong to all of that. I became a proud loner, flaunting my independence and freedom— sneering at my friends' piano and horseback riding lessons, Sarah Lee puddings in their fancy lunch kits, family dinners, and summer vacations in Hawaii.

2. CLASS IS ABOUT **INHERITED CAPITAL**: SOCIAL, ECONOMIC, AND CULTURAL. **IT'S NOT ENTIRELY ABOUT CASH.**

This is a tricky thing. The socio-economic class a person is born into seems to magically mold and define their future regardless of how much money is in their pocket at any given time. Research shows that most people stay in the income group they start life in. There is much less class mobility than we think. "Classes do not consist of individuals differentially achieving on the basis of ability, but of individuals inheriting the advantages and disadvantages of their parents before them" (Dennis Forcese, *The Canadian Class Structure*).

Even though I grew up on welfare, that level of poverty wasn't really my socio-economic class. My grandparents were working/lower middle class and owned a house. So when I was 11, my previous life of bouncing around many different schools, houses and cities came to an end when my grandmother sold the family home and bought two cheaper houses. My mom, brother, and I moved into our own house and my mom went back to work as a secretary, so our lifestyle changed a lot. Our economic situation stabilized and was closer to what my mom's class was growing up.

As a young adult, I raised my daughter while living on student loans and welfare. The year after finishing college and before finding full-time work, we lived primarily on white bread and fried bologna sandwiches (which were cheap, comforting, and satisfying) and I felt terribly defeated and depressed. But, we also had a stable roof over our heads and I eventually got a good union job. Because of my college degree (achieved through students loans I am still paying off) and stable housing situation I could move out of the entry-level retail jobs I started out in, and move into a job with a living wage. So, even though I have been cash-poor for most of my life and carried with me the first-hand lessons of welfare-style poverty, I have still managed to maintain a working/lower middle class lifestyle—largely due to the property my grandparents passed down... and my white skin.

3. CLASS IS **COMPLEX, SUBTLE, AND COMPLICATED** BY OTHER INTERSECTING FACTORS.

I was a white, 5th generation Canadian girl born in an urban centre on the west-coast and grew up in the '70s era of free love and new social movements. Life would have been very, very different for an Indigenous girl growing up on a reserve in the Canadian North. And different again for the daughter of a migrant farm worker living in the Canadian prairies on a temporary work permit. Class analysis alone doesn't begin to illuminate the differences in our realities and our opportunities and futures. I work hard to listen to people's stories and imagine their experiences rather than make assumptions. It's essential to comprehend our own standpoints and recognize our particular privileges and barriers; that way we can discover real commonalities and not gloss over or minimize important differences.

4. RADICALIZE CLASS:
NAME IT, OWN IT, GET ON WITH IT.

Name and explore your class: as best you can, understand how it has played out in your life. Comprehend the invisible structures that maintain it. Try to tease out the privilege and power your social class affords you, as well as the other factors that enhance, dilute, and complicate it: race, gender, mental and physical health and ability, personal history, sexuality... understanding this intersectionality is key to understanding oppression and helps us get closer to not being oppressive to others. Nothing else really matters.

Aiming to not replicate class privilege in your day-to-day life, and learning from your screw-ups is the best you can do. Keep your heart open.

"Anarchism? You bet your sweet betsy. The only cure for the ills of democracy is more democracy. Much more."

—Edward Abbey

What's Liberalism?

With the word "neoliberalism" so much in the air these days, it is sort of strange that it seems to mean something so far from what "liberalism" or liberal means in everyday conversation (in North America, at least). If being "liberal" means being open-minded, tolerant, and seeing the need for a state-supported social safety-net—which is basically what it is taken to mean today—then how can "neoliberal" mean "leave everything to the market" and "protect profits, lower taxes"? That does not sound like a "new version" of liberalism.

The reason for this disconnect is that the meaning of the "liberalism" in neoliberalism comes from Europe. In Europe, the term "liberal" still has its original meaning: a European liberal is an advocate of individual liberty, free trade, small government, minimal taxes, and private property. This liberalism originated in Europe in the sixteenth and seventeenth centuries, and although it sounds "conservative" today, at the time it was considered extremely radical. In a time when kings, clergy, and aristocrats made the all the rules and all the money, it was very bold to say that rulers should let their subjects say what they felt, buy and sell what they liked and with anyone they chose, pay less tax, and claim their own property. The American Revolution was a liberal revolution.

Today, liberalism as a political philosophy is usually associated with a commitment to individualism, egalitarianism, universalism, and progressivism (in the sense that liberals believe in the "progress" of society over time). On the face of it, a lot of this sounds pretty attractive. In fact, some of it sounds a little like how some anarchists describe anarchism. The problems with liberalism, though, and the reasons it is the main source of neoliberalism, come from the fact that this description of liberalism is based on a very superficial assessment. In fact, this description of liberalism is the one liberals rely on. So its flaws come from the flaws of liberalism itself, and we have to step outside the liberal frame to see them. When we do, its connection to neoliberalism becomes clearer.

The key flaws in liberalism are its abstraction and its idealism. In other words, liberalism only makes sense if we abstract from the real world enough to pretend that in some imaginary way, everyone is the same. In that imaginary place, everyone shares these ideals, and everyone enjoys them just as much as everyone else. If political doctrines were best judged based on their imaginary places, then liberalism would be as good as it thinks it is. But the problem is the real world. Everyone is not the same. When you say to a homeless person "You are as free as anyone to make your way in the world," you are only right in the most abstract, meaningless way. And not everyone shares these ideals either. Many aspects of real cultural life do not fit too easily with it—sometimes in bad ways, like the fact that men oppress women all over the world, and sometimes in ways we admire, like some indigenous communities' reverence for the wisdom of elders. So liberals either have to accept that some people in some places are free to impose unfreedom on some people, or, like the neoliberal powers of today, they have to force-feed "freedom" to millions of people who don't necessarily want it. Either choice is a massive inconsistency.

The key is to drop the abstract idealism, and think about liberalism as a real historical movement, and not merely as a set of ideas. While liberalism is associated with the popularization of these very appealing claims—liberty, egalitarianism, universalism, progress—it seems pretty useless to base an understanding of something purely on the "ideals" its own advocates claim it is "supposed" to achieve. If we look at what liberalism has actually achieved—since thinking up these really appealing ideals is not really an achievement, since they have existed for thousands of years—what we find is that its substance is a lot more complicated. It is true that in many places more and more people have come to enjoy these "rights." But it is also true that liberalism's abstract ideals have justified the arrival of a lot of suffering and unfreedom in the world: the destruction of traditional social supports in the name of individual liberty, the end of customary exchange for "free markets," the rejection of collective solidarity for selfish aggrandizement, and the justification of indefensibly unequal human welfare as the product of individual choice.

What's Neoliberalism?

Neoliberalism is certainly one of the "keywords" in conversations among anti-capitalists today. Yet, at least at first glance, it almost seems unnecessary, since it is generally used as just another word for contemporary capitalism, a capitalism "turned up to 11." In fact, though, neoliberalism is a very helpful term because it actually describes some very specific dynamics in contemporary capitalism that make it different from previous capitalist regimes.

We can think about neoliberalism's distinctiveness in two ways. On the one hand, it describes a package of policies that have become increasingly common to countries all over the world since the 1980s. This package is basically what the International Monetary Fund (IMF) demands low-income countries adopt as a condition for receiving a loan. The package has three main components:

Liberalization: the country receiving the loan must eliminate tariffs and subsidies for local industries, it must remove restrictions on trade that protect domestic businesses, it must remove rules restricting foreign ownership and flows of investment funds, etc.

Privatization: the country receiving the loan must sell its state holdings, which in many developing countries are substantial, including national transportation infrastructure, natural resources, energy generation and water provision, etc.

Stabilization: the country receiving the loan must not attempt to manipulate the exchange rate of its currency, but must allow it to trade at its value as determined on international financial markets—which almost always means that the currency will plummet in value and prices inside the country will skyrocket.

Together, these three policy goals are the core of neoliberalism as an international capitalist order. But an important question is what this order is supposed to achieve. This policy package is neoliberal because it is supposed to produce a global arrangement that makes the world friendly to a particular kind of capitalist order, and this brings us to the second way of thinking about neoliberalism.

In this more fundamental sense, neoliberalism is the ongoing effort to construct a regulatory regime in which the movement of capital and goods is determined as much as possible by firms' short-term profits. Because the world is very complex and ever-changing, neoliberalism is also complex and ever-changing, since it has to adapt itself to the changing situation. This means that neoliberalism is not just about "deregulation"—capital gets rid of the rules that prevent it from realizing profit. It is actually much more complicated and flexible than that, and it changes depending on time and place. Often it is about deregulation—getting rid of tariffs of taxes, for example. But often it is about "reregulation": making new rules where sometimes there were none before: intellectual property laws that allow corporations to own information and even life-forms across the planet, for example.

The final defining feature of neoliberalism is the unusual role the state plays in trying to make it work. In neoliberal regimes, deregulation, and reregulation are organized so that markets will do the work that tradition, or laws, or ethics, or force did before. In other words, neoliberalism gets rid of some rules, and creates others, so that the market will decide who gets what and how much. So, in addition to its other features, neoliberalism is distinctive in that the state tries as much as possible to regulate not with law, police, and persuasion, but via "market mechanisms" that are supposedly "neutral" and more "natural." That they are neither is obvious to the people who have to live with the results.

—**Geoff Mann** (see page 53 for bio)

12. RACE

If you're the type of kid who, like me, reads, listens to, watches, tells, and invents stories daily, and your migration's single gentle landing gets more violent the more you arrive into this state, try to keep doing what you love most instead of sacrificing it because you lost almost everything else. Recognize the way darker people are portrayed in your comic books, myths, legends... all the mediums through which you absorb stories. Notice which characters you are attracted to and become aware of the types of attraction fostered in these stories, the ones that are un- or less available, or just plain missing. For many of you this won't be a choice, for some a skill you must cultivate. Notice which heroes draw you, who usually dies first or is ridiculed the most, which characters' emotions are deemed most dangerous, which villains repel you most or secretly speak to you. Notice how in the best stories, everyone is flawed, struggling with some inner contradiction and external obstacle to their full humanity.

What is amazing about race is this: it is possible to hate another person or accept or even justify their suffering without ever meeting anyone *like them*. Also this: racism is so big it operates independently of interpersonal acts of violence and exclusion, the way institutions operate on longer wavelengths than human relationships. Long before racism became one of the primary forces through which our world's social, economic, and environmental realities work, we have been inventing ways to dehumanize each other and make people into objects. The race concept has evolved into one of the most effective tools for dehumanization ever invented by the human mind. Racialization is the process through which people are placed into racial categories. It happens at the personal, interpersonal, and institutional levels. Colonization, imperialism, capital, the nation state, policing, war, genocide, occupation, apartheid, slavery, exploitation, exclusionary practices, borders, security, military/prison/education/media industrial complex, indigenous, settler, refugee, migrant, status.

If you grew up in the type of neighbourhood I did, you will hear transmissions of racism daily from people your age, mostly from fellow sufferers. This does not mean we are its engine, though we are intimate with it. This intimacy can be a fuel for understanding that you should not ignore.

Get really good at the things you love. For example, pool. Try playing with the 8-ball and cue ball reversed. Don't take the metaphor too seriously; real life is never as easy as this. When you read Gwendolyn Brooks by mistake, it will be pool that tells you poetry has something to do with you. There are days when beating an ornery asshole at this game can give you the deepest joy. When you beat another man of colour and he throws down a hundred on the next game, remember, he's been here before. You are not the defeat he's looking for, or maybe it's the other way around.

More importantly, learn about the struggles inside your family, the hierarchies, the sexism, the heteronormativity, the relations of caste, class, and ableism: these are part of every act of violence you will ever commit and work against.

Each oppression gives permission to the rest. There is so much work to be done.

In your first P.E. class, guys of all shades boisterous and together; when the one indigenous youth arrives and their mostly uncracked voices start to chant Oka! at him, wonder why you are gutted so easily. Days later, his quarried grimace won't be there to show you the courage to tell them stop. Later, you will march. Where you live, women disappear in the streets, mostly indigenous, mostly poor. No matter what they were doing, they deserve better. You will have to take it upon yourself to learn about your relationship to the keepers of the land you came to, to become more accountable.

There are statistics to back up all those feelings that singe your gut. When they seem too easy, it's probably something you ate when you shouldn't have, or the ache of good food you let go to waste.

A friend from your neighbourhood will move away. When he returns to visit, he will tell you there are brown boys who grew up without the consistent threat of a fight around so many corners. At first you'll laugh because you don't believe him. You need to believe him, to believe they also grew up round the corner from you, that more of them will. One day this image will make you cry.

As long as there has been oppression, there has been resistance. Think of ally as a verb instead of a noun. Guilt will never offer freedom. Punishment is one of the only words I am wary of putting in the same sentence as deserve.

In your struggle, break down to break open, it is the only way to have something fresh to offer. Something not in between unsettled and building, fear and passion, self and other, reflection and action, conviviality and battle, self-determination and solidarity.

There is a story in the Panchatantra in which a clever rabbit tricks the jungle's despotic king by describing an imaginary rival lion lurking at the bottom of the well. The shallow water and the walls' amplifying echo chamber make this fabrication's unflinching snarlface and roar come alive. It wasn't his own mis-recognized reflection that killed the lion, yet—even if he didn't believe rabbit's talk—the mirage was already waiting for him, waiting to grow as he leaped down toward its calm surface and through to the hard rock floor underneath.

The face you see in the mirror, those flaws you keep noticing, ask where you heard about them before. If you are me, don't take too long, your sister is facing things too and you should probably begin to have solidarity with her against them sometime, like now. Pay attention to the stories she identifies with and the ones that try to identify her. By the way, she is stronger than you, in part because of the pressure cooker that marred her tiny body years ago and the way her personal growth was a stretching of those scars towards her adult skin: resilient and beautiful.

OTHER STUFF TO CHECK OUT:

- **BLACK SKIN, WHITE MASKS**, Frantz Fanon
- **BLACK FEMINIST THOUGHT**, Patricia Hill Collins
- **HALF WORLD**, Hiromi Goto
- **DROWN**, Junot Díaz
- **JOY LUCK CLUB**, Amy Tan
- **STILL I RISE**: A Graphic History of African Americans, Roland Laird, Taneshia Nash Laird, & Elihu Bey
- **AUTOBIOGRAPHY OF MALCOLM X**
- **"ANARCHIST PANTHER"** (zine)
- **RACE IS A FOUR-LETTER WORD** (film)

AUTUMN BROWN is a mother, facilitator, health justice organizer, and anti-racism trainer based in Minnesota. A mixed-race woman of color who has spent her entire life in multi-cultural contexts, Autumn believes deeply in the healing power of talking openly about racism. Visit www.iambrown.org for more info.

In any conversation about race and racism, one inevitably experiences a point where the dialogue (or debate or screaming match) devolves into what is sometimes called "oppression olympics." It's the competition for whose ancestry or identity group has experienced the most sordid and horrific oppressions. For folks with white skin privilege, an example of this would be drawing attention to their family history of poverty, their parent's lack of a college education, or their personal experience of being lesbian or gay, so as to draw attention away from the social and economic access they are afforded based on the color of their skin. For people of color, an example of this is saying that no one else could ever understand the terror and violence they have experienced at the hands of the rich and powerful.

On both sides there is a strong desire to negate any current experience of privilege by fervently claiming another aspect of personal identity that is fraught with a history of fear and pain. This desire is dangerous because as soon as we enter into this kind of conversation, we have submitted to the divide-and-conquer tactics that keep racist systems in power. Racist systems are propagated by a powerful dominant culture based on competition and on the value of advancement at the expense of others. When "winning" and "losing" become the terms of the conversation about race, we automatically lose, because we have allowed a racist system to define the terms of the conversation.

It's our responsibility to change the very nature of the conversation, and it's of critical importance that we get to define the terms so that we don't get stuck in destructive patterns of competition. The easiest way to define new terms is to determine what the purpose is for having the conversation at all. Why talk about race and racism? My answer is that we can only begin to dismantle racist systems and heal racial injustice if we begin by naming. This requires us to be in conversation about our identities, but the purpose of that conversation is not to prove our oppression. If our desire is to experience racial and economic healing, then our new goal is getting to a deeper understanding of how each of us experiences the multitude of identities we have.

Ask yourself this: how, why, and when do you get to be comfortable and at home with yourself? How, why, and when are you alienated and endangered by your identities? *If you know who you are, you know what you have to give to this brave new world we are building.*

MICHELLE ALEXANDER is a civil rights lawyer, legal scholar, and associate professor of law at Ohio State University. Her book *The New Jim Crow: Mass Incarceration in the Age of Colorblindness* challenges people of conscience to build a racial justice movement to end mass incarceration in America.

When I was fifteen, I wish someone had told me how much power I have.

And I wish more people in my life, especially people I admired and trusted, would've had the courage to speak to me openly and honestly about race. About how much race matters—still. About the caste-like systems that exist right here at home, including the system of mass incarceration that was being born during my teen years.

During the past few decades our nation's prison population has exploded—quintupled—for reasons that have stunningly little to do with crime or crime rates. Thanks to the War on Drugs and the "get tough" movement, millions of poor people—overwhelmingly poor people of color—have been swept into the criminal justice system, primarily for non-violent and drug-related offenses, the very sorts of crimes that occur with roughly equal frequency in middle-class white communities and college campuses but go largely ignored. They've been swept in by the millions, branded criminals and felons, and then released into a permanent, second-class status—a parallel social universe—in which they're stripped of the very rights supposedly won in the Civil Rights Movement, including the right to vote, the right to serve on juries, and the right to be free of legal discrimination in employment, housing, access to education, and public benefits. Today there are more African Americans under correctional control—in prison or jail, on probation or parole—than were enslaved in 1850, a decade before the Civil War began. Race acts much like a virus in America, mutating into different institutional forms: first slavery, then Jim Crow, and now mass incarceration.

I could not see what was unfolding right before my eyes when I was young—the new caste system being born. I didn't understand that a backlash against the Civil Rights Movement was inevitable and that a new caste system was predictable if people like me remained quiet, more interested in their personal achievement and advancement than the fate and well-being of all.

I wish that someone had told me—straight up—that Martin Luther King, Jr. was a revolutionary, not a reformer, and that racism, poverty, militarism, and consumerism will continue to divide and oppress with unspeakable cruelty if people like us—people who care about justice—do not find our voice and learn to use our power well.

YVONNE YEN LIU has a BA in cultural anthropology from Columbia University and a MA degree in sociology from the CUNY Graduate Center, where she pursued a PhD. Yvonne considers herself part of the post-Seattle generation, global justice activists both influenced and critical of the anti-WTO mobilizations. She cofounded NYC Summer, a youth of color organizing school, and served on the boards of WBAI 99.5 FM and Seven Stories Institute. A native New Yorker, Yvonne lived for several years in Oakland, California and her family lives in Shanghai, China.

Growing up, I always felt like I was different.

Maybe it was because I was an only child, dragged around to events by my parents, often the sole person in her single digits in the room. The adults would gather around the dinner table, chain smoking Marlboros and drinking *Maotai* (a lethal Chinese form of rice liquor), discussing politics, while I sat off the to the side, busying myself with a book or illustrations that I concocted stories out of.

Maybe it was because every Saturday morning, my parents bundled me off to Chinatown, to attend four hours of classes where we learned about *pinyin* and how an inflection when pronouncing *ma* could meant either mother, horse, or to scold. I missed Saturday morning cartoons.

Maybe it was because the little boy with brown hair and freckles that I sat next to, starting from first grade to third—we were the shortest in the class—would turn to me, holding the far corners of his eyes back with his fingers, and call me "Dragon Lady!" Or "Ivan Lendl," which greatly mystified me, because in my family, we did not follow tennis.

Maybe because when we moved from the working class neighborhood of Woodhaven, where most of my neighbors were Black or brown, to the middle class enclave of Bayside, most of my classmates were Korean. My friends' families ate kimchee with their food, we ate pickled chilies. They drank barley tea, we green. My best friend's parents were Christian. Mine were Marxists.

Maybe because when I started my junior year in high school, my friends and I had starved ourselves, trying to look like the supermodels gracing the fashion magazine covers. (It was the 1990s, heroin chic was in. So was anorexia.) We also contemplated eyeshadow techniques that made our almond shaped eyes rounder. At 17, I started a zine with my friends, by and for Asian American women. Within the mimeographed pages, we extolled the beauty of fat rolls and single lidded eyes.

Maybe because I interned at *A Magazine*, a national publication aimed at Asian Americans, in my first year in college. I blanched when the publisher told me about our marketing kit, selling our community as an upwardly mobile demographic, into brand labels like Johnny Walker Whiskey. I left the internship, mid-semester.

Maybe because I blundered into the anarchist movement by attending a Reclaim the Streets action, where we blocked off traffic on Broadway in downtown New York for three hours, because I was a club kid, attracted to the mobile sound system. More than once, over the years, I would look around the room during a meeting or a direct action in the streets, feel my difference as the sole person of color, woman of color, Asian American in the room.

Maybe because I found my home, finally, in the racial justice movement. Where among my brothers and sisters, people of color, my difference is recognized and also reflected in the faces around me. Together, in our variety, we build towards a more equitable world, one in which who we are as youth, elders, whites, Blacks, Latinos, Asians, undocumented, LGBTQ, the colonized, the third world within, and the darker nations are celebrated precisely because of our multiplicities.

"The gift of loneliness is sometimes a radical vision of society or one's people that has not previously been taken into account."
—Alice Walker

LUAM KIDANE is a writer, organizer, consultant, and educator. she has developed and facilitated programming and workshops on the prison industrial complex, anti-black racism, and art as resistance. Luam is currently based in the Occupied Territories of Mississauga of New Credit and Haudenausonee.

how do you write survival as a Black womyn in a society built to erase you? the difficulty of creative production between the boundaries of black ink is never as apparent as when you are trying to communicate something you are still in the processes of learning how to articulate.

language often runs dry but even then i must remind myself to write.

this piece is about Blackness.

it is about calling racism by its first name—white supremacy.

this piece is about stories still being written.

new york on a late summer night. i'm sitting on the stoop of a brooklyn storefront with a group of Black organizers. we spoke of the ways in which whiteness trespassed on the ancestral grounds of our very being, when we were first made to learn that the Blacker you are the more society attempts to criminalize you, marginalize you and dehumanize you.

my first memory of this was when i was six. a young Black girl in a refugee camp.

someone called me a nigger at school. assault, blast, break in, break open, burst, bust open, defile, extort, propel, pry, push, ravish, spoil, squeeze, thrust, twist, unravel, violate, wrench, wrest, wring, writhe.

at six i was caught in the webs of white supremacy; a system that defines itself by exploiting, murdering and disposing Black bodies. at twenty six i am just starting to understand what fighting these webs can mean.

moving through various organizing spaces, and being Black in a world i was never meant to survive in has taught me the importance of being intentional with words. i use white supremacy instead of racism because our society is built on colonial and imperial foundations that posit Blackness as inferior, savage, as something to be feared.

the more inoffensive your Blackness is to whiteness, the easier you are able to navigate the systemic imbalances of a society held up by exploitation. or so the story goes. this link to Blackness is not coincidental. the vilification of Blackness occurs because it is diametrically opposed to whiteness.

so i say white supremacy instead of racism. i say this so that i can understand what it is that i am opposing with clarity.

white supremacy is woven intricately into our everyday interactions. many 'radical' spaces, including people of colour only spaces, are so focused on being anti-white (here understood as fighting white supremacy) that they fail to realize how they are being anti-black.

as bell hooks has said "the raft is not the shore." calling out white supremacy is only the first step in combating anti-black sentiments in non-Black spaces. the transformative element lies in eradicating anti-black patterns from our discourses, organizing models and ways of relating to each other.

Black communities and allies have to actively learn what it means to disassociate darkness from inferiority. this happens, for example, in analyzing how to stop using darkness/Blackness as a connotation for undesirability or negativity. the active unlearning of our distancing from Blackness to prove that we are worthy, intelligent, and something to not be feared is central to modeling behaviour and actions that are liberating.

as Black people who are in and of the front lines we must always remind ourselves that we are warriors.

we must continue to build and organize in the most militant tradition of our ancestors.

we are ancestral beauty in the flesh.

our stories must be told.

ANTONIO TE MAIOHA is Maori from Aotearoa (New Zealand). His Maori heritage comes from his father's side of the family. School performances, busking, and street performance piqued his interest in performing arts which led to him attending Te Kura Toi Whakaari o Aotearoa (New Zealand Drama School) in 1992 and 1993. After graduation he joined acclaimed Maori theater project, Te Rakau Hua O Te Wao Tapu, run by well known Maori actor Jim Moriarty. As an actor he has appeared in several television series, and now lives on the west coast of his homelands North Island, Anatonio is also an active environmentalist and spoken word poet who includes themes of indigenous solidarity within his work.

Ki Nga Wahine Toa (a walk in progress)

In reflection of our cores
Carve your chinskin;
Grind the Poroporo* between jawbones teeth;
Bide your purple tongue,
For now...
In time,
From your Sacred House
Mountains of oratory-
Rivers of spite
Will transform to hot lava flows from between your bluesed lips.
'Once more <u>out</u> of the breach dear friends, once more'
Lead with the heart, follow with your feet,
Because the dried seeds of our dormant tree's
have been set too light,
And like the Tii- Kouka**
Despite the fire,
We will rise,
Despite the reign,
We will rise,
Despite the storm, winds,
siege, heil,
We will rise!
We will not baton down to your batons up,
We will pop out like hundreds of Tiger*** worms at the sound of your surface pecks
And under instructions from our foremothers
echoing through the her stories of our blood
We will fight! Fight! Fight!
"Ka whawhai tonu maatou- Ake! Ake! Ake!!!"****

Notes

* When Tuuhoe came to assist Maniapoto fight the colonisers, because they wouldn't fight while they had their mate/iikura, the Wahine Toa ate the Poroporo berries to delay menstruation so they could carry on fighting. The "Jawbone" of Wahine is a symbol for stored knowledge and whakapapa.

** If a Tii Kouka tree is burnt in a bush fire, afterwards it still grows on... as we Maaori/Indigenius people always have and as we always will. It's also a reference to those seeds that never change until they've been burnt and then they grow up and into themselves... like lots of us.

*** "Tiger worm": The seed of this poem is in reference to my Ngaa Puhi whanaunga's recent imprisonment. Tiger worms are surface feeders but have evolved to be distasteful to birds or other predators, they also take others waste products and change them into beneficial substances for the soil, and therefore for everyone—so it's also a reference to 'what's good for Maaori is good for everyone.' We're too often the first line to be attacked and the last line to defend, especially when it comes to offshore takeovers of our nations lands and assets. Through a lot of the media the majority of people uninformed to the real truths of our country are polarised into believing we're screaming radical protesters out for our own gain, when in fact we're actually out there trying to preserve a better future for their grandchildren and for the grandchildren of the policeman who are terrorising us too!

**** I use these words well aware that there are many ways to skin a cat as you walk to the summit. So by "fight" I also refer to fighting in courts, fighting thru Art, fighting thru writing, waiata, poems, email, everyday conversation, Whaikoorero, fb, doco, just fighting or offering alternative stories to the sensationalised tripe of the system by making other information available by whatever means we can.

ALAN GOODMAN is vice president of academic affairs/dean of faculty and professor of biological anthropology at Hampshire College, Amherst, MA. He teaches and writes on the health and nutritional consequences of political-economic processes such as poverty, inequality, and racism. Goodman co-directs the American Anthropological Association's public education project on race and is a past president of that association.

Race is a Myth; Racism is Real.

Look around a room of individuals. We humans come in a variety of shapes and colors, abilities and temperaments. We are a highly visual species and our eyes detect differences and our cultural brains make meaning out of difference. Race is the folk idea most often used to explain human biological differences. But what we think is visually obvious—that humans group into convenient racial boxes—is a cultural myth. Moreover, it is a myth that hurts.

At the genetic level of DNA letters, or nucleotides, we can directly compare individuals of the same and different so-called races. Imagine two strings of DNA set side by side. Two Europeans are different from each other: less than 1 DNA letter per thousand, as are two Asians as well as a European and an Asian. Europeans and Asians differ slightly more from Africans. On average we are 99.9% genetically similar. But two Africans differ the most from each other: about 1.2 letters per thousand! On average, two Africans are more different from each other than from a non-African. Race (or continent of origin) does not explain human biological variation.

Why? Evolution and history explain human variation. Humans evolved and first lived in Africa. If we imagine genetic variation as nested Russian dolls, the European and Asian dolls fit inside the genetically more diverse African doll. In a genetic sense *we are all Africans under the skin*. Our eyes have interpreted a few genetic variations like skin color and assumed they have deeper meaning. They do not.

Yet, race is still a powerfully ruinous idea, leading directly to deplorable racial inequalities in health and wealth. In the US, black babies still die at a rate that is twice that of white babies and the average wealth of a white family is nearly eight times that of a black family. These statistics show how racism gets into institutions and bodies. And that is why we need to understand human biological variation as distinct from race, as well as the continuing power of the idea of race and racism.

IJEOMA MADUBATA, 19, was born in Riverdale, Maryland. She currently studies at Princeton University, majoring in psychology. Ijeoma hopes to have a future involving child psychology as well as working with education reform.

IMANI OLIVER studies Psychology, African American, and African Studies at Princeton University. She is originally from Brooklyn, New York, where she lives with her Jamaican parents and two older brothers. She intends to move into education reform and educational policy law after graduation.

Both Imani and Ijeoma were interns with the **YOUNG PEOPLE'S PROJECT** in Jackson, Mississippi for the summer of 2012 through a project with Princeton University. The YPP was founded in Jackson in 1996 by former Algebra Project students and current AP students at the Brinkley Middle School. YPP has grown in the spirit of the work of C.C. Bryant, Amzie Moore, Fannie Lou Hamer, June Johnson, Ella Baker, Bob Moses and many others, and students from Jackson have inspired and supported the expansion of YPP to cities throughout the country. YPP is a community of youth guiding youth, advocating for a quality education in traditionally poor and underserved communities through the use of math literacy and civil rights programs and workshops.

Some of yall not learnin but I'm not here to school you
I know you see the influences around you tryna fool you
and we play into it,
think we got a poker face when they seein' through it
thinking we #winning but the stats say we stay losin
but we are a dignified ignorant people
unaware of the potential that we have
to make a difference, and remain content.
We're all born color blind
but end up blinded by the colors we see
can't see clearly into what human is in reality

But we are all slaves to our brains
locked in the ideas of race, a social construct
built by those who need to instruct
others on levels of superiority
and false notions of the "majority"
It's annoying me
How much my thoughts are responsible for the reasons I can't see
the truth:

That my demise is caused by my insatiability.
I'm not just talking satisfaction.
I'm talking about not getting what we deserve, but won't take action,
but we can't get enough of the cars, sex and fashion.
You see we were asked not to love each other.
They wanted us to curse our fathers and leave our mothers.

To disgrace our sisters and to kill our brothers. We did.
Cuz instead of pulling 'em back in we turn and shove 'em
They want us to ignore that we are all the same.
To run, forget the books and seek the fame
to want to be a part of a larger cult,
leavin' alone our families at home searching for luck

We were taught to think in this manner,
to think that this caste system is what really matters
cuz somebody thought that to get ahead we'd need it
when it really just makes us hurt, and act upon it
What happened to when we weren't classified

but the point is that we gotta learn from this world,
cuz the odds are against us from the day we're born
see the movement didn't start from one roar,
small people's peeps that made the vision sure
be a revolutionary in the smallest way first
get used to the idea that your small peeves are others' concerns
your opressor or professor giving unfair advantage?
well, tell your friends to tell their friends.
Do what you can manage.
Injustice is injustice to all,
regardless of the race, color, creed that you call
Cuz whites not just white, and black's not just black
Our one race is human, and that's a matter of fact.

13. GENDER

It's often easy to think of the world in reductionist terms, to think of people as divided into two camps: boys and girls. That's a story we have been told more or less forever and one which is often used to make sense of things. But it's also a distorting narrative and one which has a whole raft of repercussions, some of which are really damaging and oppressive. It's worth taking some careful time to think about the concept of gender, of how power is distributed across gender lines, and about how those lines leave some people in the margins entirely. Gender affects experience on a personal and global level, and can't be avoided in a discussion of power and oppression.

A good starting point is to consider the distinction between *Sex* and *Gender*. Sex refers to biological differences: your sexual organs, chromosomes, and hormones; in our society it has been arbitrarily decided that there are only two, but bodies are much more complex than that. Gender refers primarily to identity, as well as socially constructed ideas of behaviour as fitting into opposing categories of masculine and feminine. Like sex, gender has been split into a binary system, one in which folks who do not identify as male or female are ignored or targeted for all sorts of bullshit. One way to say it is that sex is between your legs, gender is between your ears. That's a cute line to express that sex and gender may not go hand in hand the way we're told they do, but it is also an oversimplification.

So what did Judith Butler mean when she said "All gender is performance?" At risk of putting words in her mouth, we'd say that she is arguing that we act out certain roles and behaviours that reflect our socially-constructed notions of what it means to be male or female (distinctions that do not and cannot represent everyone). Societies construct what it means to be "masculine" or "feminine" and then we perform certain prescribed roles, usually based on the title and pronoun assigned to us at birth in relation to our sexual organs; we behave, talk, dress, act, walk, and move like we are supposed to. Trans and gender variant folks who visibly defy gender norms are often the target of violence on many levels, sometimes subtle and often brutal. Many trans people experience a fair amount of internal turmoil trying to accommodate cultural gender expectations while struggling to express their identity honestly. Cis-gender (assigned sex and identified gender match up) people have the privilege of rarely having to make that choice.

In resisting these categories and assigned behaviours, something really important happens. It might be as simple as boys washing the dishes, listening to show tunes, or wearing a skirt. Or girls playing sports, having facial hair, or speaking in a deep voice. Those are easy transgressions of gender roles, and there are an endless number of bolder possibilities, but when gender can be systematically and constantly deconstructed it begins to carve out a space for people to act in ways that reflect their actual desires and feeling, including but not limited to sleeping with who they want.

It's crucial to resist "normalizing" tendencies and undermine the ways in which "gender" boxes people in and tries to define who people should be and what they should act like. Maybe even more critically, we have to find ways to defend everyone's ability to figure out and describe their own relationships with gender, and to change that whenever they feel like it.

OTHER STUFF TO CHECK OUT:

- **OPENING UP**: A Guide to Creating and Sustaining Open Relationships, Tristan Taormino

- **A DANGEROUS WOMAN**: The Graphic Biography of Emma Goldman, Sharon Rudahl

- **THE HIGH SCHOOL COMIC CHRONICLES OF ARIEL SCHRAG**, Alison Bechdel

- **HOWL**, Allen Ginsberg

- **DARK CONTINENT OF OUR BODIES**: Black Feminism and the Politics of Respectability, E. Frances White

- **LESBIAN AVENGERS** (online)

- **THE MALE PRIVILEGE CHECKLIST** (online)

- **SHAMELESS MAGAZINE**

- **PARIS IS BURNING** (film)

JANELLE KELLY has worked for over a decade in a variety of capacities with street involved and vulnerable youth. She is currently the Executive Director of a residential, youth, alcohol, and drug treatment program. Janelle continues to avoid "dress days."

As a kid, the males in my family embraced and encouraged my tomboy identity. They let me into their world of self-reliance, confidence, and freedom. Even as a child I knew that this world was different from the realities of my mother's lived experience, different than the experience of the other girls in my neighbourhood.

As a young child I felt most like myself. I was not thinking about who or how I was supposed to be, I just was. By the age of ten, acceptance of my non-gender conforming behaviour became conditional. I could play sports as long as I was less competitive; wear jeans to school as long as I complied with weekly "dress days." My mother and I began a dance of compromise that left us both disappointed. The males in my family retreated to give way for the young lady I was to become.

By the summer of grade eight, tolerance for my gender non-compliance halted all together. The gender "rules" were enforced by my family, teachers, peers, and eventually by me in an effort to "fit in." I lost the essence of myself and bought into the idea that I needed to be a better girl. The next few years of "fitting in" led to several poor decisions that almost cost me my life.

As a young adult I re-found myself and in doing so reconnected with my family. I realized that I did not need to follow the rules. I could be an outsider and still "fit" on my own terms. I could be myself. As it turns out, a lot of the kids I was trying to fit in with in high school, didn't actually they fit either. We were all just trying to avoid being an "other," to avoid being bullied, to avoid drawing attention to our vulnerabilities, we were all just trying to survive.

On the heels of the "It Gets Better" campaign, it's hard not to say it gets better because… it does. One of the greatest acts of resistance you can engage in is to get through being a youth in today's culture with your core values intact even if that means just hanging on, staying safe, and surviving until it does get better.

Push back against the norms when it's safe and stand up for those around you when they need an ally. Question the rules you are expected to follow. Be a critical thinker and remember that your core values are not derived from marketing campaigns or the media. Think about what it means to "be a man" or "act like a lady." Ask yourself why the rules exist; do they make sense to you?

Fit where you fit, create space where you don't, and stand up for what you know is right. It is these acts of resistance, this type of questioning, that will help you to hold your truth and your core values. In doing this, you create space for not just yourself but for those around you. In doing so you create a better world.

ALEX MAH is a mixed race trans person who currently resides in Vancouver, Coast Salish Territories. He is an organizer with No One Is Illegal and the calamites collectives. Alex currently works as a front line support worker, and enjoys writing, making posters, and working on videos.

Trans, transgender, transsexual, transwoman, transman, trannyboi, tranny, transvestite trans-spectrum, transfabulous.

To be honest, I spent a lot of time as a female-bodied, not yet "out," trans queer guy having grown up in a small town in a small brown body with frizzy hair thinking about killing myself. I would pace through high school hallways, or hide in bathroom stalls, or in the woods behind the school away from the viciousness of my classmates.

The most current statistics say that nearly half of transgendered people have attempted suicide—as though that were a useful (or easily countable) statistic for those of us still living on the planet. Not saying instead, that (whatever percent) of people were murdered by the hatred of the society around them.

Gender queer, gender variant, gender non-conforming, a-gendered, genderneutral, genderbender, cisgendered, genderquestioning, genderexploring, no gender, multiplegenders, gendered.

While each of us are born with gendered-parts (sex assigned at birth), the gender we act out in society is "performed," meaning that it's something that we act out everyday. The power of gender roles enforced by society leads to many male born men performing in oppressive ways (sexism) against women, and many cis-gendered (gender matching birth assignment) people performing in oppressive ways (transphobia) against trans-spectrum people.

When I began regularly being seen as male, the biggest lesson was, firstly, how messed up men's attitudes are when it comes to women. Secondly, I realized the incredible beauty of the people around me, who continued to act with love and respect towards me, to fight with me and grow radically in their own understandings of trans struggles.

Crossdresser, intersex, two-spirited, drag queen, drag king, female to male, male to female, butch, femme, sissy, he-she, hermaphrodite, hijra, kathoey, androgynous.

Radical people have made the decision to embrace the responsibility to find ways to work together to impact the world for our generation, and future generations, to live in dignity. To be a radical ally to trans people, it means that you find ways (big and small) to challenge yourself and the people in your world on how they behave towards other genders. This doesn't mean feeling guilty, but wanting people to feel comfortable, respected, safe, and supported.

A couple of pointers to start you off:

183

★ If you've just met someone, don't ask questions you wouldn't ask anyone else you just met.

★ If you knew someone as one name and it changed, do your best to use the chosen name.

★ Ask the person, in private and gently, if you have questions about:

- Whether to use he, she, they, ze, or another pronoun;

- How they identify gender-wise;

- Whether they want other people to know their trans status or not.

Educate yourself on trans issues:

ALLY BASICS:

www.gendertalk.com/info/tgism.shtml

web.mit.edu/trans/alliestoolkit.html

TRANS INFO:

www.genderadvocates.org/Tyra/TYRALinks.html

www.genderspectrum.org

JAMIE HECKERT lives on the south coast of England where he listens, writes, organises and invites the impossible. He's co-editor (with Richard Cleminson) of *Anarchism & Sexuality: Ethics, Relationships and Power* and contributor to numerous other publications. An earlier version of this poem appeared at www.anarchistdevelopments.org.

Listen to yourself,
to the subtle flows
of emotion, desire
coursing through your body.
You need not conform
to any boxes, any borders.
Desires overflow
these simple lines
designed
to control,
to contain.

Love yourself,
what you bring to the world.
Voices may say,
"You're not good enough,
you're not doing it right."
They speak
from anger
from fear.
You need not hold
these words
in your belly.
Let them go,
when you are ready.

Practice yourself;
do what moves you.
Feel your breath, your body.
Touch your heart.
Caress your skin.
Take the gifts
of wind and water,
earth and sun,
food and drink,
hands and mouths.

REG JOHANSON teaches writing and literature at Capilano University, located in North Vancouver on the occupied territory of the Tsleil Wa Tuth people. He writes poetry in the Grandview-Woodlands neighbourhood of Vancouver, Coast Salish territory.

There have been many times in my life when people felt the need to correct the way I was "acting" my gender: there was that girlfriend who didn't like the way I crossed my legs when I sat, thigh-on-thigh. She thought men should sit ankle-on-knee; at a wedding shower I was supposed to go with "the men" but I didn't want to. I wanted to stay with "the women." The women commented on it: "he's hiding behind his mother's skirts!"; in the locker rooms of my life I've been teased for the shape of my chest and the thinness of my arms; I've endured many finger-crushing squeezes from men who think you can tell a man's character by the firmness of his handshake; it diminished me a little in my grandfather's eyes that I was frightened by noisy small engines, like the ones on motorbikes, chainsaws, skidoos, motorboats; I've been told that my sexual orientation is ambiguous—some folks can't decide if I'm gay or straight just by looking at or listening to me.

There have been a hundred small ways in which I acted "wrong" somehow. But the penalties for failing—or refusing—to perform gender in the culturally specified way can be much more severe. Many people have been killed for having bodies that don't fit their performance.

The oppression of gender is a subtle one. Because it's not only forced upon us. We also act up to it. Living in a male body, for example, means one has access to certain privileges. I remember how my mom used to force my dad to deal with certain people/situations, because as a woman she had many experiences of not being taken seriously. Even something as simple as moving around the city requires different considerations for women than it does for men: is it after dark? Is the neighbourhood safe? Will I be alone in an isolated place?

Sensitivity, compassion, and caring are virtues; toughness, a fighting spirit, and the ability to act decisively are virtues. Gender is oppressive when it tries to deny us one or the other of these sets. We want both, in the same body.

As an exercise, you might take some notes on the following questions: Who taught me how to be a man/woman? What did they teach me about these roles? How do I feel/what do I think about that learning now? Which lessons were positive, which were negative?

CYNTHIA DEWI OKA is a poet, community, educator and young mama currently based in Vancouver, unceded and occupied Coast Salish Territories. She is a member of the Press Release collective of movement poets and her articles have been published in *Left Turn: Notes from the Global Intifada* and *Briarpatch Magazine*.

I was raised as a girl by conservative Christian parents, who came from a long line of displaced, landless people. Throughout my youth, my movements were limited by a dogmatic standard of womanhood and heterosexuality, which were also intimately tied to my racial identity. As a Southeast Asian immigrant, it was through surviving rape and becoming a teen single mother that I finally realized: nobody will give me the right to choose what I do with my body and who I choose to love. Nobody can make me sacred.

There are some inheritances that we enter the world with, that we have no memory of being without. From the beginning, they give others permission to perceive, tell stories, and make decisions about us. Gender is one of these inheritances. It shapes what we believe we can think about, what we should be afraid of, whether and how we can be safe, when and by whom we can be heard, and who we should desire.

It is a gift and responsibility to self-define out of a striving to understand ourselves, each other, and the world(s) we co-create with our choices. To be some way simply because it is what has been handed down to us is to dispossess ourselves of the power that makes us human. I am talking about the power to experience the fullness and breadth of life because of how we work our bodies and yearn in a relationship to others that honour their right to do the same. There is no more native country than the bodies we carry and the intimacies we permit to inhabit them.

There continues to be incredible violence visited on people who transgress dominant hetero-patriarchal norms—whether through ostracism, impoverishment, neglect, murder, or incarceration. We need to name these violences and articulate what kind of world is realized and foreclosed by their occurrences. What kinds of names are available in that world? What kinds of thoughts? What does love look like in it?

To unravel our circumstances and conjure ourselves anew is an act of magic. Language, art, music, fashion, science, technology, architecture, law, medicine—all ingredients of potent human activity where dominant gender/sexual norms can be transgressed and humanized.

All of us should be able to live in our bodies. All of us should be able to thrive through our yearnings. I want my life to multiply possibilities for freedom, fulfillment, love. And you?

MARTY FINK's work explores comics, zines, and cultural production to represent transgender identity, homo desire, and HIV/AIDS. Fink also works with Prisoner Correspondence Project and teaches English, Sexuality, and Women's Studies at Concordia University.

JOSIANE ANTHONY-H is a/the Togo-born and Ghana-bred youth who now resides on Coast Salish Territory. She is a self-proclaimed young-Black-Feminist, STUBBORN, passionate activist, poet and storyteller who enjoys Art and uses it to…break barriers and make change.

Dear Black women
You are Black, you are beautifully gorgeous
You are not just beautiful,
Your skin is very beautiful
Have i told you that Black is beauty? Well please permit me to do so

Your features are spectacular
From head to toe
Your head uniquely shape
filled with knowledge
Covered with types of hair that cause admiration and eager to touch
Your neck all ringed out
Uniquely shaped
Your skin and personalities

Yes you are the "angry Black woman" they say
But when you walk in to a room
It feels like heaven just drop on angel the halo

Your skin radiant and glowing
You embrace cultural diversity
You are brave, talented and strong

You tolerate bull shit everyday, every night, hour, minutes and seconds
From the men in your lives, ignorant non Blacks and the people in power

You are full of wisdom, talent characters

With all the bull shits and frustrations they put you through
For the sake of your color, gender and whatever else it may
Your heart, still and always strong like rock of ages
Yet warm and full with caring, love, hospitality and forgiving

Yes you are always the last people any will like to include
and talk to about human right
You were and are rejected among your fellow women of other races
They said you weren't yet aware of sexism
Or were too busy fighting against racism
And do not have time to deal with "being a woman"

Because you were taught not to use your mouth but only your ears
Not to cry but swallow your pain
You look up to the skies and say ain't i a woman too?

Dear Black woman
Look into the mirror and tell me what you see

A woman
A Black woman
A Golden woman
(Lines highlighted in blue are what you say with me)

For the black woman and girls who bleach, weave and self mutilate
And put on the contacts to have the bluest eyes,
This is for you

For the Black women racism never allowed us to save,
This is for you

For all the Black women&girls in here right now,
This is for you

For all the self-identified Black women&girls all over the world,
This is for you.

14. DISABILITY

It's tempting to think about disability in terms of what certain people can't do, and in some ways that's true: some folks have certain kinds of limitations that restrict them in specific, sometimes painful, sometimes invisible, sometimes very public, and sometimes pretty heavy-duty ways.

Anyone who has particular kinds of challenges needs solidarity not charity, and empathy not paternalism. And they also need specific allowances made for their (in the context of our ableist world) limitations whatever those might be.

Where is the line between "abled" and "disabled?" We are all "limited" in our own ways, and each of us has our own needs, physicalities and capacities. Who decides if you are disabled? (Is disabled a state of mind? A physical check-list? What about those people who have nothing physically wrong but are disabled from phantom pain?) The goal is to trust and respect other people in their diagnoses, evaluation, and/or identification of themselves, and to decide for yourself how you want to identify yourself.

But more than that it's also important to perceive each other as worthwhile human beings. It's not about "getting over" or "looking past" the specific configurations of individual bodies. How about figuring out ways to appreciate and honour everyone's bodies.

When it comes down to it, you cannot and will not ever know what it's like to live in someone else's body. It is key to trust folks when they say they can or cannot do something, do or do not have the energy for something you may think is simple, and to treat each person as an individual with different challenges than the ones you have. To be in solidarity with disabled folks is the same as to be in solidarity with any person or group. You have to go into it knowing that you know nothing but yourself.

More grass means less forest; more forest less grass. But either-or is a construction more deeply woven into our culture than into nature, where even antagonists depend on one another and the liveliest places are the edges, the in-betweens or both-ands..... Relations are what matter most."

—Michael Pollan

OTHER STUFF TO CHECK OUT:

- **SINS INVALID** (organization)

- **THE PAIN CHRONICLES**, Melanie Thernstrom

- **BLIND GEEK ZONE** (online)

- **DISABILITY POLITICS AND THEORY**, A.J. Withers

- **WHEN THE BODY SAYS NO**, Gabor Maté

- **THE FAULT IN OUR STARS**, John Green

- **THE EMPOWERED FE FES AND DIVAS** (online)

- **THE EXAMINED LIFE**, Astra Taylor (film)

SUNAURA TAYLOR is an artist, writer, and activist living in Oakland, CA. Her artworks have been exhibited at venues across the country and she is the recipient of numerous awards. She publishes extensively and is currently working on a book on animal rights and disability, forthcoming from the Feminist Press. She graduated from the University of California, Berkeley in the department of Art Practice with her MFA in May 2008.

I didn't like other disabled people growing up, but at the same time, I was secretly fascinated by them. "How do they survive?" I'd wonder. "Do they have jobs? Partners?... Do they ever have sex?"

I was a teenager deeply rooted in a narrative of overcoming. Clearly my disability was a drawback, a *negative*, but I could overcome it. I wouldn't let it define me. Even as a radical bohemian homeschooler, a childhood with virtually no TV and socially conscious parents, ableism creeped its way into my family's home and my own self-perception.

Of course I didn't call it ableism then. It wasn't until I was twenty-one that I realized the prejudice and discrimination I had internalized into hatred and fear of my own disabled body, had a name: Ableism.

Ableism is prejudice against those who are disabled and against the notion of disability itself. This prejudice is manifested in many ways—from inaccessible environments, to a lack of access to education, jobs, housing, and so forth, to discriminatory language and stereotyping, to hate crimes.

If there is one thing I wish I had been told growing up it's this: disability is not your problem. A long and enduring history of discrimination and marginalization of disabled people is the problem.

I also wish I had been told that I have a future. A future filled with politics, amazing friends, travel, career, love and romance, sex, humor, and a remarkable community. If people are patronizing or pitying to you, or treat you as if you don't have a future, remember that it's discrimination. You deserve respect, rights, justice. You deserve access to where you want to go. You deserve a fulfilling life. You deserve love.

I now proudly identify as a member of the disability community. A community that is nothing like the stereotypes I once imagined as a young adult. These disabled people are radicals: demanding justice and fighting oppression. They are incredible artists, activists, scholars, and writers. They are funny. They are thriving.

This community has helped me realize that what I was taught to think of as my own individual problem, a medical problem, is in fact largely a social and political identity. Disability scholars call this the "social model" of disability. Our bodies may be frustrating and painful sometimes, but discrimination, prejudice, and ableism are often the things that are most disabling about being disabled.

Sometimes I wish I could go back in time to tell myself that it will be ok. Since I can't, I'll say it to you instead: "You will survive… In fact, chances are you'll love your body and your life."

I also asked a group of my disabled friends what they would have wanted to know as a teenager about being disabled. Here are some of their replies:

> "I wish I'd understood disability as my culture and not a medical diagnosis… the sooner one learns they are fortunate to be part of this amazing community the more time we have to enjoy it in this life!"—Kara Ayers

> "I wish I had been told that physical and mental disabilities are beautiful examples of nature's wonderful habit to demonstrate diversity, as that would have spared me many moons of excruciating, internalized ableism."—Ruth Sarah Jones

> "I wish I had been told… that there was a social model, a political model, a cultural model, etc. in addition to the pity-heavy charity nonsense. Oh, and that I, too, would someday be a professional dancer, travel the world, become friends with some of the greatest people on it and marry the person of my dreams. All, not in spite of my disability, but rather because of it."—Lawrence Carter-Long

> "I wish I'd been told that my body belonged to me, not to the medical establishment or to my parents, and that I deserved to not only understand but be involved in the decision-making process about surgeries. Also, more inclusive sex education… And, I wish that I'd been encouraged to connect to peers with disabilities, rather than to prove myself stronger/closer to" normal."—Leslie Freeman

> "Where to start?! Actually, simply, that it WOULD be ok—just never easy… :-) Also it really IS possible to remain under 3ft tall and yet be a Grown(ish!)-Up!"—Sophie Partridge

"I wish I had been told… You are not alone. Really. Even if it feels that way. So don't fall in love with being the only one, keep looking for community… and then you are not alone."—Petra Kuppers

"As a person you have power. Power as an individual. Power in a community."—Maria Town

"There are other people who share your experiences."—Alisha Maria

"I wish I had been told… Plan for the future, because you may in fact have one. Of course you can dance [fill in activity of your choice, for me it was dance]; you just have to find the right adaptive tools. Adaptation isn't weakness—nor is it shameful. If you have been isolated, if you have been lonely, if you have been objectified, teased, neglected, victimized, shunned, shamed, or deprioritized because of your disability or its effects, it is not your fault, and there is *an entire world* of people here ready & waiting to love you—teach, support, listen to, talk with, love you."—Toby MacNutt

"I wish the term neurodiversity had existed. I wish adults had bothered to tell me the advantages of dyslexia or ADD. But they didn't."—Iris Mcginnis

"Not to overpower Dan Savage but it DOES get better (unless it is pretty awesome now…) and to paraphrase (Laura) Hershey—it does so by practicing, and finding community, whatever that is for u (queer, crips, mad, spastic, all of the above)."—Liat Ben-Moshe

BETHANY STEVENS JD, MA is a disabled sexologist and lawyer teaching in the Center for Leadership in Disability, within the Institute of Public Health at Georgia State University (GSU). Before teaching at GSU, Stevens was a 2008 Center of Excellence for Sexual Health Scholar at Morehouse School of Medicine under 16th Surgeon General of the United States Dr. David Satcher.

As a disabled sexologist, looking back on my teenage years I wish I had the chance to go say a few things to myself. Here, I offer the sexual insights I would have loved to have known so I could have avoided years of self-hatred and emotional turmoil from feeling lack of desirability and the belief that would never change.

I was born with a congenital disability that makes my bones brittle. In my 31 years of living, I've had over 60 fractures and 16 surgeries, intended to strengthen my bones through the insertion of metal rods into them. With all the fractures and surgeries, I spent much of my young life isolated in bed healing from injuries, amounting to about 7 years of life alone in bed healing. That created a huge gap in my socialization process and my educational experience. When I was 15 years old, I had a surgery that took me well over six months to heal. I was incredibly depressed, even when my friends would come visit me, because they told me stories of going to parties and out on dates. I didn't get to experience any of that as a teenager, due to healing from injuries, an overprotective mother, and friends who really didn't want their disabled friend tagging along to "cool" parties.

Naturally, I had to find something to do with my time, so I escaped into the land of fiction—in books, television and movies. For years, I considered those images to reflect reality—and none of those images included people like me. I knew all the stories about the guy getting the girl in the end, even the one who was deemed ugly in the story would end up happily with a partner in the end. I had my heart set on living that fiction, yet wondered how I could possibly do so in the body I am in. I would often ask my mother would I ever fall in love and would I ever have sex. She assured me some wonderful man would, at some point in the far off future, be able to see past my disability and see me as the attractive, brilliant person I am. I didn't know then that it is absolutely ridiculous and oppressive to suggest someone would see past such an important part of me.

If I could go back and counter the dialog that my mother and all the fiction I consumed taught me, I would tell me the truth about sex. The truth that media conceals with its over-sexualization of everything and its overemphasis on a body beautiful standard that most people cannot live up to. And an even bigger truth about sexuality is that it is something we all have with us. Sexuality is not just sexual activity, and it certainly is not just heterosexual penetrative sex. Sexuality is intertwined in our whole personhood, it is an experience we have for a lifetime (or as sexologists often like to say "sexuality is a womb to tomb experience"). So to feel sexual urges and want to explore your body at a young or old age is perfectly typical. My focus on masturbation for years was a great outlet for me and a good teaching tool—though I didn't know that at the time. I thought I was doing something wrong touching myself because of religious teachings but now I teach my students—of all abilities—that exploring your body is one of the best ways to know what you want when/if you decide you want to engage in sexual activities with others.

One big lesson I cannot stress enough is that sexuality is a human right that EVERYONE is worthy of and EVERYONE can find someone to be interested in them. This may sound like a lie when you are struggling to get through troubling teen years (I would have thought it was a lie) but it really is true. Especially, when you move out of your house and start building an identity of your own—whether it is in the context of college or work or whatever else keeps you busy—you will start finding there is momentum to your own sexual appeal.

It took me until my late teens, when I moved away to college that I could even grasp that people wanted to engage in sexual activities with me. After that recognition, my sexual ball started rolling. I knew what I wanted and I hunted for it. This method does not work for some and many find it off-putting, but it worked for me. More subtle approaches that are recommended by my less aggressive friends include meeting people with similar interests and building friendships into something more. Additionally, online dating websites are increasingly wonderful ways to meet people and their minds, not just their bodies. I spent years exploring different types of people to see who would best fit me. As it turned out, it was me that needed to get to the stage of wanting to settle down. When I finally reached that period, only three years ago, I found my wife on Craigslist (a free online source for various activities, including dating and casual hook-ups).

AJ IVINGS is a Canadian artist whose work primarily focuses on the relationship between nostalgia, heredity, and the body. She is a co-founder of the Memewar Arts & Publishing Society, Memewar Magazine, and Meme-Press. Her work has been shown in Australia, the United States and in Canada, and has been featured in the films *Tunnel Vision* (2005), and *As Slow as Possible* (2008).

"Disabled" is a series of digital photographs that document a performance that took place in 2009. The subject of the documentation is the able-bodied performer Elliott Lummin—whose body movement was restricted, for the purpose of the performance, by a corrugated plastic sign that simply read "disabled." The photos show Lummin performing tasks such as crossing a city street, dining at a restaurant, boarding a bus, and shopping while having to negotiate his disabled body. The concept that the word "Disabled" is capable of impairing an individual refers to the social model of disability—which proposes that "systemic barriers, negative attitudes, and exclusion by society (purposely or inadvertently) are the ultimate factors defining who is disabled and who is not in a society."

CARMEN PAPALIA is an educator and radical social worker. His participatory projects create the opportunity for productive conversation on topics
such as the accessibility of urban design and perceptions surrounding
impairment and disability. Papalia is currently a MFA candidate in the Art &
Social Practice program at Portland State University.

I want the International Symbol of Access to be more accurate.
I want the cane and the hat to be "my" thing.
I want to star in a short film set in Paris in which Natalie Portman is my love interest and I am visually impaired.
I want to play with a handicap.
I want to be mistaken for a paralympic athlete.
I want my friends to buy me a Braille Playboy as a joke.
I want to address the wrong person and for it to seem intentional.
I want to use the library.
I want everyone to know when they should help me and when they should not.
I want to be able to choose what I can see.
I want to be the face of blindness in North America.
I want to drop witticisms like "hear you later."
I want my mobility instructor to have a Masters in Orientation and Mobility.
I want to offer expensive seminars on how independent I am.
I want to be able to see my caller ID so I can dodge calls.
I want this to be in a literary magazine and not in an academic journal.
I want to be prayed for while shopping at Banana Republic.
I want one of those gadgets that beeps when a cup is full.
I want to wear a huge sign that reads "DISABLED" when I'm out in public.
I want complimentary carnitas and horchata because I'm visually impaired.
I want songwriters to ask me before they use metaphors for blindness.
I want to make a living as a visually impaired writer.
I want to find a way around non-verbal communication.
I want to be recognized as a hero.
I want to tell the guy from Blind Justice that I wasn't laughing at him.
I want to go to a monthly Friday night social for blind adults ages 21—35.
I want my visual impairment to help me make friends on the bus.
I want to eat organic vegetables that were grown by disabled people.
I want my drunkenness to be mistaken for blindness.
I want a card that confirms that I am indeed visually impaired.
I want to be the subject of a Just for Laughs gag.
I want to have my retinas scanned at the airport.
I want to write a column about my adventures in blindness.
I want to walk without a white cane and for everyone to know that I'm visually impaired.
I want to hang out with Michael J. Fox.
I want to be a pro at something visual, like archery.
I want to go on a blind date with a blind person.
I want my visual impairment to increase the value of my artwork.
I want an assistant to read my mail.
I want to brush off awkwardness with witty comments and sarcasm.
I want first dibs on tickets to see the Blind Boys of Alabama.
I want everyone that I meet to have an attractive voice.

I want to give a special name to poetry that is written by people who are disabled.

I want to join a dragonboat team with a name like "Eye of the Dragon" or "Blind Ambition."

I want to develop a symbol that communicates partial sight.

I want to launch a campaign that focuses on hope, not disability.

I want to wear a t-shirt that sports the slogan "fuck the color blind."

I want to represent the Diversity Committee.

I want my blindness to make me invisible.

I want to ride a media circuit.

I want my eyeball cane to make me the coolest guy at the CNIB.

I want to use a special bathroom.

I want to work as an actor and for my disability to add an intangible element to my performances.

I want to develop a cutsie word for my disability so I don't have to say the word for my disability.

I want a telescopic phallus that I can show off on the bus.

I want everyone that didn't talk to me in high school to ask me questions about my disability.

I want people to tell me about their disabled friends and family.

I want my white cane to be a utility knife of sorts.

I want my mannerisms to be studied by film producers while I camp at Bowen Lodge.

I want to receive endorsements from Blind Skateboards.

I want my disability to attract women with fetishes.

I want to indicate my medical history by checking all of the boxes that apply.

I want to be the only person with a disability at school and on the bus.

I want every film to have an interesting script and dialogue.

I want to wear headphones so I can see museum exhibits.

I want to offer a walking tour in which I guide blindfolded participants across busy intersections.

I want to go to Ryerson or York University so I can talk about Critical Disability.

I want to test drive a Ferrari with reckless abandon.

I want to spy on people and steal things.

I want to be the lead male role in a Hollywood film that does not focus on my visual impairment.

I want to replace the word "crip" with the phrase "are you fucking kidding?" whenever it's used for empowerment.

I want the university to pay me for all the time that I spend securing accommodations.

I want my white cane to get me media access at events.

I want to watch the Olympics in HD.

I want to be able to make fun of people who are hearing impaired.

I want to live by a transit line.

I want an apology from Don McKellar.

I want coverage for pre-existing conditions.

I want my autobiography to be available at airport bookstores.

I want a talking mirror.

I want "special needs" support.
I want to celebrate Braille literacy week with events and a free t-shirt.
I want people to talk a bit louder because I can't see them.
I want a kissing tutorial because I don't think I'm doing it right.
I want to use my visual impairment as an excuse for cutting in line.
I want every crosswalk to be equipped with an audible signal.
I want to wear huge sunglasses and a talking watch.
I want Shia LaBeouf to play me in a film about my life.
I want to be handled by strangers.
I want the fact that I'm visually impaired to be mentioned somewhere in my bio.
I want attractive people to stand in my field of vision.
I want this to be relevant right now.
I want to star in a film directed by James Cameron in which I portray a blind former marine that is able to see by means of an artificial hybrid body.
I want a dollar for every eye on me.
I want to be commended by Jon Stewart for my strength.
I want a seeing eye monkey that I can dress up in little clothes.
I want to pretend to be reading from a newspaper at the coffee shop.
I want to rewrite Dawn of the Dead so it has something to do with disability.
I want to be the artistic director of the opening and closing ceremonies for the 2010 Paralympic Games.
I want to be considered in debates regarding climate change.
I want to be a piano tuner or a masseuse.
I want a license and insurance.
I want to touch tactile representations of random works from the Louvre.
I want to be marketable.
I want to launch a motivational speaking career in which I teach business professionals how my achievements can help improve their business strategies.
I want to be the first person to do (something) with a disability.
I want to bump into something and start a chain reaction.

White, disabled, and genderqueer, **ELI CLARE** lives, writes, and rabble-rouses in the Green Mountains of Vermont. He is the author of a collection of poetry, *The Marrow's Telling: Words in Motion* and a book of essays *Exile and Pride: Disability, Queerness, and Liberation.*

Tremors

Hands burled and knobby, I tuck them
against my body, let tremors run
from shoulder blade to fingertip. Tension
burns the same track of muscles, pencil slows
across blue-lined paper, words scratch
like sandpiper tracks at low tide.
Kids call cripple. Bank tellers stare silent.
Doctors predict arthritis. Joints crack
in the vise grip: my hands want
to learn to swear.
Late at night
as I trace the long curve of your body,
tremors touch skin, reach inside,
and I expect to be taunted, only to have you
rise beneath my hands, ask for more.
everyday encounters, written 1992

Retard, Cripple, Defect

If only we had taken
the boys on, those
who knew the litany best—
rocks and erasers,
bruising words. Instead
the taunted turned:
her paper-thin voice reached
across the school yard, my shaky
fists answered back.
Lonely bodies, we were
the only two.
grade school 1975, written 1994

How to Talk to a New Lover About Cerebral Palsy

Tell her: *Complete strangers*
have patted my head, kissed
my cheek, called me courageous.

Tell this story more than once, ask
her to hold you, rock you
against her body, breast to back,

her arms curving round, only
you flinch unchosen, right arm trembles.
Don't use the word *spastic*.

In Europe after centuries
of death by exposure
and drowning,
they banished us
to the streets.

Let her feel the tension burn down your arms,
tremors jump. Take it slow: when she asks
about the difference between CP and MS,

refrain from handing her an encyclopedia.
If you leave, know that you will ache.
Resist the urge to ignore your body. Tell her:

They taunted me retard, monkey,
defect. *The words sank into my body.*
The rocks and fists left bruises.

Gimps and crips, caps
in hand, we still
wander the streets but now
the options abound: telethons,
nursing homes, welfare lines.

Try not to be ashamed as you flinch and tremble
under her warm hands. Think of the stories you haven't told yet. Tension locks behind
your shoulder blades.

Ask her what she thinks as your hands shake
along her body, sleep curled against her,
and remember to listen: she might surprise you.
everyday encounters, written 1992

MIA MINGUS is a writer, organizer, and community caretaker working for disability justice and transformative justice to end child sexual abuse. She identifies as a queer gimp woman of color, Korean transracial and transnational adoptee, and longs for home, belonging, and peaceful nights for all of us.

I didn't grow up knowing many other physically disabled folks. There was another girl in my grade who was visibly physically disabled, like myself, but we never talked about it. Ever. I often wonder if we would have even known how to talk about it. I wonder if I would have had the consciousness to even recognize what I was experiencing. Since I was disabled from the time I was a baby, I didn't know that there was any other way to exist outside of people staring at me, making-do with things being inaccessible or pity. It was so normal, I don't know that I would have been able to identify that there was anything wrong with it or that it could ever change.

On good days, I was a secret superhero. I took inaccessibility and used it to build connection with people, making it fun, instead of lonely. I sliced through pity and used its debris to build an air of mystery and awe. I took staring and turned it on its head, transformed it into pride, and used the opening it provided for a deeper swagger, a more powerful swing, and a sweeping sway to my walk. People weren't just staring at me, I commanded them to look at me. I met their gawk and gaze with my own absolute joy of the sun on my skin and the air filling out my movements.

I was an activist, even as a child, but I never talked about disability. I talked about what it was like as a girl of color, but never as a *disabled* girl of color, even though I wore a brace from my hip to my heel, even though I spent my summers in the hospital.

I would fight my parents each day about wearing my brace and in fifth grade I started taking it off the moment I got to school and hiding it in my bag. I hated it. It hurt and gave me blisters; it was hot and itchy. I loved the way my body swung without it, the lightness of a limp that was free to inhabit itself; the way I could curl into myself to break a fall.

If only I had known how magnificent I actually was then. If only I had known that I was part of a legacy of powerful disabled women of color who fought for their dignity and resisted against a world that saw them as disposable. That doctors don't know everything and *no one knows your body better than you do.*

That there is no "normal" or "better" way to be. No body is right or wrong. You are not wrong. *You are not wrong. You are not wrong.*

You are magnificent.

SYLVIA McFADDEN is an activist, knitter, and all around lovely person. She loves spending her free time in dog parks. She has three jobs, several invisible illnesses, and a (generally) good attitude. She can be found protesting against anti-choice folk where ever they are found.

I didn't know I had chronic pain.

I'd had chronic pain for nineteen years and I didn't know it.

I was in so much denial. It's just the way life is for me. I can take care of myself. Hide it. Don't tell anyone.
What? How the fuck did that happen? How could I be in denial so far that I didn't notice that my life was filled with chronically debilitating pain?

It's okay, I had ways of dealing with it.

Don't drink

Don't pee

Don't walk too much

Don't stand too much

Don't tell anyone

Don't go anywhere

Eat

I did go to the doctors about it once and a while when it got really bad.

They looked, they said there might be something wrong, here's some cream, the pain probably wasn't that bad, that it would probably go away. I guess it could be your urethra. I guess it could be the skin on your vulva. But I think it's probably all in your head. Let's just put you on anti-depressants and see how that works out.

My therapist was shocked when I told her about the pain.

One day I said "it sort of hurts when I pee... pretty much every day... and has since I was four years old"

"Oh? How bad? You've mentioned your pain before, but you've never told me it has been happening for years."

"Sometimes I can't stand up for hours afterwards"

"What? Sylvia, why haven't you told me this?"

"I don't know, I don't really talk about it"

By the time I mentioned my pelvic pain to her, I had something like 15 years of denial under my belt. We had been seeing each other for over a year (moving from CBT for panic disorder to therapy around early childhood trauma). She told me that pain can affect lots of things.

"Like what?"

That's when I began to explore the affects of pain on the body and mind.

I read books about the affects of pain[1] and books about how trauma can translate into chronic pain.[2]

Those books changed my life.

I started to make connections between my pain, my trauma, my panic, and my body.

I get that I'll always have pain of some sort in my life but I understand it now. I have some autonomy from it, some control.

I understand when I have flares, I understand why my body does this.

I used to say "my body hates me" but I don't think that any more.

[1] *The Pain Chronicles*

[2] *When the Body Says No*

MELANIE YERGEAU is an assistant professor of English at the University of Michigan. Active in the neurodiversity movement, she serves as Board Chair of the Autistic Self Advocacy Network, an organization run for and by Autistic people. In her spare time, she blogs semi-regularly at aspierhetor.com.

"Can you blame others for not wanting to talk to you?" asked my former shrink. "If I weren't your therapist, I wouldn't want to have a conversation with you."

I spent my childhood wanting to outgrow myself. My eyes bounced across humans and objects and air molecules; I wanted them to rest, to focus, to remain fixed on someone else's pupils. Other kids played, milled seamlessly across playground spaces, talked and gathered and wrestled and laughed. And I watched, on the outer edge of the grounds, wondering what was so horrible about me.

The fallacy in my childhood mind was the I. I wanted to outgrow myself—or so I thought I did. Since toddlerhood, well before I'd even been diagnosed with autism, neurotypicality was represented as something both to reminisce and worship. My third-grade teacher somberly informed my parents that I had the social skills of a three-year-old. Bullies chased me with lit cigarettes and shocked my bare arms with exposed batteries from a disposable camera. Doctors floated one possibility after the next, ideas ranging from cerebral palsy to lactose intolerance. According to them, there was something "wrong" with me, something seriously wrong with me. I was variously a robot, a brat, a retard, and a spaz. From all directions, I was pathology and blight.

And yet, despite my supposed neurological "problems," there was "hope." Hope that I would someday cease to be me. And like any faith-based narrative, I needed only to want it for myself. If I worked hard enough, if I trusted enough in God/shrinks/educators/the kids who liked to beat me up at recess—if I trusted in these things, Neurotypical Melanie would arise from Autistic Melanie's ashes. She would saunter over to a bar counter. She would order vodkatinis in a suggestive voice, sans autistic inflection. She would know absolutely nothing about the Electric Light Orchestra.

This was my narrative. Or rather, this was their narrative, a narrative I'd convinced myself into telling. I memorized it. I'd sit on the bus and gaze longingly out the window. I'd invent plot lines and visualize my transformation into a non-autistic character, a character with friends in greater number than my record collection. I'd imagine the new me, the me I would become if only—yes, if only—

I am now a college professor. I am now an activist and member of many thriving cross-disability communities. My bodymind is my bodymind. There is no if only—there is simply only. I am only me. I am autos, I am neurologically atypical, I am a stim fiend, I am stiffer than ironed polyester. I am autistic, and my narrative is one of reclamation and protest, of obscure '70s music, and occasionally misused prepositions. My narrative is parallel and stimmy and developmentally pervasive.

As any autistic person knows all too well, Neurotypical Lore persists. It persists with my ex-therapist, which is reason for his ex- affix. It persists with teachers and relatives and doctors. It persists with society writ large. And sometimes, in moments of despair and crushed spirit, it persists with me. In these moments, I summon my autistic pride self—an autistic self that isn't singular, an autistic self that belongs to a powerful community of autistic selves, plural.

"To be truly radical is to make hope possible rather than despair convincing."
—Raymond Williams

15. INDIGENOUS STRUGGLES

All over the world the struggles of indigenous people are largely invisible within mainstream media and popular discourse. If you were only to read major newspapers, watch network television, and peruse corporate internet sites it might be easy to believe that indigenous people are dead and gone. In fact many people still hold that native struggles for land, sovereignty, and justice are relics of the past, reduced to John Wayne movies, tourist gift shops, and new age fantasia. And, the story goes, if native people survive, they are fully assimilated into dominant culture and any vestiges of traditional life have disintegrated.

But it's not true. All over the globe indigenous people are still struggling and resisting dominant society and holding on to culture, community, and teachings. From Bolivia to Chiapas, Coast Salish territory to Six Nations, Philippines to Indonesia, Burma to India, New Zealand to Australia, on every continent and in all kinds of ways, native communities are finding new ways to resist colonization: from language revival to blockades, local economic development to legal challenges, scholarship to ceremony, direct action to reoccupation of traditional territory, native peoples are challenging dominant colonial narratives and asserting millennia-old traditions and sovereignty.

Whether you are of indigenous or settler heritage, it is critical to understand that native struggles for self-determination are not an isolated struggle for identity. All colonial culture is founded on land theft: the wealth of the West is predicated on vicious occupation and illegal capture of indigenous territory, land, and resources from one end of the Americas to the other. But that story is still being written and the acknowledgment of indigenous rights to land and self-determination is the foundation upon which a just society has to be built. That is the basis we can and should build from.

This is really to say that a liberatory politics that takes its lead from the exigency of native self-determination requires solidarity between settler and indigenous communities. But this is no easy task: finding routes to trusting relationships and shared action is complex and fraught. Indigenous people are capable, determined, sophisticated, and articulate, but our struggles are entwined and the heart of native self-determination is facing the reality of land theft, and that means settlers giving something, and sometimes a lot, back.

OTHER STUFF TO CHECK OUT:

- **WRETCHED OF THE EARTH**, Frantz Fanon

- **ALL OUR RELATIONS**: Native Struggles for Land and Life, Winona LaDuke

- **FROM A NATIVE DAUGHTER**: Colonialism and Sovereignty in Hawaii, Haunani-Kay Trask

- **ANGEL WING SPLASH PATTERN**, Richard Van Camp

- **ALTERNATIVE**: An International Journal of Indigenous Peoples (magazine)

- **FUNNY YOU DONT LOOK LIKE ONE**, Drew Hayden Taylor

- **FIRST NATIONS 101**, Lynda Gray

- **THE LONE RANGER AND TONTO FISTFIGHT IN HEAVEN**, Sherman Alexie

- **SNAG MAG** (magazine)

TAIAIAKE ALFRED is a professor in Indigenous Governance and in the Department of Political Science at the University of Victoria, Canada. He specializes in studies of traditional Indigenous governance, the restoration of land-based cultural practices, and decolonization strategies. Taiaiake is a Bear Clan Mohawk.

GLEN COULTHARD is an assistant professor in the First Nations Studies Program and the Department of Political Science at the University of British Columbia. Glen has written and published numerous articles and chapters in the areas of Indigenous thought and politics, contemporary political theory, and radical social and political thought. Glen is Yellowknives Dene.

There are over 350 million Indigenous peoples in the world and our struggles are redefining what it means to be radical today.

As land-based societies, Indigenous peoples have always been the prime targets of capitalist expansion and colonial domination. By colonial domination we mean the relationship between Indigenous peoples and settler societies where power—in this case, interlocking features of economic (capitalism), gendered (patriarchy), racial (white supremacy), and political (state) power—has been structured into a relatively secure set of hierarchical social relationships that continue to enable the theft of Indigenous lands and political authority. In this respect, Canada and the United States are no different than any other colonial power: in these contexts, colonial domination continues to be geared toward the settler-state's commitment to maintain—through force, fraud, and more recently, so-called "negotiations" over land and self-government—ongoing access to the land and resources that provide the material and spiritual nourishment of Indigenous societies on the one hand, and the foundation of colonial state-formation, settlement, and capitalist development on the other.

Through our struggles, Indigenous peoples are redefining what it means to resist the colonial condition that we have all inherited. Contemporary colonialism rarely maintains itself solely through the blunt forces of capitalist exploitation and overt land theft. In order to achieve so much political control and physical destruction, colonialism has had to solidify its gains by normalizing the injustices it has perpetrated against Indigenous peoples. This means that Indigenous resistance must confront not only the illegitimate exercise of settler-state and corporate power, but also the colonial ideas, values, and beliefs that have seeped into our cultures and psyches. Our freedom is not only constrained by the structural relations of power that we face on a daily basis—grinding poverty, white supremacy, violence against Indigenous women, state domination, and environmental destruction; it is also undermined by the reproduction of these forms of power by and within our own communities.

These aspects of empire impede our capacity for self-determination, sabotage our health, and destroy the spiritual and physical well-being of our communities.

Today's Indigenous warriors understand and practice resistance as a means of transcending these destructive forces. In this sense, "resistance" is no longer a sufficient term to describe what is happening among our people; personalities are being reconstructed, lives re-made, and communities re-formed in a process more akin to "regeneration" and "resurgence."

Indigenous peoples are aware that we cannot defeat colonial aggression alone. A coherent and transformative strategy of Indigenous resurgence requires that we actively promote solidarity and cooperative action with those who share similar commitments. But solidarity is hard work. It requires a great deal of critical self-reflection and commitment to action on the part of the settler population. Coming to grips with colonial privilege by acknowledging the role that settlers play in the maintenance of empire must be seen as a necessary aspect of the struggle to decolonize, for Indigenous peoples and for everyone.

Indigenous peoples today are articulating a new vision of a human existence for the 21st century. We are critically rethinking and refashioning the basis of our social and political lives toward the realization of our freedom as the original peoples of this land. We invite anyone with the courage and commitment to create a genuinely just society to join us in this struggle.

GORD HILL's first book, *The 500 Years of Resistance Comic Book*, is now in its second printing. He is a member of the Kwakwaka'wakw nation whose territory is located on northern Vancouver Island and adjacent mainland in the province of "British Columbia." He has been involved in anti-colonial and anti-capitalist resistance (i.e., Indigenous people's and anti-globalization movements) since 1990. He lives in Vancouver's Downtown Eastside. This story reprinted with permission from *The 500 Years of Resistance Comic Book* by Gord Hill (Arsenal Pulp Press, 2010).

THE HEAVIEST FIGHTING WAS IN OCOSINGO, WHERE OVER 50 EZLN WARRIORS MAY HAVE BEEN KILLED...

SOME WERE FOUND WITH THEIR HANDS TIED BEHIND THEIR BACKS—THEY WERE EXECUTED BY SOLDIERS.

BY JANUARY 4, ZAPATISTA UNITS HAD ALL WITHDRAWN TO THEIR BASES IN THE LACANDON JUNGLE.

BY JANUARY 12, 14,000 MEXICAN TROOPS HAD BEEN DEPLOYED. THEY RAIDED TOWNS + VILLAGES, WITH HOUSE-TO-HOUSE SEARCHES + MASS ARRESTS.

ZAPATISTA WOMEN WARRIORS

BUT THE ZAPATISTAS ESCAPED. COMPRISED OF MAYAN INDIANS, THE EZLN HAD TRAINED AND ORGANIZED IN SECRET FOR 10 YEARS...

THEY TOOK THEIR NAME FROM AN INDIGENOUS LEADER IN THE 1910 REVOLUTION: EMILIANO ZAPATA.

BY SPRING, HUNDREDS OF OCCUPATIONS + LAND SEIZURES HAD OCCURED. MANY NATIVES WERE INSPIRED TO REBEL...

ALL ACROSS MEXICO, WORKERS, STUDENTS, THE POOR, + OTHER SOCIAL MOVEMENTS RALLIED IN SUPPORT OF THE INSURGENTS.

MANY TOWNS IN CHIAPAS DECLARED THEMSELVES AUTONOMOUS FROM THE STATE + ALLIED WITH THE ZAPATISTAS.

THEY SELF-ORGANIZED SCHOOLS, LOCAL GOVERNMENT, HEALTH CLINICS, AND WORKER'S CO-OPS TO SELL FOOD AND CRAFTS (INCLUDING CORN + COFFEE).

THE ZAPATISTAS HAVE ALSO ORGANIZED INTERNATIONAL GATHERINGS WITH DELEGATES FROM AROUND THE WORLD.

NATIONAL MOBILIZATIONS UNDER THE EZLN BANNER HAVE INVOLVED TENS OF THOUSANDS - FOCUSING ON LAND AND THE RIGHTS OF INDIGENOUS PEOPLE.

AS PART OF MEXICO'S COUNTER-INSURGENCY WAR, MASSACRES, ASSASSINATIONS, TORTURE + IMPRISONMENT ARE USED.

IN 1997, 47 PEASANTS WERE MASSACRED BY RANCH-HANDS ORGANIZED INTO A PARAMILITARY FORCE IN ACTEAL...

I'M AN INSURGENT. I HAVE DEDICATED ALL MY LIFE AND TIME TO THE CAUSE.*

* MAJOR ANNA MARIA, EZLN

DESPITE THIS, THE EZLN CONTINUES TO EXIST, ORGANIZE + MOBILIZE AMONG MEXICO'S INDIGENOUS PEOPLES...

TODAY, THE ZAPATISTA SPIRIT OF INSURGENCY HAS SPREAD THRU MEXICO AND THE WORLD. IN 2006, THE EZLN LAUNCHED THE 'OTHER CAMPAIGN' TO UNIFY SOCIAL MOVEMENTS. THAT YEAR, REVOLTS AT ATENCO & OAXACA SHOOK THE COUNTRY, AS DID PRESIDENTIAL ELECTIONS MARKED BY FRAUD...

WARD CHURCHILL is of mixed racial and cultural descent. A member of the American Indian Movement since 1972, he is the author of more than twenty books and well over two hundred articles and book chapters. Since retiring from his professorship at the University of Colorado in 2007, he has functioned as an independent scholar. This article was originally written as an official paper of the Autonomous Confederation–American Indian Movement.

During the past couple of seasons, there has been an increasing wave of controversy regarding the names of professional sports teams like the Atlanta "Braves," Cleveland "Indians," Washington "Redskins," and Kansas City "Chiefs." The issue extends to the names of college teams like Florida State University "Seminoles," University of Illinois "Fighting Illini," and so on, right on down to high school outfits like the Lamar (Colorado) "Savages." Also involved have been team adoption of "mascots," replete with feathers, buckskins, beads, spears, and "warpaint" (some fans have opted to adorn themselves in the same fashion), and nifty little "pep" gestures like the "Indian Chant" and "Tomahawk Chop."

A substantial number of American Indians have protested that use of native names, images, and symbols as sports team mascots and the like is, by definition, a virulently racist practice. Given the historical relationship between Indians and non-Indians during what has been called the "Conquest of America," American Indian Movement leader (and American Indian Anti-Defamation Council founder) Russell Means has compared the practice to contemporary Germans naming their soccer teams the "Jews," Hebrews," and "Yids," while adorning their uniforms with grotesque caricatures of Jewish faces taken from the Nazis' anti-Semitic propaganda of the 1930s. Numerous demonstrations have occurred in conjunction with games—most notably during the November 15, 1992 matchup between the Chiefs and Redskins in Kansas City—by angry Indians and their supporters.

In response, a number of players—especially African Americans and other minority athletes—have been trotted out by professional team owners like Ted Turner, as well as university and public school officials, to announce that they mean not to insult but to honor native people. They have been joined by the television networks and most major newspapers, all of which have editorialized that Indian discomfort with the situation is "no big deal," insisting that the whole things is just "good, clean fun." The country needs more such fun, they've argued, and a "few disgruntled Native Americans" have no right to undermine the nation's enjoyment of its leisure time by complaining. This is especially the case, some have argued, "in hard times like these." It has even been contended that Indian outrage at being systematically degraded—rather than the degradation itself—creates "a serious barrier to the sort of intergroup communication so necessary in a multicultural society such as ours."

Okay. Let's communicate. We are frankly dubious that those advancing such positions really believe their own rhetoric but, just for the sake of argument, let's accept the premise that they are sincere. If what they say is true, then isn't it time we spread such "inoffensiveness" and "good cheer" around among all the groups so that everybody can participate equally in fostering the national round of laughs they call for? Sure it is—the country can't have too much fun or "intergroup" involvement—so the more, the merrier. Simple consistency demands that anyone who thinks the Tomahawk Chop is a swell pastime must be just as hearty in their endorsement of the following ideas—by the logic used to defend the defamation of American Indians—should help us all really start yukking it up.

First, as a counterpart to the Redskins, we need an NFL team called "Niggers" to honor Afro-Americans. Half-time festivities for fans might include a simulated stewing of the opposing coach in a large pot while players and cheerleaders dance around it, garbed in leopard skins and wearing fake bones in their noses. This concept obviously goes along with the kind of gaiety attending the Chop, but also with the actions of the Kansas Chiefs, whose team members—prominently including black members—lately appeared on a poster, looking "fierce" and "savage" by way of wearing Indian regalia. Just a bit of harmless "morale boosting," says the Chiefs' front office. You bet.

So that the newly-formed Niggers sports club won't end up too out of sync while expressing the "spirit" and "identity" of Afro-Americans in the above fashion, a baseball franchise—let's call this one the "Sambos"—should be formed. How about a basketball team called the "Spearchuckers"? A hockey team called the "Jungle Bunnies"? Maybe the "essence" of these teams could be depicted by images of tiny black faces adorned with huge pairs of lips. The players could appear on TV every week or so gnawing on chicken legs and spitting watermelon seeds at one another. Catchy, eh? Well, there's "nothing to be upset about," according to those who love wearing "war bonnets" to the Super Bowl or having "Chief Illiniwik" dance around the sports arenas of Urbana, Illinois.

And why stop there? There are plenty of other groups to include. "Hispanics?" They can be "represented" by the Galveston "Greasers" and the San Diego "Spics," at least until the Wisconsin "Wetbacks" and Baltimore "Beaners" get off the ground. Asian Americans? How about the "Slopes," "Dinks," "Gooks," and "Zipperheads"? Owners of the latter teams might get their logo ideas from editorial page cartoons printed in the nation's newspapers during World War II: slanteyes, buck teeth, big glasses, but nothing racially insulting or derogatory, according to the editors and artists involved at the time. Indeed, this Second World War-vintage stuff can be seen as just another barrel of laughs at least by what current editors say are their "local standards" concerning American Indians.

Let's see. Who's been left out? Teams like the Kansas City "Kikes," Hanover "Honkies," San Leandro "Shylock," Daytona "Dagos," and Pittsburgh "Polacks" will fill a certain social void among white folk. Have a religious belief? Let's all go for the gusto and gear up the Milwaukee "Mackerel Snappers" and Hollywood "Holy Rollers." The Fighting Irish of Notre Dame can be rechristened the "Drunken Irish" or "Papist Pigs." Issues of gender and sexual preference can be addressed through creation of teams like the St. Louis "Sluts," Boston "Bimbos," Detroit "Dykes," and the Fresno "Fags." How about the Gainesville "Gimps" and the Richmond "Retards," so the physically and mentally impaired won't be excluded from our fun and games?

Now, don't go getting "overly sensitive" out there. None of this is dreaming or insulting, at least not when it's being done to Indians. Just ask the folks who are doing it, or their apologists like Andy Rooney in the national media. They'll tell you—as in fact they have been telling you—that there's no harm done, regardless of what their victims think, feel, or say. The situation is exactly the same as when those with precisely the same mentality used to insist that Step 'n' Fetchit was okay, or Rochester on the Jack Benny show, or Amos and Andy, Charlie Chan, the Frito Bandito, or any other cutesy symbols making up the lexicon of American racism. Have we communicated yet? Let's get just a little bit real here. The notion of "fun" embodied in rituals like the Tomahawk Chop must be understood for what it is. There's not a single non-Indian example used above which can be considered socially acceptable in even the most marginal sense. The reasons are obvious enough. So why is it different where American Indians are concerned? One can only conclude that, in contrast to the other groups at issue, Indians are (falsely) perceived as being too few, and therefore too weak, to defend themselves effectively against racist and otherwise offensive behaviour.

Fortunately, there are some glimmers of hope. A few teams and their fans have gotten the message and have responded appropriately. Stanford University, which opted to drop the name "Indians," has experienced no resulting drop in attendance. Meanwhile, the local newspaper in Portland, Oregon recently decided its long-standing editorial policy prohibiting use of racial epithets should include derogatory teams names. The Redskins, for instance, are now referred to as "the Washington team," and will continued to be described in this way until the franchise adopts an inoffensive moniker (newspaper sales in Portland have suffered no decline as a result). Such examples are to be applauded and encouraged. They stand as figurative beacons in the night, proving beyond all doubt that it is quite possible to indulge in the pleasure of athletics without accepting blatant racism into the bargain.

JOI T. ARCAND is an artist, writer, and designer from Muskeg Lake Cree Nation, SK and among other things, a plains Cree/Métis/German hybrid prairie-girl on the west coast. This piece is adapted from a larger story published in *Pacific Rim Magazine* in May 2011 profiling Khelsilum Rivers and his work to revitalize the Skwxwú7mesh language.

Skwxwú7mesh Sníchim is the language spoken by the Skwxwú7mesh people, whose traditional territory includes some of Vancouver. Both the Skwxwú7mesh language and nation are colloquially referred to as Squamish. As one of British Columbia's 32 distinct First Nations languages, the Squamish language is traditionally passed down orally from generation to generation; it is the way its speakers have related to each other and the world around them since time immemorial. However, since European colonization reached the West Coast, the number of fluent speakers has dwindled to an estimated 0.01 percent. Today, it means that in a nation of approximately 3,324 people, Khelsilum Rivers estimates, there are four fluent speakers left.

The First Peoples' Heritage, Language, and Culture Council (FPHLCC) released a report in April 2010 outlining the status of B.C.'s First Nations languages. The report has brought to light some dismal statistics: only 5.1 percent of B.C. First Nations people are fluent speakers of their language, which puts all 32 of the languages included in the study as severely endangered, nearly extinct, or already sleeping (extinct).

The dramatic loss of fluent speakers began with colonization and the Canadian government's historic policies to assimilate First Nations people into English-speaking, non-First Nations society. A major part of the assimilation process was the forced removal of children from their families and placement into church-run residential schools, where First Nations languages were strictly banned from use. Part of the process included brutal physical and emotional punishment, resulting in children feeling fear and shame for speaking their language. As the report states, "many residential school survivors, their children, grandchildren and great-grandchildren still feel the effects of the loss of their traditional First Nations languages."

For a nation whose way of life has been drastically affected by the development of Canada's third largest city within their traditional territory, there are some challenges in creating environments where the Squamish language is spoken exclusively—the influence of the English language is everywhere. Because there aren't many fluent speakers left, there aren't many opportunities for the language to exist without the influence of English. "It is difficult at times, because English is my thinking language. It requires a conscious thought to really switch over [to Squamish]," says Rivers. Creating environments where only Squamish is spoken triggers the mind to operate in that environment. "And those don't exist right now."

You could say it started with a tweet. That is how Rivers learned about the language-learning method called Where Are Your Keys (WAYK). Based out of Portland, Oregon, WAYK was developed by Evan Gardner and his associate Willem Larson to get people speaking their language as quickly as possible. During a phone conversation from Bend, Oregon, Gardner describes WAYK as "an open-source, community-based method designed to accelerate the language-learning process." The game incorporates sign language, special rules, and techniques that help transfer language faster from one person to another. A typical game has players sit around a table where they interact with simple objects, such as rocks, sticks, and pens. Players learn by passing questions and answers about the objects back and forth.

Larson and Gardner had been working with First Nation communities in Oregon and Washington for about 10 years when they began to develop a larger web presence. About two years ago, Larson spotted a tweet from Rivers on Twitter. "[Rivers's tweet] said something like, 'I want to learn my language within the next such and such timeframe,'" Gardner explains, "We emailed him back and said, well, we know a way. Any community that actually wants to bring their language back just needs to have someone that says, 'Okay, I'll do it.'"

For the Squamish nation, Rivers has become a leader for those who want to learn their language. With the help of Gardner and Larson's method and mentorship, Rivers has organized community language nights for his people. The language nights are attended three times a week, by up to 24 dedicated learners ranging from 10 to 64 years of age.

The language nights are also bringing his community together. "I noticed people that wouldn't normally interact with each other are now in an environment where they have a shared interest and they are interacting and building a relationship, becoming friends or community members again," Rivers says. And they're having fun while learning, he adds: "When there is laughter present, people tend to learn a lot more. So if it's fun and there are a lot of funny and silly moments—and people are laughing, it means that people are learning."

So what is needed to bring a near-extinct language back to life? Ten percent. One in 10 members of the Squamish Nation need to be fluent in the language in order for it to remain safe from extinction. Rivers has a plan to make that happen. "I have an eight-stage strategy that I'm following, developed by American linguist, Joshua Fishman. His strategy helps you identify where your language is on the scale, so you can appropriately accomplish the next step." Rivers says that Skwxwú7mesh Sníchim is still in the early stage: getting an adult generation of speakers who act as language apprentices, and as bridges between elders and the youth. He says, "if we're there and we start creating newspapers in Squamish or writing books in Squamish, they're not going to be entirely useful until there are people who are able to read them." He says that time and resources spent on producing written learning tools could be better used to address the issue of where the language is at now, and getting it to the next level, which is creating an integrated group of active speakers where the language is used habitually or exclusively.

ANDREA LEE SMITH is a co-founder of INCITE! Women of Colour Against Violence, the Boarding School Healing Project, and the Chicago Chapter of Women of All Red Nations. She is currently an Associate Professor in the Department of Media and Cultural Studies at the University of California, Riverside. This essay was originally published in the *New Socialist* (October 2006).

We often hear the mantra in indigenous communities that Native women aren't feminists. Supposedly, feminism is not needed because Native women were treated with respect prior to colonization. Thus, any Native woman who calls herself a feminist is often condemned as being "white."

However, when I started interviewing Native women organizers as part of a research project, I was surprised by how many community-based activists were describing themselves as "feminists without apology." They were arguing that feminism is actually an indigenous concept that has been co-opted by white women.

The fact that Native societies were egalitarian 500 years ago is not stopping women from being hit or abused now. For instance, in my years of anti-violence organizing, I would hear, "We can't worry about domestic violence; we must worry about survival issues first." But since Native women are the women most likely to be killed by domestic violence, they are clearly not surviving. So when we talk about survival of our nations, who are we including?

These Native feminists are challenging not only patriarchy within Native communities, but also white supremacy and colonialism within mainstream white feminism. That is, they're challenging why it is that white women get to define what feminism is.

DECENTERING WHITE FEMINISM

The feminist movement is generally periodized into the so-called first, second, and third waves of feminism. In the United States, the first wave is characterized by the suffragette movement; the second wave is characterized by the formation of the National Organization for Women, abortion rights politics, and the fight for the Equal Rights Amendments. Suddenly, during the third wave of feminism, women of colour make an appearance to transform feminism into a multicultural movement.

This periodization situates white middle-class women as the central historical agents to which women of colour attach themselves. However, if we were to recognize the agency of indigenous women in an account of feminist history, we might begin with 1492 when Native women collectively resisted colonization. This would allow us to see that there are multiple feminist histories emerging from multiple communities of colour which intersect at points and diverge in others. This would not negate the contributions made by white feminists, but would de-center them from our historicizing and analysis.

Indigenous feminism thus centers anti-colonial practice within its organizing. This is critical today when you have mainstream feminist groups supporting, for example, the US bombing of Afghanistan with the claim that this bombing will free women from the Taliban (apparently bombing women somehow liberates them).

CHALLENGING THE STATE

Indigenous feminists are also challenging how we conceptualize indigenous sovereignty—it is not an add-on to the heteronormative and patriarchal nation-state. Rather it challenges the nation-state system itself.

Charles Colson, prominent Christian Right activist and founder of Prison Fellowship, explains quite clearly the relationship between heteronormativity and the nation-state. In his view, same-sex marriage leads directly to terrorism; the attack on the "natural moral order" of the heterosexual family "is like handing moral weapons of mass destruction to those who use America's decadence to recruit more snipers and hijackers and suicide bombers."

Similarly, the *Christian Right World* magazine opined that feminism contributed to the Abu Ghraib scandal by promoting women in the military. When women do not know their assigned role in the gender hierarchy, they become disoriented and abuse prisoners.

Implicit in this analysis is the understanding that heteropatriarchy is essential for the building of US empire. Patriarchy is the logic that naturalizes social hierarchy. Just as men are supposed to naturally dominate women on the basis of biology, so too should the social elites of a society naturally rule everyone else through a nation-state form of governance that is constructed through domination, violence, and control.

As Ann Burlein argues in *Lift High the Cross*, it may be a mistake to argue that the goal of Christian Right politics is to create a theocracy in the US. Rather, Christian Right politics work through the private family (which is coded as white, patriarchal, and middle-class) to create a "Christian America." She notes that the investment in the private family makes it difficult for people to invest in more public forms of social connection.

For example, more investment in the suburban private family means less funding for urban areas and Native reservations. The resulting social decay is then construed to be caused by deviance from the Christian family ideal rather than political and economic forces. As former head of the Christian Coalition Ralph Reed states: "The only true solution to crime is to restore the family," and "Family break-up causes poverty."

Unfortunately, as Navajo feminist scholar Jennifer Denetdale points out, the Native response to a heteronormative white, Christian America has often been an equally heteronormative Native nationalism. In her critique of the Navajo tribal council's passage of a ban on same-sex marriage, Denetdale argues that Native nations are furthering a Christian Right agenda in the name of "Indian tradition."

This trend is equally apparent within racial justice struggles in other communities of colour. As Cathy Cohen contends, heteronormative sovereignty or racial justice struggles will effectively maintain rather than challenge colonialism and white supremacy because they are premised on a politics of secondary marginalization. The most elite class will further their aspirations on the backs of those most marginalized within the community.

Through this process of secondary marginalization, the national or racial justice struggle either implicitly or explicitly takes on a nation-state model as the end point of its struggle—a model in which the elites govern the rest through violence and domination, and exclude those who are not members of "the nation."

NATIONAL LIBERATION

Grassroots Native women, along with Native scholars such as Taiaiake Alfred and Craig Womack, are developing other models of nationhood. These articulations counter the frequent accusations that nation-building projects necessarily lead to a narrow identity politics based on ethnic cleansing and intolerance. This requires that a clear distinction be drawn between the project of national liberation, and that of nation-state building.

Progressive activists and scholars, while prepared to make critiques of the US and Canadian governments, are often not prepared to question their legitimacy. A case in point is the strategy of many racial justice organizations in the US or Canada, who have rallied against the increase in hate crimes since 9/11 under the banner, "We're American [or Canadian] too."

This allegiance to "America" or "Canada" legitimizes the genocide and colonization of Native peoples upon which these nation-states are founded. By making anti-colonial struggle central to feminist politics, Native women place in question the appropriate form of governance for the world in general.

In questioning the nation-state, we can begin to imagine a world that we would actually want to live in. Such a political project is particularly important for colonized peoples seeking national liberation outside the nation-state.

Whereas nation-states are governed through domination and coercion, indigenous sovereignty and nationhood is predicated on interrelatedness and responsibility. As Sharon Venne explains, "Our spirituality and our responsibilities define our duties. We understand the concept of sovereignty as woven through a fabric that encompasses our spirituality and responsibility. This is a cyclical view of sovereignty, incorporating it into our traditional philosophy and view of our responsibilities. It differs greatly from the concept of Western sovereignty which is based upon absolute power. For us absolute power is in the Creator and the natural order of all living things; not only in human beings... Our sovereignty is related to our connections to the earth and is inherent."

REVOLUTION

A Native feminist politics seeks to do more than simply elevate Native women's status—it seeks to transform the world through indigenous forms of governance that can be beneficial to everyone.

At the 2005 World Liberation Theology Forum held in Porto Alegre, Brazil, indigenous peoples from Bolivia stated that they know another world is possible because they see that world whenever they do their ceremonies. Native ceremonies can be a place where the present, past, and future become co-present. This is what Native Hawaiian scholar Manu Meyer calls a "racial remembering" of the future.

Prior to colonization, Native communities were not structured on the basis of hierarchy, oppression, or patriarchy. We will not recreate these communities as they existed prior to colonization. Our understanding that a society without structures of oppression was possible in the past tells us that our current political and economic system is anything but natural and inevitable. If we lived differently before, we can live differently in the future.

Native feminism is not simply an insular or exclusivist "identity politics," as it is often accused of being. Rather, it is a framework that understands indigenous women's struggle as part of a global movement for liberation. As one activist stated: "You can't win a revolution on your own. And we are about nothing short of a revolution. Anything else is simply not worth our time."

ANDREW CURLEY is a member of the Navajo Nation and a Ph.D. student in the Department of Development Sociology at Cornell University. He is interested in energy politics, climate change, and economic development on American Indian reservations.

A few cautionary notes about radical organizing in indigenous communities:

The difficulty with work in and around indigenous communities has something to do with cultural politics—that is how culture and politics relate and overlap in these places. It is important for young radicals and organizers to be aware of two things; these cultural politics are both sensitive and disputed. Building an alliance with one group of actors in an indigenous community might mean alienating yourself from another. There is not a singular indigenous perspective on these issues that you work on. Like all communities, there are factions. One should be aware of the political faultlines inherent in these struggles before proceeding.

In a broader sense, how politics is done outside of indigenous communities and what they mean for you might be fundamentally different from how these debates translate for indigenous peoples. Don't expect the same political frames or cultural references to work within tribal communities as they do in your milieu. Talking about radical politics for indigenous peoples might mean something entirely different than your understanding of it. Put simply; be aware that you will not fully understand the cultural and political frames through which indigenous peoples think through your politics. Try to make space within your work for organic solutions that come from tribal peoples themselves who know their political and cultural terrain.

Finally, all of these cautionary notes are not meant to negate the potential of radical politics across indigenous communities. It is not to suggest that cultural politics is antithetical to radical politics. Rather it is to make the small but important observation that these two types of politics originate from different experiences and consequently take on unique trajectories. The former is the outcome of centuries of resistance against colonialism, whereas the latter is more or less rooted in class struggle against exploitation. There are areas where class struggle and anti-colonial resistance bridge, but places where they diverge. In a pragmatic sense, it's important for your work and the work of indigenous peoples to find spots where they naturally meet rather than toil furiously at fording areas where there are large gulfs and torrent waters.

STAY **SOLID**

ANGELA STERRITT is a Television and Radio Journalist and Reporter with the Canadian Broadcast Corporation. She is also currently a writer for *Maclean's Magazine* and a graduate of the University of British Columbia. Sterritt's broadcast and print journalism career in Canada has spanned over a decade. She is a proud member of the Gitxsan Nation.

RICHARD J.F. DAY is an autonomy-oriented practitioner and theorist, who is interested in creating and linking radical alternatives to the currently dominant order. To get a sense of where he's coming from, you can read his book *Gramsci Is Dead: Anarchist Currents in the Newest Social Movements*, and keep an eye out for a new project called *The Equations of Insurrection*.

When I think about my experience with settler-indigenous solidarity, I'm brought back to a conference on anti-imperialism that I attended some years ago. The meeting involved mostly settlers, and was being held on a university campus, but the organizers had done the right thing and asked an elder from the local indigenous nation to welcome us to the land.

It was the first day, most people didn't know each other, and we were just kind of sitting around, waiting for something to happen. It was pretty obvious when the elder came into the room, as he was carrying a drum and was wearing some items of traditional dress. He stood near the front of the room, to the side, looking around, but looking more comfortable than most of us.

At this point in my life I didn't have a lot of experience in working with indigenous people. I knew that I felt, somehow, that what I should do was go over and introduce myself. But I wasn't sure of the protocol, and didn't want to screw things up. I felt that other people felt the same, and wondered why none of the organizers were stepping in.

Finally, one young person stood up, walked over to our host, shook hands, and chatted a bit. Right after that the welcome ceremony began, and proceeded in the usual formal way. Then something more informal happened. The elder talked about indigenous protocols of meeting, being open, how to make for good relations. Then he called up the young person who'd come over to talk with him, and said: "This one, he did the right thing. And I want to thank him for that."

At the time, I thought that what he did that was "right" was to know the protocol and act appropriately. If I had only known it, I could have done the right thing too! But since then, I've come to believe that the elder was trying to teach us something different. I think he was trying to get us to trust ourselves, even when we don't know the protocol, to act from our intuition.

I think he was trying to teach us that while it can be very hard to reach across the colonial divide, as communities and as individuals, it's absolutely necessary to try, again and again, if we are to have any chance of working well together. I also think he was trying to show us that, in taking up this difficult, but very rewarding task, a little bit of courage, humility, and willingness to make mistakes, goes a long way.

16. ECOCIDE

It is totally clear that the world is in the midst of an ecological crisis. All over the world the ways in which dominant cultures interact with the land and the natural world are deeply unsustainable, no matter what the label on your paper towel dispenser says. There is widespread agreement on this, but little agreement on what to do, from green capitalists to those who argue that we must destroy civilization as we know it. But how can we work towards an ecological future while living happy, healthy lives without collapsing into nihilism, panic, apathy, or debilitating rage? Is there any way to live in this world that nurtures the land and our non-human friends? What are some ecologically sane ways to live that are being practiced by happy/healthy people? Are there any?

It is hard sometimes to think that your own actions can have any impact on slow-moving, mind-bendingly global catastrophes, but it's not going to do anyone, maybe most of all yourself, any good to live in denial. Climate change really does exist, species really are being extinguished, the oceans are on the brink of a massive die-off, brutal pollution is everywhere, ecosystems really are collapsing. There are huge and powerful interlocking systems of disinformation and lies (like, say, Fox News, or the petro-chemical industry, or oil companies) that want you to believe that everything is OK, that the environment is just fine, but the scientific, cultural, and common-sense consensus is that we're in deep shit and things need to change pronto.

There are lots of root causes that people can (and do) point to: monotheistic religions that claim dominion over the natural world, overpopulation, industrialism, patriarchy, racist oppression, agribusiness, a society predicated on burning fossil fuels, massive over-consumption, colonialism—and there are good arguments to be made that each of these are major underpinnings to the ecological crises we find ourselves in. Each deserves to be analysed, understood, and confronted, and all of these factors have converged in the 21st century under (post)modern capitalism where environmental domination exists hand-in-hand with social domination: they are two sides of the same coin. Ecological thinking has to be anti-capitalist thinking.

Our argument is that there are many targets to point your energies at, but the imperative is to continually deepen your own analysis so that you are not "going green" by turning off the lights when you're not in the room, but honestly assessing the deeper root causes of the environmental crisis and acting accordingly.

There are incredible people and vibrant projects all over the world, right where you live, who are developing better ways to think and act. Maybe most powerfully, there are traditional societies and indigenous cultures that have lived in place for millennia without fucking their ecosystems up. We have a tremendous amount to learn from them, and right now almost everything should be on the table when we think about what a better world might look like.

OTHER STUFF TO CHECK OUT:

- **THE ECOLOGY OF FREEDOM**, Murray Bookchin

- **FROM THE GROUND UP**: Environmental Racism and the Rise of the Environmental Justice Movement, Luke Cole, Sheila Foster, and Samuel Slipp

- **FIELD NOTES FROM A CATASTROPHE**, Elizabeth Kolbert

- **DEMOCRATIZING BIOLOGY**: Reinventing Biology from a Feminist, Ecological and Third World Perspective, Vandana Shiva

- **LISTENING TO WHALES**, Alexandra Morton

- **INDIGENOUS ENVIRONMENTAL NETWORK** (organization)

- **EATING ANIMALS**, Jonathan Safran Foer

- **NAUSICAÄ OF THE VALLEY OF THE WIND**, Hayao Miyazaki (movie or comic)

- **THE GARDEN** (film)

HILARY MOORE, 26, works as a nanny and lives in Oakland California. She organizes, writes, and teaches on climate justice, reproductive labor, and white, working-class strategies.

Dear Hilary,

I could give you some winning lottery numbers from the future, or offer a lucrative heads up on this thing called an iPod. Yet, we have more pressing matters to discuss. I want to talk to you about your new best friend, Punk Rock. Right about now, you two are getting well acquainted. Pretty exhilarating, isn't it? The music wraps you up, spits you out, and still, you crave more!

I'm writing you, not to change your mind, because I like where you've ended up—me—but to encourage your curiosity. I want you to imagine punk rock as a *thrift store of ideas*. It's a rather funky place, dingy with a tinge of body odor lingering around your nostrils, but nonetheless, it's inviting. Soon you will peruse the aisles, finding ideas that complement you: to your right, we have the vegan straight-edge section tagged with militant animal rights pamphlets; to your left, we have the drunk-punk, fuck-the-world section that offers a studded belt for no additional cost; just ahead, the all-inclusive tough-guy hardcore section that will beat anyone and everyone up; and just beyond the stab-you-in-the-junk riot grrrl section, we have our anti-authoritarian accessories. So many options! Spend some time looking around, try things on. Most of what you find is shit, but occasionally there is that one ideological t-shirt that feels shockingly good and you will wear it forever.

The more time spent inside this punk rock thrift store, the more pissed you might become. Perhaps you'll get mad that nothing fits you, or that everything outside punk rock is so bourgeois! Either way, it seems like the shopping bag you're toting across the aisles is laced with anger towards someone, if not everyone else; after all, isn't that what being punk is all about?

In about three years, you're going to become intoxicated with the eco-aisle, a patch-work of anarchism, feminism, and environmentalism. Get curious about the ideas, like how legacies of domination and hierarchy have shaped our ecology, cultures, ethics, bodies, politics, and even our ability to imagine a better world. Please, nerd out and dive deep, but remember: it's too damn simple to blame "people" or "society" for the way things are. There are systems at work and *organizing with people*, especially those outside our drab thrift store, is our only hope for creating a truly free society.

STAY **SOLID**

DERRICK JENSEN is the author of twenty books, and holds a degree in creative writing from Eastern Washington University, a degree in mineral engineering physics from the Colorado School of Mines, and has taught at Eastern Washington University and Pelican Bay State Prison. This piece is excerpted from *Endgame* (Seven Stories Press, 2006).

The Squamish people, who live near what is now Vancouver, British Columbia, tell this story: A long time ago, even before the time of the flood, the Cheakamus River provided food for the Squamish people. Each year, at the end of the summer, when the salmon came home to spawn, the people would cast their cedar root nets into the water and get enough fish for the winter to come.

One day, a man came to fish for the winter. He looked into the river and found that many of the fish were coming home this year. He said thanks to the spirit of the fish for giving themselves as food for his family, and cast his net into the river and waited. In time, he drew his nets in and they were full of fish, enough for his family for the whole year. He packed these away into cedar bark baskets, and prepared to go home.

But he looked into the river and saw all those fish, and decided to cast his net again. And he did so, and it again filled with fish, which he drew onto the shore. A third time, he cast his net into the water and waited.

This time when he pulled his net in, it was torn beyond repair by sticks, stumps, and branches which filled the net. To his dismay, the fish on the shore and the fish in the cedar bark baskets were also sticks and branches. He had no fish, his nets were ruined.

It was then he looked up at the mountain and saw Wountie, the spirit protecting the Cheakamus, who told him that he had broken the faith with the river and with nature, by taking more than he needed for himself and his family. And this was the consequence.

And to this day, high on the mountain overlooking the Cheakamus and Paradise Valley, is the image of Wountie, protecting Cheakamus.

The fisherman? Well, his family went hungry and starved, a lesson for all the people.

This piece was contributed **ANONYMOUSLY.**

 The three arrows imply that that which is put into the recycling is simply re-created, that the whole process is neutral and benign, and that it could go on forever. A simple look into the facts about industrial processes, when separated from the myths created by marketing, gives us a very different view into this greenwashed process.

Recycling is not sustainable, as it does not meet the fundamental definition of what can be "sustained." Its not that we should not recycle things, it's that we need to have a greater awareness of the production and the "recycle sector" so that we can resist their poisonous, destructive culture and consider how to undermine their existence.

Recycling also perpetuates the myth that the consumer is somehow responsible for, and can alter, the global situation in which we find ourselves.

Recycling is another brick in the wall of pacification of the population towards capitalism's anti-moral procedures. The destruction of the world is ongoing, and we are sold packaged solutions such as recycling to make us feel like we are "doing our part" or even "saving the planet." These slogans portray it as though, if we were to take one less napkin, that would somehow save a tree. The ludicrous presumption behind this tagline is that "if everyone did it, it would stop the production of napkins." In truth, when compared with the reality of industrial manufacturing, government subsidies of failing industries, and coercive advertising, a picture emerges of activities that are utterly ecologically and socially destructive, masquerading as morally and environmentally superior choices.

Al Gore recommends that you plant a tree, and try meatless Mondays. Thanks Al, but you can go fuck yourself. Here's some of our ideas:

★ Organize yourself with a small, trusted affinity group and take direct action against the industrial sector: www.youtube.com/watch?v=fNGpulnkLvI.

★ Support someone who takes direct action against the industrial sector. Donate legal funds to an "eco-terrorist" who is on trial in your area. Or write one of these imprisoned warriors letters. A list of imprisoned comrades can be found here: www.abcf.net/abcf.asp?page=prisoners.

★ Ally with Indigenous people who understand the need to undermine dominant culture.

★ Forage your food: Dumpsters are full of viable food (www.ranprieur.com/misc/dumpster.html), and medicinal and edible plants are everywhere (www.ranprieur.com/misc/dumpster.html).

★ Transform conventional forms of advertisement into art for social change.

★ Educate, educate, educate, yourself, others, and your community.

★ Create public art to educate, engage in poetic terrorism (hermetic.com/bey/taz1.html#labelPoeticTerrorism).

★ Create, support, and become part of alternative local economic systems to exchange goods.

★ Occupy Land and make a home.

★ Grow your own food, frequent potlucks, eat local, volunteer for a meal.

★ Make your own clothes, re-use your old ones, connect with people who make clothes as a revolutionary art form.

★ Reduce, reduce, reduce consumption.

★ Build a like-minded community.

★ Support local, alternative, and independent media.

★ Brew organic beer, wine, etc.

★ Create an internet network co-op.

JO-ANNE McARTHUR hails from Toronto, and has been working as an animal rights photographer for a decade and is founder of the international award-winning documentary project *We Animals*. She has documented the complex relationships between human and non-human animals on all seven continents and has contributed her photographs to over 60 campaigns. You can see more of her work at www.weanimals.org.

Do you dream about saving the world?

I do. Unabashedly so.

Don't lie; you've dreamt about it too. Think back. For some, it was when you saw the devastating reality of pollution in your city or in the water around it. Or maybe it was when you found that injured bird and, helplessly, you resolved to become a veterinarian or an advocate on behalf of animals. Perhaps it was when you realized there were people starving to death in many countries around the world and your heart screamed out as you vowed to help. Maybe it was when you saw your first clear-cut.

For me, it was when I was a young girl and witnessed a dog tied by a chain outside of someone's home in the cold winter months. In my distraught anger, I vowed that I could, and would, help all unfortunate and abused animals everywhere. I dreamed of speaking out for them.

If you want to save the world, you are not alone.

But you will be made to feel so.

As the pressures of school, parents and social conformity propel you towards the well-worn path of mediocrity, you might find your senses dulling. You might find things of less importance taking precedent, and "reality" replacing your creativity with practicality. You might find the dreams you once had a little naive. Who, after all, could possibly "save the world"?

You can. We all can, if we nurture our dreams and our vision for a better world.

Your dreams are what make you, and the world you create, beautiful and unique.

Hold fast to those dreams. Hold them out before you like the apple of your eye. Steady now; keep your eye on that prize. It depends on you as much as you depend on it. Nurture that precious vision, however bold. As Goethe famously wrote: "Boldness has genius, power, and magic in it."

The planet needs you.

Go forth and treat your dreams with the respect they deserve.

OLIVER KELLHAMMER is a Canadian land artist, permaculture teacher, activist, and writer. His botanical interventions and public art projects demonstrate nature's surprising ability to recover from damage. For more information about his various projects, check out his website at www.oliverk.org.

To You, Young Permaculturalist of the Future: Permaculture is a design philosophy that tries to create more functional relationships between people and nature. It can apply to gardens, cities, or just how you organize your life. As an artist, and urban activist, I've been using permaculture for over 25 years and along the way, I've picked up a few tips I thought I'd share with anyone who might be just starting out.

Care of people, care of the Earth:

★ This is the main thing, the basic ethic. If you're not doing *both* of these things, you're not doing permaculture.

Observation first, action later:

★ Spend lots of time watching and learning before diving in with what you think is the obvious solution.

Work where it counts:

★ It is the contaminated, damaged and fucked-up places that need your love the most. Concentrate your efforts there and the rest of the world will take care of itself. Leave wild areas alone. They are fine just the way they are. Always ask yourself: "What can I not do?"

Incrementalism:

★ Small, adaptive interventions are better than grand gestures. There are no "one-size-fits-all" answers. Also, remember things often work homeopathically—tiny interventions can have big, sometimes unintended effects. Take the time to learn from what you've done.

Plan for catastrophe:

★ Next time anyone complains about your compost piles or sheet-mulched lawns, remind them of the very important service you are providing—potentially saving their asses! A secure neighborhood is a food secure neighborhood. In the event of a disaster, North American cities have at most just a few days worth of food before they run out. It will be the eggs from your backyard chickens and the kale from your guerrilla garden that might help you and your neighbors eat until help arrives. Remember: in a disaster zone: permaculture = less looting!

Get to know your neighbors:

★ Yes, some of them might be annoying but most aren't and you might be surprised at how much support you really have—from people you wouldn't have guessed. Old timers and immigrants and people who grew up on farms can have a wealth of information on forgotten or locally unknown sustainability tricks. Many of the skills and materials you need to transform your neighborhood probably already exist right on your block.

Generate a yield, share your surplus, and close waste streams:

★ Permaculture isn't just about theories or good intentions. It's about creating on-going yields, i.e. food and *fun* from small-scale, intensive systems. Fast growing annuals like squashes, beans, potatoes, and greens can feed lots of people and bridge the gap between right now and when your long-term plans are closer to getting realized. Share your surpluses with those who are in need and you will build connections and a better world. And remember: pollution is just unused resources. Find ways to channel waste back into productivity.

Politicians and bureaucrats are followers not leaders:

★ Don't expect much creativity from them regardless of their political stripe. Their job is to maintain whatever *status quo* got them into power and yours is to push the envelope. Sometimes, it's easier to ask for forgiveness than permission. If you ask and they say "no," just start your project and see what happens. Yes, there is the risk you will get shut down but now you are defending something real and not just an idea and you will have had some time to organize community support.

Nature knows best:

★ You can't force nature to do anything. It always does what it wants. Learn to work with it and not against it and you'll be richly rewarded.

BEN WEST has explored various avenues to make change for the better ranging from film-making and slam poetry to political organizing and campaigning for the Wilderness Committee. In all his work, Ben hopes to find meaningful solutions to address his passion for environmental justice, green jobs, and eco-literacy. In his spare time Ben is a juggler, scriptwriter, and wannabe stand-up comedian.

Did you know that Exxon-Mobil is now the wealthiest company in the history of industrial civilization? This might seem strange, given that this is the company infamous for the Exxon Valdez oil spill in Alaska, but they aren't alone. BP, now forever internationally associated with the horrible oil spill in the Gulf of Mexico, has also been making record profits along with most of the other giant oil companies. These companies collectively have been responsible for numerous spills and disasters worldwide with horrible consequences especially for the most poor and vulnerable.

We should consider the implications of these facts when attempting to answer the critical environmental question of our generation: Why is it we know global warming is happening yet we continue to burn more oil and make things worse? As it turns out, Exxon funded 90 percent of reports that claim global warming isn't taking place.

Like the tobacco industry before them, these guys will stop at nothing to convince us that their products aren't harmful. That, of course, is not the only thing tobacco and oil have in common. Living in a big city exposes you to the daily equivalent of half a pack of cigarettes worth of cancer-causing human carcinogens from automobile exhaust.

What seems clear is that we must recognize what we are up against and who our allies are. There is a powerful elite who are driving the climate crisis. This is significant because it's a reminder that this isn't really just about us changing our light bulbs; it's about changing who has power.

The future of the environmental movement depends on seeing the difference between allies and enemies. We need to move beyond a view of environmentalism that pits the environment against the economy. What good is an economy that only serves the interests of a small minority and puts us all at risk?

Working together with social justice activists, the labour movement, and other progressive people, another world is possible. Let's get to work creating good "green jobs" that provide housing, transportation, and energy without poisoning and polluting our air and our atmosphere. Let's create jobs that benefit people and undermine the ability of big oil and the big banks to exploit us and the planet we depend on. It's only by seeing how we are all connected that we can all succeed.

MADHU SURI PRAKASH is currently involved in 7 revolutions inspired by Gandhi, Berry, Illich, and Tagore. Each one of these four is a PHILOSO-PHER OF SOIL inviting us to abandon our OIL WORSHIP FOR SOIL RE-GENERATION. These seven revolutions involve making and regenerating soil. All of these we may start: 1) right now 2) in our own backyard and 3) in community with kindred spirits. She works with *YES! Magazine*, kindred spirits in Dehradun India, Bija Vidyapeeth [the University of the Seed–for Seed Satyagraha], and is a professor at Penn State.

Take care of your shit. Please.

This invitation/injunction not only honors a colorful American colloquialism; it goes much further than mere talk. It responds with moral imagination, intellectual vision, and plain, practical common sense to a growing challenge today: to stop World Water Wars being waged by Superpowers and Super Corporations against common people; even as trillions of gallons are flushed away by "developed peoples" to transport urine and shit to polluting and violently toxic treatment plants: poisoning rivers, ponds, oceans, and millions of acres of fields growing food for billions across our desecrated, raped Mother Earth.

King Edward and Thomas Crapper collaborated with others to liberate royalty from their responsibilities to "take care of their shit" by flushing it "out of sight, out of mind." Middle and upper classes, mimicking royalty as usual, began claiming the flush toilet as a human right to be enjoyed by non-royalty: thereby universalizing Royalty's prerogatives and predispositions towards social irresponsibility and ecological illiteracy.

Thanks to peasants' common sense and respect for their soils, fields, and traditions in every indigenous culture, today's innovators in architecture, engineering, and Green Design for every aspect of sustainable living have centuries of knowledge of soil and water regeneration to draw upon. Young bioneers are turning to diverse indigenous alternatives to the global colonization by British Royalty's flush toilet: for which corporations, always hungry for profits, continue creating demands in every nation today with strong support from the Global Education System.

Young and old Innovators alike, including school dropouts, are regenerating the ancient knowledge of Guatemalan and Vietnamese peasants to design and manufacture Dry Composting Toilets. The skills and teaching required to manufacture and build Dry Composting Toilets are being mastered by ten-year-olds and teenagers right in their backyards. In Mexico and other countries, young "school dropouts" are decades ahead of the Emperor of Microsoft, Bill Gates, now interested in amassing liquid and solid gold: urine and feces. Instead of learning from young and old peasants as well as school dropouts for disseminating toilets that do not waste a single drop of water on the transportation of feces and urine, Emperor Microsoft is giving billions to German scientists.

Happily, he could spread those research monies employing millions of young people across the world, while simultaneously producing liquid and solid gold in our toilets for the food grown in our backyards, kitchens, and community gardens. Along with creative, autonomous employment opportunities, Dry Urine-Diverting Toilets offer economic support and useful employment to young and old alike for growing and cooking clean, uncontaminated food—protected from the poisons and bacteria of expensive and fossil-fuel-dependent Treatment Plants.

Autonomy and freedoms are being enjoyed by all the millions making and using these dry toilets, in their communities and schools. By separating Shit from State rules and regulations (forcing commoners away from their traditional, indigenous ways of shitting and urinating), revolutions at the grassroots are extending people's power: home-grown decades back through the separation of Church and State.

Take care of your shit! As a young doctoral student landing in the United States four decades ago in hot pursuit of the American Dream, I could not have imagined I would be challenging the moral decency or the ecological irresponsibility of the Flush Toilet as I aged.

A half century of living has begun liberating me from the conservatism of Global Development Economic and Education paradigms. Instead of chasing the unsustainable American Dream, I find myself celebrating the young, leading entrenched and closed-minded elders to radically question the universal right to the poisoning and poisonous Flush Toilet. Thanks to these young, we are winning back our original freedoms through the contemporary separation of Shit from State. Ecological literacy is growing at the grassroots in conjunction with new understandings of political economy that require disconnecting our intestinal tracts from the bureaucratic machinery of State institutions fully ignorant of soil making and the riches spread and shared through society through the backyard creation of liquid and solid gold.

17. IMMIGRATION & MIGRATION

Immigration: is the act of foreigners passing or coming into a country… for the purpose of permanent residence.

We intended to talk about Immigration in this chapter. It was, initially, going to be about settlers, colonists, and imperialists, and how they forcefully displace "other peoples." This chapter wanted to explain how the imbalance of power and wealth within nation states creates internal refugees out of its "own peoples" and indigenous peoples.

We wanted to look at how *they* "accept" political refugees from conflicts they've themselves orchestrated, cracking down on immigrants they conveniently desecrated as illegal, while opening doors to economically-invested immigrants actively participating in their own willful assimilation. This chapter wanted to look how those in power are supporting wars, economic policies, and global corporatism, creating massive dislocation, displacement, and immigration of peoples everywhere. It also wanted to mention "those people" crossing imaginary borders, people coming from different climates and different cultures, looking and talking differently. This chapter wanted to be about those foreigners who do not *feel* like us, about the "alien"-labeled Mexican, "the terrorist-look-alike" much-feared Muslim, the undocumented but highly efficient baseline workforce of the north, and all the other illegal runaways. This chapter was going to talk about borders enforced with strategic militaristic stratification. It was going *to use and subtext "the other"* and the way we almost tediously *identify* it, as the immigrant.

But this chapter is not about immigration. Fuck Immigration. This chapter is about you. It is about your identity within, between, and across identity intersections, (immigration being one of them). This chapter is about deconstructing how you see immigrants as "the other" and how you may fail not to see yourself as an immigrant in a globalized world in which we are all foreigners. Hence, we are all immigrants. Whether you are a privileged Caucasian middle-class, heterosexual, young, academic male activist born in North America with a blood line of "colonist/Settler grandparents," or whether you are an exploited war-child trafficked from Iraq across the imaginary borders as a result of post-/neo-colonial wars and oppression, you are still an immigrant. Even if you are a working-class two-spirited indigenous woman living in a North American reserve with a history of "colonial oppression," the forceful displacement from your ancestors' land into the industrial city makes you an immigrant.

Know your battle. Know the struggle you want to fight for in today's world. *This is not optional, it is a must.* As capitalism, globalization, and world economic powers consolidate their control over states and full continents you need to to define yourself politically in a way that makes sense to you, so that you can widen your common solidarity grounds with the rest of the peoples of the world. Whether you want to take a progressive approach through the *system*, an activist stand in opposition the system or an insurrectionist revolt against the *system*… or even if you want to become part of the oppressive minority elites in order to accumulate economic power, it is now a good time to start defining yourself in a global context where you can identify yourself in a world beyond nation-state borders.

If you cannot identify yourself among or between any of these, you are in *"no-man's land"*—caught up as a cog in the machine you cannot see yourself clearly, nor can you really see "the other" for what she is. Before labeling "the other" as an *immigrant*, there are multiple identity borders that one needs to begin to recognize in order to expand our capacity to connect with the world and other human beings. The most common identities for resistance and oppression, connection and division are Class, Gender, and Racialization. These are by far the most pronounced identities to acknowledge as a basis for division or connection.

Without first constructing a politics within a frame of power, privilege, inclusiveness, and oppression, to discuss anything about immigration becomes a meaningless and oppressive task. Therefore, know yourself, know your battle. Know the struggle you want to fight for in today's world and define yourself fluidly as you figure yourself out.

OTHER STUFF TO CHECK OUT:

- **NO ONE IS ILLEGAL** (organization)

- **A PEOPLE'S HISTORY OF THE UNITED STATES**, Howard Zinn

- **NATIONAL IMMIGRANT SOLIDARITY NETWORK** (organization)

- **CREATE DANGEROUSLY**: The Immigrant Artist at Work, Edwidge Danticat

- **PERSEPOLIS**, Marjane Satrapi

- **BORDER ACTION NETWORK** (organization)

- **ORIENTALISM**, Edward Said

- **NATIONAL YOUTH IMMIGRANT ALLIANCE** (organization)

- **ANDOLAN**: Organizing South Asian Workers (organization)

ALEXANDRA HENAO-CASTRILLON is a Latina woman learning from every single day. She has only been in Vancouver for two years and already she is sick of the world-wide structural violence.

You know, there are thousands of people that dream of coming to Canada. People with different stories, jokes, experience, adventures, knowledge, fears, likes, and dreams. A very privileged group of them are already here studying, working, partying, shopping, having fun, and making friends. Another group, not so privileged as the former, can barely stay here trying to find a grocery store or to have money to buy in it; they beg for hearing an identifiable word or sound, for making a new friend, for receiving at least a smile; they believe the effort is worthy for helping their left-behind families. Some of this last group work in occupations requiring lower levels of formal training, like those called agricultural workers. No matter how similar you find these groups there is lots of difference between them.

Do you know that foreign agricultural workers bring stories, jokes, experience, adventures, knowledge, fears, likes, dreams from their hometown in Mexico and Guatemala? Do you know that they are commanded to do their job with no proper protection or training in working with dangerous substances? ...they are forced to live crammed in small places? ...they are threatened to lose their job if they raise concerns about their labour conditions? ...they can be threatened either by employers or consulates when requiring medical attention or reporting any injuries or accidents at their workplace? ...Canadian employers can cancel their contract at any moment and send them back to their home country? ...they have to accept danger and exploitation if they want to work? ...their voice is silenced simply because they are still learning the language of the employer?

All of these workers come with a dream, or many dreams. They want to realize their dreams and do their best to make them come true, just like us. They move around to look forward to get them. They leave their families and friends behind in order to provide them better life conditions. They do not want to take anything from us. They are willing to tell us their stories, to share with us their life experiences, the good ones and bad ones too. They just want to share who they are with us. What would you do to achieve your dreams? Wouldn't you like people around giving you a hand, at least just one?

SOZAN SAVEHILAGHI is a Kurdish anti-authoritarian organizer based in Vancouver–Coast Salish Territories. She immigrated to Canada as a refugee at the age of 9. She is engaged in migrant justice, anti-racist, and anti-capitalist activism and she strives to stand in solidarity with indigenous and queer communities of struggle.

exhaled whispers overheard on a crisp night on the slopes of the zagros mountains

exile: you travelled a long way. how did you get here?

child: i crossed the merz with a smuggler on the back of a fearless donkey.

exile: you crossed the merz, huh? was there a line on the ground - like on a map?

child: no silly. there was only a line of men with guns.

(im)migrants subsist

undertake long difficult journeys in search of a better life. moved by a need to escape from poverty and/or violence, to re-unify with their families or simply a chance to thrive on this planet. they cross borders and check-points by planes, boats, cars and on foot in search of safety and a better life. poor people and people of colour are seen as undesirable (im)migrants. their movement across the planet is restricted.

immigrants in the americas flourish on the lands of indigenous peoples. turtle island was never ceded to colonizers. indigenous people and (im)migrants alike are constrained by colonial systems of oppression that seek to assimilate and erase their histories.

who decides who can move from one place or another?

are there people who are more deserving of a better life?

how can we be accountable as guests on this land?

. pursue your dreams . connect with community and family . hold cherished memories and invite new ones to be made . know your roots . speak the tongue your soul knows best . insist on how your name is said . welcome your identities . embrace your skin . belong and feel safe .

. learn the history of the land . uphold the struggles that came before . take responsibility for privilege . work in solidarity . create safe space . stand up to injustice . defend the earth .

. bask in laughter . eat home cooked foods . seek truth . acknowledge the ancestors . find comfort . search out hidden beauty . challenge your heart and mind . move your body . feed your soul . find peace . summon courage . protect loved ones . hounour yourself .

. trust . love . always subsist .

moving against

rivers rushing

narrow paths

along cliff sides

through lines

of questioning gunmen

pressing forward

i carried you

for three days and two nights

i was fearless

because you were

afraid of the future

unaware you contained

the promise of

hope

GUILLERMO VERDECCHIA is an Argentinian-Canadian theatre-maker and scholar. He has won many awards for his acting, directing, film, and screen-writing, including the 1993 Governor-General's Award for his play *Fronteras Americanas.* He lives in Toronto with his partner and their two children.

★ You came from Somewhere Else. Now you're Here.

★ Maybe, like me, Somewhere Else haunts you. You carry a piece of it, invisible in your pockets, sometimes under your ribs. Sometimes it aches. Sometimes you forget it's there. But it's there. In your skin and eyes, in the way you smile—or don't. It's in the shapes your tongue likes to make; in the sounds your ears pick out. In the way your mother touches your hair, the way your father folds his hands.

★ You feel you have two hearts, two tongues, two memories. Or more.

★ You feel you live between two worlds, Here/Now and There/Then.

★ This can be a pain in the ass. Or it can be a beautiful and important thing.

★ Some people will try to tell you that you're not-neither, that you don't really/can't ever belong.

★ But here's what I've learned: your culture, your ethnicity, your identity is not a set of rules, not a script to follow slavishly. There is no test to pass or fail.

★ Anyway, you ARE not-neither. You are betwixt and between. You cross over, slip between worlds and words.

★ You are a border zone.

★ The border is encounter, overlap, contact, sparks, the trembling that comes with the possibility of something new.

★ The border is the fleshy interface of difference.

★ If there's one thing humans have in common, it's difference.

★ If there's one thing we need to get better at, it's difference.

★ Not erasing it. Or undoing it. Living with it.

★ You who came from Somewhere Else and now live Here, you with two or more tongues, with eyes in the back of your heart, with the secret beneath your ribs, you, there, on the border, you are an expert in difference.

★ You are possibilities. You are contradiction. You are unfolding. You are multitudes.

★ From your border zone, you can see two or three or four sides; you can see there and back; you recognize other border people and zones. Because the world is full of fault lines, people on the move, with two or more homes, hearts, and tongues.

★ This is the future.

★ You are the future. And the future is now.

BUSHRA REHMAN's mother says Bushra was born in an ambulance flying through the streets of Brooklyn. She co-edited *Colonize This! Young Women of Color on Today's Feminism.* Her book of stories, *Bhangra Blowout,* is forthcoming through Upset Press.

Rapunzel's Mother, or, a Pakistani Woman Newly Arrived in America

And with a cabbage, a box of eggs so clean she could easily forget
the source of their existence, my mother filled her silver cart
and moved in line to make her purchase.

The cashier turned a sharp glance at the small brown woman
with the pierced nose and covered head. She didn't fit
into this, an American supermarket.

"And what?" asked the cashier, "Are you willing to pay for this?"
She held the head of lettuce in the air. It reflected
off her rhinestone glasses and the hairspray in her hair.

"But this," said my mother, "Is America. I thought there was no barter here."

"Hmmmph," said the cashier, "There's give and take all over the world.
What made you think it would be different here?"
She shook her head and her plastic hair.

"But I have money." My mother tried to act like she didn't care.
Her English broke all over her and fell apart in the air.

But the cashier cackled, "No, no, no, my dear, what I want is here."
And she jabbed a nail, silver-painted and crooked at my young mother's stomach
which I had just begun to share.

"That is the price you'll have to pay, my dear, for this fresh lettuce
each egg that erupts into a new-blown head will be the property
of this here supermarket, country, and nation.

"And don't even think of running because we've got the goods on you.
Along with every other immigrant, we've got your passport
your foreign passport right here."

She made to reach into her too tight jeans, but my mother, she ran out of there.
The shopping girl openly laughed behind her, and the lines and lines
of customers just stood there with their stupid grins.

My mother ran, the door opened by itself.
My mother ran, but she still found herself
in a foreign land, far away from home.

"Rapunzel's Mother" appeared in *Mizna: Prose, Poetry, and Art Exploring Arab America* (Winter 2004).

NO BORDERS is an international network of groups working towards freedom from border controls, state authority, and capitalism. This comic was produced by No Borders Northeast (nobordersnortheast.org).

Every time you are asked to prove where you are from or what citizenship you have, your entitlements are dependent on what your background happens to be. Border controls like visa requirements, immigrations, and right to work rules reinforce inequalities and protect privileges.

If you happen to come from outside the European Union (EU), typically you are not allowed to work in any country within the EU, unless there is a job that no other national citizen could do. State controls have created this system where, for example, wealthy company directors are able to travel and live internationally, while other people are prevented from freely traveling to live or work in countries that they would like to visit.

States benefit from controlling who is allowed to live where by having a source of easily exploitable cheap labour in less privileged countries while also creating undocumented people in their own country who do not have access to the same employment rights as people with legal status.

Europe (along with the U.S., Canada, etc) actively entices people from other countries when it suits them (eg. qualified professionals whose training has been paid for in other countries and overseas students who subsidise national students' university course fees), while enforcing brutal and inhumane border and immigration controls (eg. detention centres, prison, no right to work or state benefits) on people who want to migrate but are not considered economically beneficial.

No Borders groups are particularly active in Europe; they work with the aim of building societies free from border and immigration controls and for freedom of movement for everyone.

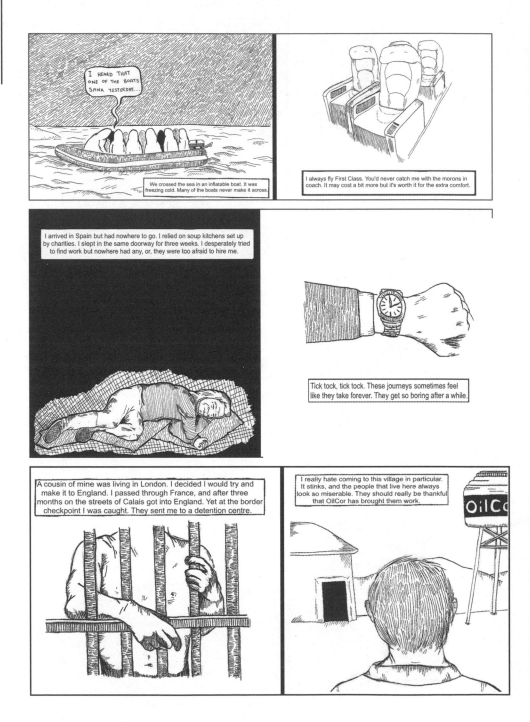

CARMEN AGUIRRE is a Vancouver-based theatre artist who works across North and South America. She has written or co-written eighteen plays, has sixty film, television, and stage acting credits, and has just published her first book, *Something Fierce: Memoirs of a Revolutionary Daughter* in North America and the United Kingdom. She is an acting instructor at Vancouver Film School and facilitates Theatre of the Oppressed workshops around the province.

Nobody wants to leave their home. Period. End of story.

However.

I believe that if you are a monocultural Canadian who has lived here your entire life, you should move to another country. Somewhere you don't speak the language, don't get the social signals, and don't know a soul. Do it with no money. No job waiting for you. No house. Arrive there. Get a job. Stay. No matter what. For at least a year.

Then come back. And as you walk down a Vancouver street, remember that many of the people you pass are in the middle of doing what you just did. Some are doing it because they had no choice. Most are from homes they never wanted to leave. They are walking around with broken hearts, grieving their losses, and the last thing they want to hear is how lucky they are to be here.

If you're lucky enough to have an immigrant tell you his or her story, and if that story is about persecution, refrain from saying: "I can't imagine that." Remember: the last residential school in Canada was closed in 1996. Remember: an estimated 150,000 native children went through the residential school system. Many suffered physical, sexual, and emotional abuse. Remember: the aim of the residential school system was to assimilate the native population to the mainstream. Remember: the United Nations has recognized the Canadian residential school system as ethnicide.

I've written this assuming that you, the reader, are neither native nor an immigrant. I've written this assuming that you, the reader, are a mainstream person who is becoming radicalized. And it is to you I speak: oppression exists here and everywhere. Compassion is the ability to put oneself in others' shoes. Compassion can lead to solidarity. And just as there is oppression here and everywhere, so there is resistance. And an active resistance demands an active solidarity. If you want to live a life of passion and purpose, there is nothing more fulfilling than fighting for the rights of all peoples; and in so doing, in revolutionizing your very self.

So give yourself the core-shaking, devastating, and at times exhilarating experience of being an immigrant yourself, know your own history, and begin the life-long journey of fighting to change the world. Because if you don't do it, someone else will change the world for you.

18. COPS & COURTS

No matter who or where you are, the police are always part of our consciousness. Whenever we're in public (or in private even) there is always a part of our brains wondering if a real or imagined officer or security guard or transit cop is going to come and interrogate us, or worse. There is a constant hum, a ubiquity to their presence, whether via patrol cars or surveillance cameras. Figuring out how to respond to the police, and thinking about your direct and indirect relationships with them is a key piece of youth culture.

Cops and courts are a central part of the state apparatus; their primary job is to protect private property and those with the most economic and political power. While both are in place to provide protection for many who are being victimized, hurt, and even committing crimes, it can be argued that their ultimate job/mandate, especially cops, is to protect those with the most material wealth and power from those with the least amount of wealth and power. That's why they call it "keeping order."

But wait, some cops are nice! You may have a parent, aunt, friend, brother who's a cop and a super great person, and they probably are, and for sure they became a cop to protect and serve their community. That's great in theory, but once they're in their uniform, they have a code to work and act by. Cops are trained to be and should always be expected to be brutal in carrying out their job: to ultimately protect the state, and the owners of property, and capital. Radical social change is exactly what cops are there to prevent, and they are frequently violent in doing it.

How as a radical youth, can you navigate this oppressive system, be a solid activist, stay out of jail, keep your dignity: that is, ward off the police state? We'll suggest three guidelines:

★*Always stand up to the cops*: speak truth to power, never let them intimidate you or anyone around you, never take their BS, know you have rights.

★*Never stand up to the cops*: just avoid them, cops habitually violate rights, do everything you can to never get arrested, eschew confrontations unless absolutely necessary, you will always lose anytime you try to stand up to cops.

★*1 and 2 are dependent* on where you live, how much money you have, and how you look. Another way to say it is, it's going to be affected by your race, gender, class, and geography, how brash you're feeling that day, how much time you have, what your family is like, and tons else.

So be strategic! Engage with the police if you have to but know who they are. Maybe it makes sense to call in the cops if there is a violent domestic dispute next door that you and your neighbours can't handle. Maybe if a cop pulls you over while riding your bike it just makes sense to answer their questions and keep moving. But there are other times to fight back, to argue, to gather friends and resist, to be sneaky, to run away, to holler.

But no matter what, understand what the cops' job is and do not be naïve about their role. If you are interested in safety and security, look instead to your community, family, friends, and neighbours. They are the people you can rely on and trust to take care of you, and in return you need to do the same. Always think about how you and the people around you can take care of each other and keep each other healthy and safe.

OTHER STUFF TO CHECK OUT:

- **CRITICAL RESISTANCE** (organization)

- **IRON CITY**, Lloyd Brown

- **ABOLITION DEMOCRACY**: Beyond Prisons, Torture, and Empire, Angela Davis

- **ANARCHIST BLACK CROSS** (organization)

- **THE COMING INSURRECTION**, The Invisible Committee

- **A PLAGUE OF PRISONS**: The Epidemiology of Mass Incarceration in America, Ernest Drucker

- **LETTERS OF INSURGENTS**, Freddy Perlman

- **JUSTSEEDS** (organization)

- **DISCIPLINE AND PUNISH**, Michel Foucault

- **COPWATCH** (online)

- **V FOR VENDETTA**, Alan Moore

VICTORIA LAW is a writer, photographer, zinester, and mother. She is the author of *Resistance Behind Bars: The Struggles of Incarcerated Women* (PM Press 2009) and the co-editor of *Don't Leave Your Friends Behind: Concrete Ways to Support Families in Social Justice Movements* (PM Press 2012). She also edits the zine *Tenacious: Art and Writings from Women in Prison* and photographs Hong Kong fishing villages and Coney Island.

When I was fifteen, my friends started getting arrested, going to jail, then getting sentenced to prison. Guilt or innocence wasn't the issue; my friends all did what they were convicted of—robbed a place at gunpoint, stole from someone, assaulted someone. Looking back, I wish that I'd had resources or people to help me make sense of both their actions and society's belief that justice was served and harm was healed by locking up sixteen-, seventeen- and eighteen-year-olds.

Although cops, court, and jail played a big role in our lives, we had no person or resource to help place it all in context. The term "school-to-prison pipeline" had yet to come into being and none of us could see that we were part of a cycle: Children from poor communities of color go to schools that seem like prisons. Gang recruiters who understand that the "education" offered is meaningless offer them quick and easy money. These kids are then arrested for acting out their own version of the American Dream.

When I was fifteen, I wish that I had had knowledge about the prison-industrial complex and its impact on people of color, particularly poor people of color in urban areas. None of us had ever heard the term "prison abolition"—the idea that prisons do not ensure safety and so people and communities have to prevent and address harm in other ways. None of us had heard the term "transformative justice"—the idea that one has to not only address the harm done but also the causes behind this harm.

I wish that there had been ways for me and my friends to know about and join in these conversations rather than believing that our only two choices were to stay in school and get good grades or drop out, get money the easy way, and most likely pick up a criminal record that limits our options in the future.

When I was fifteen, the Internet wasn't widely available and so, even living in New York City, we didn't have access to these resources. It took me three years, much violence, and my own arrest to find these conversations.

Today, you can type "prison abolition" or "transformative justice" into any search engine, find these conversations, and join these movements.

HARSHA WALIA is a South Asian community organizer, facilitator, popular educator, and writer currently based in Vancouver, Unceded Coast Salish Indigenous Territories in Western Canada. Over the past decade she has been active in grassroots movements including migrant justice, Indigenous solidarity, Palestinian liberation, anti-racism and feminist collectives, South Asian community organizing, and anti-imperialist and anti-capitalist struggles. Her writings have appeared in alternative and mainstream publications, magazines, journals, and newspapers.

We are told that the police are a peaceful force who maintain "law and order" and are here to "serve and protect" us when others get out of hand. In reality, the history of the police force has been written in blood. The Canadian national police force was created in 1873 in the Northwest Territories as a quasi-paramilitary force to establish colonial sovereignty over Indigenous lands by forcing Indigenous communities to settle on reserves and by quashing rebellions and the "Indian Wars."

The cops (hell even transit police!) are armed with guns and tasers, and routinely patrol low-income neighbourhoods and arbitrarily arrest youth who are street-involved, homeless, of colour, trans, or otherwise considered "deviant." The reality of profiling by the police—for example being stopped in a car because you are Black or being followed in a store because you are Native—has been confirmed in dozens of academic and even police studies.

Similarly, the law is not neutral. It is a product and a reflection of our hierarchical social organization. As philosopher Anatole France said, "The law, in its majestic equality, forbids the rich as well as the poor to sleep under bridges, to beg in the streets, and to steal bread." The Courts have decided that it is illegal to squat an abandoned building. The Courts have repeatedly upheld the immorality of the Indian reserve system. The Courts have determined that protesting in a mall is a violation of the Trespass Act. It is therefore no surprise that marginalized people are over-represented in the in-justice system.

So what do you do when you find yourselves in contact with the cops, and subsequently, the court? As a general rule of thumb, you do not have to identify yourself or answer questions by the police unless you are being detained. If the police stop you and start asking you questions, ask if you are free to go before you answer anything. Do not be unnecessarily confrontational, but be assertive. When you are with a crew, be aware of who is more vulnerable to police violence (because they are of colour, have a previous record, etc.). De-escalate and avoid conflict with the cops if those friends are uncomfortable. Even if you do not anticipate it, create and share an arrest-plan with friends: who they should contact (family and employment), your date of birth and address for the lawyer, any medications you need in jail. Memorize the numbers of at least two rad lawyers who will take your calls any time of the night. When you find yourself in the Court system, do not panic, it is meant to make you feel embarrassed and powerless. Tell your friends about your charges and take them along for your Court dates.

If you become vocal in social and environmental justice movements, expect that the state will attempt to weaken you. Always go to demonstrations with friends so you can look out for each other and leave together. While dealing with the cops and courts can be traumatizing, the strongest weapon we have is our collective solidarity to overcome the fear that the state instills within us. Remain steadfast alongside friends and allies and do not let labels such as "criminal" or "bad protester" isolate us from each other and from the movements that we believe in and belong to. Challenge the dehumanizing social organization around us that normalizes a lack of responsibility to one another and to the Earth. We destroy the state by forging relationships that overgrow its logic.

The first time I was arrested was one of the most terrifying experiences. I did not know how long I would remain in custody, I worried that my boss would fire me, and I was certain that I would jeopardize my immigration status. However, being released from jail at 3AM to a group of friends—who have now over the years spent countless hours in front of prisons and organized legal and court support— was one of the most significant affirmations of community and kinship that has sustained me in my activism. Remember, they cannot jail our hearts.

"To make a thief, make an owner; to create crime, create laws."

—Ursula K. Le Guin

MARLA RENN is most proud of her (un)learning through the Purple Thistle, loves to garden collectively, loves to cook and eat with others, and she wants a world we are proud of. She lives in Vancouver with her stellar partner and angry cat.

"Nonconformity and discontent are not enough. Neither is critical awareness. People mobilize themselves when they think their action may bring about a change, when they have hope. And that is what more and more people have today."

—Gustavo Esteva, Celebration of Zapatismo

The following terms describe ways that people organize themselves in protest. Their purpose, as with all protest, is to up the costs which are felt by powerful decision makers when they attempt bad policies. Their goal is to interrupt, change, or eliminate those policies and the institutions that carry them out.

DEMONSTRATION: An all-encompassing term. Street theatre, a road block, and a candlelight vigil are just a few examples. A demonstration is a public, disruptive, or attention-grabbing political action. It might include the tactics of a rally, march, or protest.

RALLY: A gathering of people that demonstrates power and common purpose. It might be more general in message or it might make a clear statement or demand, and usually includes speakers, performers, and information sharing. It is not necessarily disruptive or transformative to space, but it can be. May Day rallies are a long-standing tradition and way to celebrate labour history, as well as make demands related to workers and labour struggles.

MARCH: A rally that moves. It will itself have specific tactics, like a snake march, or it may itself be a tactic to make other actions possible. A march can make a statement in opposition to something, but it could also be a supportive or celebratory action—like a march in support of transgendered people and their allies. Marches have the advantage of being an effective way for a crowd to demonstrate power, and to keep people together and active for long periods of time.

PROTEST: Its purpose is to register opposition in a symbolic manner. A protest doesn't have to be public, but it does have to have some audience even if the powerful never hear about it.

BOYCOTT: A refusal to interact with a business or other entity so as to pressure it into some policy change. Some time ago, there was a boycott called to pressure Nestlé to cease their illegal marketing of baby formula in poor countries.

SABOTAGE: Done anonymously, usually in the workplace: work slow-downs, theft, breaking equipment, etc. The intention is to gain leverage in a struggle while communicating dissatisfaction.

STRIKE: Usually at workplaces or schools, a strike is essentially defined by non-compliance. It is used as a tool for the strikers' to gain leverage and have their demands met.

DIY: Taking direct action as an approach to problem solving. It is guided by a spirit of basic rejection of following leaders, or in seeking solutions from the very same institutions that are contributing to problems.

ARLIN FFRENCH is an artist, tattooist, and illustrator in East Vancouver. He bicycles and creates in the safety of night's dark blankets.

PAMELA CROSS is a long-time activist involved in numerous civil disobedience and direct action campaigns in Ontario, Quebec, and New York State. She now works as an activist-feminist lawyer, primarily on issues related to violence against women.

WHAT ARE COURTS?

Once the police have laid criminal charges, they pass the file on to the prosecuting lawyer (in Canada, this person is called the Crown Attorney, in the US, the District Attorney), who is responsible for managing the case from this point on.

The prosecuting lawyer (PL) has a lot of power over your case. She or he will try to settle the case without having to go to court. This process, which is informally known as plea bargaining, involves meetings between the PL and your lawyer, who is called the defence lawyer. The two lawyers meet outside the courtroom and try to negotiate a resolution. For example, if you have been charged with several things, the PL may offer to drop some of the charges if you agree to plead guilty to some of them, or your lawyer may tell the PL that you will plead guilty if the PL agrees to a minimal penalty. If the two lawyers come to an agreement, they take this to the judge who can approve or not approve of it. If the judge does not approve, either the lawyers try again or the case goes to a trial.

Your lawyer should be consulting with you during this process. You do not have to agree to any settlement you don't want, but if you turn down something that seems reasonable to the PL, this can have a negative impact on your case when it goes to trial. Still, it is important to remember that your lawyer works for you and that you do not have to do what your lawyer recommends.

If you don't have a lawyer, these meetings don't happen and your case moves along towards a trial.

How trials are managed, the roles of different people, the actual trial procedure—all of these things are different depending on where you are. In Canada, the "administration of justice," which is the term used to describe how courts are run, is the responsibility of the Attorney General of each province. You can find out a lot about how the courts in your province are run by checking out the Attorney General website. Also, there is a very helpful website—www.courtprep.ca —that answers lots of questions about criminal court and has an interactive courtroom where you can find out what the different people in court do.

All the rules and procedures about criminal court are important, but I think it is more important to understand the power of the court and the implications for you of different kinds of strategies you might use in the courtroom.

In Canada, judges are appointed by the government. They are independent and are not accountable to anyone. In the United States, most judges are elected, so are accountable to the public. Really, it is not much different than not being accountable to anyone. What is important about this is that judges have an enormous amount of power and not all of them use it in an appropriate or respectful way. This can have a big impact on the outcome of your case.

PLAY BY THE RULES

There are lots of rules when you are in court. Mostly these rules are in place because people are supposed to show respect to the court process and to the judge. For example, you are supposed to stand up every time the judge enters or leaves the courtroom, you are not allowed to wear a hat, you are not allowed to take pictures or record what is happening, you are not allowed to chew gum, and so on.

Criminal courts are seriously overextended, and cases can take a long time to get from start to finish. There is an unwritten reward and penalty system in which people who don't take up much of the court's time (enter a guilty plea, behave in court, follow the rules) are rewarded by such things as having charges dropped or being given less serious penalties and folks who take up time by presenting a full defence or not following the rules find themselves receiving a more punitive attitude.

ACTIVISM AND THE COURTS

Some activists see the law as part of the system they are fighting against, whatever the specific issue might be that led to their arrest. For these folks, the court process and the judge are not worthy of their respect and they see the experience as highly political and part of their activism. They challenge the authority of the court, refuse to follow the rules, and confront the power of the judge.

This is a completely legitimate form of activism, but it can have a very significant impact on the outcome of the case. If you refuse to follow the rules of the court, you are more likely to be found guilty and to receive a more serious penalty. You might even be found in contempt of court as a result of your courtroom behaviour.

Other activists see the law as an opportunity to bring the political issue that led to their arrest into the courtroom. These folks generally follow the rules and present a strong legal and political defence to the charges they face. This can be very time consuming, because the criminal process moves very slowly. They are hoping to persuade the judge that they were right to do whatever they did and to get an acquittal (not guilty). It is very hard to use political arguments successfully in criminal court, so activists using this strategy are usually still found guilty, but because they have followed the rules they sometimes find that the judge is a bit less strict in giving a penalty. Sometimes in these cases judges will say something like: "You have broken the law, which is very serious, but I believe you did so out of a strong conviction that you were trying to make the world a better place, and I will consider that when I am imposing the penalty on you."

Still other activists try very hard to avoid being arrested because they see the whole criminal process as an intrusion into their lives that they want to minimize as much as possible. These folks sometimes plead guilty as early as they can so they don't spend weeks or months or even years involved with the court, all while their freedom is limited by bail conditions. They hope they will get a less serious penalty as a "reward" for not tying up the court's time with a long trial.

None of these approaches is wrong. They each are equally appropriate. What you need to do, hopefully before you get arrested and hopefully with a group of like-minded people, is to decide which approach you want to take.

Making this decision will depend a lot on your personal circumstances. For example, if you do not have legal status in Canada or the US, you need to think about deportation. If you are a single parent, you probably don't want to go to jail for any length of time. If you are an Aboriginal or racialized person, you need to anticipate the racism that is part of the criminal court process. If you are trans or queer, you need to think about what spending time in jail might be like for you. If you are under 16, you need to consider the possible involvement of child protection authorities. If you have disabilities, you should think about the barriers you will face in the courtroom and as part of any penalty you may receive.

Whatever your personal circumstances and whatever court strategy you decide you, working within a group of both arrested and non-arrested people is really important.

TEST THEIR LOGIK aka **ILLOGIK** is an established Toronto-based revolutionary artist. With a decade of production under his belt, as well as eight years of rapping, ILLOGIK has long been using the musical medium to spread revolution and liberation.

TESTAMENT is a Toronto and London-based anarchist hip-hop artist and organizer. During the past four years, Testament has toured coast to coast throughout Turtle Island, and has performed shows in such international hotspots as Oaxaca and Palestine.

no one is illegal we're all people
we're all equal no fences
no borders no nations
no prisons no deportations

who's illegal who's indigenous?
talk about immigrants are europeans serious?
the government instrument it's stolen land insidious
borders and orders children imprisoning

face it this is a racist state
built on genocide apartheid and hate
colonized native peoples and the land was raped
now the white boys are the ones guarding the gate

gimme a break they take and take
pay less then minimum wage how you supposed to keep food on the
plate
you got 3 jobs and always on the alarm
or shipped in to pick all the food for them on their farms

in your community at home the land was robbed
by the capitalist bastard international mob
what choice do you have when your family's starved
but make the trek to the north to babylon

see the city is a sweatshop you gotta be strong
no rights or status exploited and harmed
working under the table without any papers
the system maintained by this stolen labour

this trade arrangement wage enslavement
diaspora on the pavement searching for payment
but to pay rent is where most your time wen
all the money spent what's left barely a dime or a cent

face it the system is racist the basis
is classist most the poor have brown faces
fact is class is tied to what race is
a perception twisted into what hate is

i can't take it see no one is illegal
we're all equal the system is evil
so shake these nations and break the borders
reunite families and stop deporting

ADAM LEWIS is a settler anarchist working towards decolonization in social movement and academic contexts. He is finishing his MA on anarchist engagements with Indigenous struggles of resistance and anarcha-Indigenism as a form of anti-authoritarian and anti-colonial politics, before beginning his PhD. He was arrested on conspiracy charges in 2010 for engaging in anarchist resistance against the G20 in Toronto. In November 2011, he and 5 others accepted a plea deal to a lesser charge of counseling that resulted in the dropping of charges for 11 others. He finished serving a 70-day provincial jail term on February 5, 2012 (see conspiretoresist.wordpress.com). He gardens, drums, bikes, and heartily partakes in vegan baked-goodness.

Given that engaging in political work, especially of the radical variety, inevitably leads to clashes with the law—whether police, lawyers, courts and prisons—we need to expand our understandings of the potential risks of doing political work. This isn't to scare us away or to focus only on playing it safe within the rigid rules of the law, but rather to understand how prison systems are part of a larger system of injustice. It is important to understand what occurs in these sorts of institutions and how prisons play into other aspects of control and policing on behalf of the state—and because our politics might bring us there at some point.

Prisons are complex places, filled with lots of rules both formal and informal that differ from institution to institution and from level to level (i.e. federal, state, provincial, etc.). There are power dynamics that affect what your experience will be like at every turn. The guards use the creation of informal hierarchies to turn prisoners against one another rather than against the prison or guards. They also enforce this by sending "troublesome" prisoners to segregation, subjecting them to beatings, or by punishing the whole unit through the use of searches, and removal of "privileges" (TV, telephone, visits, yard time).

There is very little to do while inside—read, workout, watch TV, or play games. This constant lack of stimulation and activity means that people in jail are extremely bored, which can lead to anxiety, isolation, frustration, and violence. Prisons are designed to try and break people down, which often means that prisoners are made to take out their emotions on other prisoners.

There are specific rules on what you can receive from the outside—which is largely only letters and printed material sent in via mail, or in some cases, but certainly not all, books that have come direct from the publisher. Everything is screened by security. Inside you can purchase a select number of items from the canteen or commissary—which is mostly junk food, personal hygiene products, and a dismal number of books or magazines. Many prisoners rely on having funds in their canteen account in order to purchase food because they do not get enough from the regular diet.

Access to the "outside world" is limited to letters, weekly visits from family/friends, the constant drone of the television, and collect/personal account phone calls. Visits are often short, 20 to 40 minutes, phones are often difficult to use because of the power dynamics that exist on specific ranges or cell blocks, and mail can take forever to arrive or is lost.

"Surviving" prison is largely about keeping busy, staving off boredom, staying out of violent tensions that are created between prisoners and prisoners and with guards, minding one's own business, and keeping a low profile. It is also an opportunity to learn from those most affected by these systems, to gain insight into one of the most controlled groups of people. It is, at the same time, an opportunity to discuss politics and the need for resistance to institutions like prisons. This needs to be done carefully, but all of the conversations I had were positive and many other prisoners agreed with the need to fight against the existence of prisons. They also respected me and others like me for taking a stand and risking our own freedom for our political beliefs. These general tips definitely made my time go quickly and relatively problem-free.

This is a small snapshot of some of the realities of prison life, but hopefully it is a starting point to get us started about thinking about the realities of prisons and how that relates to our broader social movements and political work. We need to prepare to deal with the realities of potential incarceration. We need to link prison support to struggles towards prison abolition. We need to understand what many of the reasons people end up in prison (poverty, addiction, racial targeting, immigration) are political in and of themselves. All prisoners are political and we need to build links between them and movements of resistance towards a world without prisons.

"When I dare to be powerful—to use my strength in the service of my vision, then it becomes less and less important whether I am afraid."
        —Audre Lorde

19. MENTAL WELLNESS

Sometimes thinking about your mental health can make you, well, mental. The world we are living in is so messed up, so crazy, so irrational in so many ways that maybe it's a rational response to be a little insane. There is so much inequality, such rapacious ecological destruction, so much cruelty and evil and greed and weirdness out there: how can you not be angry? What's wrong with being weird, pissed off, depressed, or sketchy?

Well, there's nothing wrong with you. We all have different styles, personalities, and reactions to the world; and we've all got to embrace that. We're not all made with the same cookie-cutter and thank goodness for that. Difference is what makes the world go round and let's celebrate that. We are all facing vastly different circumstances and challenges, and everybody has got to do what they got to do to get by. Family life, racism, school, hormones, disrespect of youth, relationships, money—all of it can wear you down. Pretty much all teenagers get depressed: some just get a little moody or blue; others slip into something more serious, but all of it is worth facing head-on. We all have to live in this world and being depressed or out of balance mostly just sucks. There's nothing inherently shallow about being in a good mood, happy, and healthy.

The first thing is to be honest and generous with yourself. Don't slough it off and don't wait for someone else to solve your problems. Deal with it. Lots of people have people have been through really tough stuff and lots of people are going through stuff right now. Be straight-up with yourself: are you happy, are you thriving, are you handling your situation the way a cool person would, are you thinking clearly?

Next, look for support. It might well be your family. Many mental health patterns have a genetic component and your family might well have encountered similar feelings. It might well be your pals. Friends are almost always the best medicine. People love to share their feelings, love to support each other, love to know that they are not alone. If it is not your friends, look around your community for support. There will be far more people than you can possibly know who will be in solidarity with you.

Third, get an analysis and respond. Think hard about the root causes of how you are feeling. There will be many, and often overlapping, issues. Some of them will be interlocking social oppressions, others will be personal issues, and sometimes it is hard to see where one ends and the other starts.

Consider your personal history: there is a clear correlation between abuse and trauma and mental health issues. Look hard at your personal habits: how you spend your time, how you eat, how much you sleep, how much time you spend online, how much you are physically active, how much pot you smoke, and figure out which ones are healthy and which ones you need to change. Mental health is almost always less about the way your brain functions than it is about context.

OTHER STUFF TO CHECK OUT:

- **MORE THAN A LABEL, MORE THAN YOU CAN SEE**: Raising awareness about mental health in racialised youth and what we can do to improve it (online)

- **THIRTEEN REASONS WHY**, Jay Asher

- **THE RED TREE**, Shaun Tan

- **DO THE RIGHT THING** (film)

- **THE BELL JAR**, Sylvia Plath

- **ONE FLEW OVER THE CUCKOO'S NEST**, Ken Kesey

- **WOMAN ON THE EDGE OF TIME**, Marge Piercy

- **SMILE OR DIE**, Barbara Ehrenreich

All too often mental health issues are reflexively "solved" with drugs that often do more harm than good. That includes everything that alters your brain: sometimes you are self-medicating with booze or dope and sometime doctors are medicating you with pharmaceuticals.

Either way, drugs are a possible solution, and you shouldn't feel bad if do end up taking them, but know that at best they are just temporary, often mask the real problems, and are powerful—they can really mess you up. Drugs should only be used to alleviate mental health issues when everything else has been tried. All too often drugs—whether it's Ritalin or alcohol—make it so you can't think clearly and take care of your own shit. Self-determination and self-reliance are what we're all after, and drugs might be part of that picture, but only when you've exhausted the other options.

Finally, while you're figuring out how to organize your own life so your mind can be at peace, get active, and respond to the social oppressions that are making you feel crazy. We live in an irrational, unfair world and we have to push back. Organizing against racism, poverty, homophobia, ecological catastrophe, and/or whatever else is most compelling to you is the surest way to maintain a certain kind of sanity. Voicing your opinions, working with people who think like you do, learning about alternatives to rampaging capitalism, speaking truth to power: all that is fundamental to your mental health.

Being a teenager is tough for most everybody. There's so much joy and excitement being a youth, but it can be hard for sure. But life will—it really, really will—get better. Despite everything, the world is a friendly place.

"Progress is measured by the speed at which we destroy the conditions that sustain life."

—George Monbiot

VIKKI REYNOLDS is an activist/therapist, university/college instructor, and "super"vises teams of activists and community workers. She's worked around the world with survivors of torture, with queer and trans communities, shelter folk, rape crisis centers, and youth struggling with substances and exploitation. See www.vikkireynolds.ca for more info.

I believe what gets understood as mental illness is directed more by pharmaceutical corporations, capitalism, colonization, homo/trans/queer phobia, sexism, and racism than by real concern for human suffering. I think it's way more accurate to think about people who struggle against exploitation and domination as being *oppressed depressed*. People need justice, not just medication. The problem is not in our minds, our brains, or our neurons, but in the world where privileged people abuse power and destroy lives, Mother Earth, and communities for greed.

Being an activist, acknowledging the suffering of others, unmasking your own privilege, holding a critical analysis of the points of your own oppression and power: All of these things can lead to stuff that looks like Depression. We can start to think we might be crazy (depressed, angry, obsessive, defiant, maladapted...). Hopelessness can make us think we can't do anything about injustice. Political awareness can be paralyzing, overwhelming, and spiritually painful. Individualism makes us think we're alone, that no one thinks like us.

Our resistance to this political violence, degradation, heartbreak, and terror is to hold each other in sacred and revolutionary love, and to work for justice: that's what solidarity is. Solidarity is belonging. You just need to figure out the best use of you, trust that you will find your people, and work in solidarity with others.

In direct actions, I experience the social divine. Belonging with others who struggle and thirst for justice is my solidarity/my spirituality. Activism is my little sanity-making project, my resistance against depression. Activism is not a sign of mental illness, but mental wellness. Survivors of torture have told me a spirited political protest is worth 100 therapy sessions! Happiness is overrated: Social Justice is underrated.

We're not crazy, another world is possible. I'm not immature or crazy because I'm 50 and don't own a house, TV, or a car. It's not that I'm idealistic, foolish, or stupid—I mean I have a PhD, a life-partner, and (share) a dog. It's that I don't want to participate in consumerism with all of my life. Environmental destruction is suicidal, greed is crazy, and I believe that willfully exploiting the lives of other human beings around the planet is a sign of mental illness. Don't let anybody tell you that because you're heart-broken about the indignities and suffering of most of the world's people you're crazy—that you should go shopping and be happy.

No justice, no peace— no peace of mind. A socially-just world is a mentally-well world. Actions for justice are acts of sanity.

SARAH QUINTER is a 25-year-old artist, writer, and activist. When she's not earning her living as an art model or professional kitchen wench, she's drawing, and when she's not drawing, she's participating in radical social movements, most recently Occupy Wall Street. She's also working on a new zine. Eventually, she plans to become an arts educator. Contact her at miss.quintessential01@gmail.com.

I'm a 25-year-old artist and activist from New York City. In high school I got into punk and radical politics, and I've done a lot of organizing with my peers around youth empowerment, self-education, the arts, and mental health.

I've been in many situations where I've lent support to others through their mental and emotional struggles, and also situations where I've needed to ask for support.

On one hand, labels of mental illness are often used to disempower young people, especially those who challenge the status quo. On the other, mental and emotional struggles are very real, and can leave people vulnerable to everything from rejection to forced hospitalization to suicide. A lot of young people get caught in the dilemma of wanting to reach out, but fearing that they will be misunderstood or punished, rather than supported.

There are numerous approaches to maintaining and regaining mental wellness, and the more tools you know how to use, the better you'll be able to care for yourself and those around you. Healthy diet and regular exercise and sleep cycles can make a huge difference. Many have found that their depression and anxiety are actually triggered by food allergies. Medication provides a lifeline to many, though for others, the side-effects outweigh the benefits. Some people have managed to cut down on or go off psych meds altogether, though this process should only be attempted gradually, under the supervision of a healthcare professional.

I feel the two most important, long-term approaches to mental health are 1) getting to know yourself, and 2) building healthy relationships. A great tactic involving both of these is called "Mad Mapping" by some of my friends in the radical mental health community. It involves writing down descriptions of how you experience both mental health and illness, healthy strategies for coping with various emotional states, names of people who will support you, and instructions for how they can help when you're not in a position to make good choices. Mad Mapping can be a great group activity and is an ongoing process. Journaling and art-making can be essential for understanding not only who you are, but also who you can be. My own creative pursuits not only bring joy to my daily life, but also a purpose that has sustained me through much adversity. Healthy relationships of all kinds are always mutual. Take the time to listen to someone today, and perhaps a much-needed hand will be there for you tomorrow.

You may find yourself in a position of having to decide how to care for someone who is seriously unwell. If professional intervention seems necessary, be sure to do your research, keep your struggling friend informed, and try respect their self-determination as much as possible. It's best to have a whole team of friends and allies ready to support someone who's struggling. The Icarus Project is a support network run by and for people labeled with "mental illness." Their site has tons of great resources and an online community as well: theicarusproject. net. Be well!

> **ANGELA "EL DIA" MARTINEZ DY** is a poet, writer, educator, activist, and hip-hop emcee. She was an original member of the isangmahal arts kollective, a seminal voice for the millennial Asian American spoken word and performance movement, and co-founded Youth Speaks Seattle, serving as organizational director from 2005–2009. Born and raised in Seattle with her heart in Manila, she is currently pursuing a PhD in the UK, studying the Network Society and the Information Age. She is the co-creator of Sisters of Resistance, an anti-imperialist pro-vegan radical feminist grime and hip-hop blog: www.sistersofresistance.org.

We are living in a time of a major shift in the cultural, economic, and socio-political workings of Planet Earth. Since the 1970s, US and UK-driven neoliberal capitalism went global but imploded in the late 2000s financial crisis. Yet profit continues to be made for the sake of a corporate and political elite at the expense of the global majority, who are exploited and excluded from true financial, and thus political power. Ten years after 9-11, the current government and media-sponsored targets of public opposition continue to be not the politicians, bankers, and entrepreneurs who murder millions of people in foreign countries while draining social programs and the masses at home via economic exploitation for the poor, tax loopholes for the rich, and endless wars, but instead, Muslim "terrorists," playing on fears in the populace in the same way that fascism and anti-semitism became the order of the day for Europe in the middle of the last century. The desperation is intense on all sides; the tension must come before the release. We are looking, as journalist Mumia Abu-Jamal suggests, at an empire on the brink of collapse.

That history repeats itself is not a new idea, but whether we are aware of its cycles is an important question. Greater empires—Roman, Grecian, Babylonian— have fallen and that this one will too is not a question of *if*, but *when*. The *how* is revealing itself at present. On an individual level, it is a personal challenge to negotiate the alienation and frustration of the self caused by the contradictions of the oppressive intersecting systems—building on bell hooks' work, namely, the white supremacist, neoliberal, consumer capitalist, imperialist patriarchy that affects humans on a global scale—without falling into the traps set up to make money while keeping us from the knowledge and real human interaction that underpins all positive forward mass movement. Some of these traps include privatizing public education, the rise of the pharmaceutical industry, demise of the unions, consumerism, celebrity culture, mass media/entertainment, video games. There are more moving parts, perhaps more dangerous: abuse and trauma, drug and alcohol abuse, porn, sex or S&M addiction, self-harm or mutilation, eating disorders, the list goes on. When humans feel lost and alone and without a sense of meaning, we can lose ourselves and our hope for better futures for humankind and the planet. An activist's journey demands a directed focus on creating, that is, laying the foundations to make possible, that alternative future. This requires honesty and a willingness to face, analyze, and challenge individual and collective histories of power relationships and domination. We can effect great change in the form of the ripple effect when we act according to the radical principles of paying critical attention to ourselves, relationships, and experiences, listening to conscience and intuition, treating ourselves and others with respect and compassion, deepening collective wisdom, and pursuing with great zeal actions which speak truth to power, build and educate community, and engage the creative spirit, source of vitality, and zest for life.

"We are living in a time of a major shift in the cultural, economic, and socio-political workings of Planet Earth.... We are looking, as journalist Mumia Abu-Jamal suggests, at an empire on the brink of collapse."

DAN BUSHNELL is an award-winning public artist, painter, sculptor, story-teller, tattoo artist, and general badass. He was born and now lives in White-horse, Yukon where he operates Molotov and Bricks Tattoo Parlour.

When I was 21 I developed an anxiety disorder.
For a long time it went undiagnosed or misdiagnosed.

At the walk in clinic they
told me I had asthma,
I started to take Ventolin,
it didn't help.

When it was finally identified
help was hard to find. I wasn't
offered any alternatives to drugs.
The doctors were busy; they
pulled out prescription pads
and sent me on my way.
What you don't hear much about
though is phobias.
Anxiety disorders often
come with phobias: fear of heights,
small spaces. I met a woman once who
developed a fear of bridges; living
in Vancouver and afraid of bridges?
Pretty rough.

I developed a fear of being poisoned, so I wouldn't accept
unwrapped candies or opened drinks. I also couldn't
bring myself to swallow a pill. For eight years I
didn't even take an aspirin.
I kept looking for a way to get it under control without medication.
Eventually I ended up at the anxiety disorders unit at the
University of British Columbia.

They explained to me that anxiety attacks
are caused by a rush of adrenaline.
Your body responds to the adrenaline
in a natural way: your heart races,
you shake and sweat. Usually these
reactions in us are accompanied by
real threat or injury, so your body searches
for those things. When it doesn't find
them, your mind starts to create them.
I always felt like I was having a heart
attack or losing my mind.

At UBC they would try to induce anxiety attacks in people
and then coach them through it. It never worked for me.
They couldn't make me have an attack.
Once they gave me a tie and told me to tighten it around my
neck until my breathing was strained.
The metaphor wasn't lost on me, but I didn't have an attack.

The folks at UBC asked me how
many anxiety attacks I had
experienced. I told them hundreds.
They asked me how many times
I had died from a heart attack
or lost my mind.
Right. It helped.
I also quit drinking
coffee and smoking, I quit all
drugs and pot. I hid small dot
stickers all over my house and at work
and every time I noticed one I would
consciously relax. I was also taught to go
with it, to face the attacks and see them as
an opportunity to learn how to get control.
Exercise was also really helpful in burning
off the adrenaline when they hit.
It all helped.

Most importantly I talked about it. The worst part for me about the
whole thing was the embarrassment.
I was ashamed.
It made me feel weak and fucked up. As I told close friends and family
about it, I began to accept it.
Most of them didn't really understand, they would say things like,
"why don't you just try to calm down?"
It was hard to hold off the sarcasm.
As I talked about it though it helped me work it out for myself, answering
other people's questions helped me to develop a better understanding.
The more I understood, the easier it became to control.
It doesn't really go away but it becomes manageable.
Today I can stop an attack before it can really build up a head of steam.
I was listed as having a severe anxiety disorder; I have never taken daily
medication for it.
For about ten years now I have been listed as "in remission".

AARON MUNRO is a queer and trans-identified activist with a degree in social justice. He has worked in the DTES in many capacities and has a strong interest in community based solutions. Aaron is currently employed with Rain-City Housing and Support Society as a community developer. RainCity Housing is an organization built around compassion, purpose and a commitment to delivering progressive housing and support solutions for people.

"Insanity is a perfectly rational adjustment to an insane world."

—R.D. Laing

Unfortunately our culture has not been very kind historically to those who seem different than those who hold the majority of the power in our society. That cruelty has been especially true for those unfortunate enough to be diagnosed with a mental health issue. I've worked in the Vancouver's Downtown Eastside for the past seven years. This is a neighbourhood known for having a large number of people labeled "disordered." It became very quickly apparent to me that the issues that plagued this community had nothing to do with these labels and everything to do with poverty, lack of housing, and stigma.

My work required me to meet a lot of people who had spent most of their lives being described as "psychotic," "dangerous," and "crazy." It didn't take me very long to overcome my own bias and start using other words to define them. "Funny," "charming," "smart," "strong," and "friend" became words that would be more likely to pop into my mind. I began to really think about where I had developed the idea that I should be afraid of those who may act differently.

I also began to think about the results of that fear being so widespread in our culture. This completely unfair idea about a group of people has allowed our society to let this amazing community be jailed, victimized, and subjected to horrible experimentation for centuries—and it's still going on today. What I also realized was that this wasn't just a loss for those people who have endured this treatment, but a loss for all of us. We have lost the benefit of these folks, who may see the world differently, contributing to our society. The people I have had the pleasure to meet would have built a kinder world than was built for them.

Let's celebrate difference. We need it.

PETER MORIN is a member of the Crow Clan of the Tahltan Nation. Peter has been working with Surrounded by Cedar Child and Family Services for the past three years helping kids and youth in-care to reconnect to their families, culture, and communities.

I want to tell you that
culture helps
culture helps us
culture can help you to feel strong again
culture helps in the bleak times if you are depressed, sad, oppressed, unheard, lonely, isolated, heart-broken, separated, over-whelmed...
culture helps in the happy times when everything seems to be working
culture is a system that supports living well
understanding and practicing these culture systems helps us to live well
understanding and practicing these culture systems gives us power to help others who may be in need also
culture makes you visible
you can choose to become a dancer
you can choose to become a singer
right now we just might not have the english words to articulate the shape of our cultural practice
and finding those english words has become a part of the journey to root ourselves back into the land we are on
I want to tell you that
our culture is more that this 'thing' you learn at school
you have to go to indigenous school to learn our indigenous culture
this could start today
if you choose
you have this power to change your own world in strong ways
if I wanted to create a picture of culture
I would say our culture is a fire that can keep you warm
In your heart
In your body
In your spirit
In your emotion
This warmth is a type of safety
It is a comfortable state of being
A memory to draw on if you are feeling unsafe in your life
Cultural practice is a self-care plan
Today you are 15 (maybe older) (maybe 18)
You should know by now that your emotions can be overwhelming
(just so you know)
(that overwhelming feeling will never go away)
(age changes is how you are able to talk about your emotions/feelings)
today I want to tell you
I am a helper for our community
I share these words as help for youth
I am able to share these words because they were shared to me
My job, right now, is to support youth to re-connect to family, community,

cultural practice, and Nation
I collaborate with youth to work through any trauma (inherited or experienced)
to co-author a map back home (home = fire/warmth/comfortable space)
I want to tell you
Life is hard work
But it is rewarding work if you choose to work hard
This choice is traditional
I want to tell you that there are many teachers
In the world
And many helpers
You don't have to feel alone EVER
There is family to help
And if there isn't family to help
Then there is cultural family to help
And if there isn't cultural family to help
Then there are helpers like me
And if there isn't any helpers
Then there are ancestors who want to help also
Ancestors want to see you succeed
I also want to tell you that Elders are people who are able to talk about the challenges they have faced in their lifetimes
Elders are able to talk about a lifetime of facing challenges
They talk about overcoming challenges with dignity
It pays to take the time to listen because it will help you to face your challenges
Cultural practice helps us to recognize that everyone has challenges
I want to tell you
Healing is work
If you break a leg you spend time healing
If you have emotional pain
If you spiritual pain
If you have mental pain
Then spend the time to heal
If the pain feels to overwhelming for you
Then find someone to help you understand/articulate/transform the pain
I want to tell you
This is the beginning of your map
This map is the first step (a plan) for you
(if you need it)
don't ever feel alone with your emotional pain
we can transform it
You don't have to do this alone

SASCHA ALTMAN DUBRUL is co-founder of The Icarus Project (thei-carusproject.net): a website community, support network of local groups, and media project by and for people struggling with bipolar disorder and other dangerous gifts commonly labeled as "mental illnesses."

Writing, for me, has always been a pretty desperate attempt at fighting off loneliness. It's never been something that flows easily out of me. My writing has always been a bit of a "dangerous gift," something that allows me to powerfully communicate with the outside world while simultaneously threatening to keep me shackled to the computer screen, all alone and feeling like a desperate animal.

When I was a kid I watched a lot of TV and read a lot of comic books. My favorite comic book was called *The X-Men*. It was about a group of mutant teenagers being trained by this older guy, Professor X, to use their superpowers so they could fight against the forces of evil. I always wished I had superpowers. When I got older, I started reading stories about shamans and medicine people in indigenous cultures—people who were born really sensitive and had had traumatic things happen to them that transformed their lives forever and gave them special abilities. In these stories, there were always mentors and guides to help train them and set them on their paths as warriors and healers. Just like in the comic books.

Years later, I started realizing that all the most amazing people in my life—the wildest ones, the ones walking the edges and pushing the social boundaries and making all the connections most normal folks were too afraid to make—all of them were people who had never really fit in when they were young, had been through their share of rough times, and had somehow figured out their own ways of blazing through the world. All the people I knew who had been considered "mentally ill" and "mad" were like the mutants in the comic books, the misfits who had to carve their own paths or else be eaten by the world around them. The mutant teenagers were me and my friends. But most of us never had mentors and guides to lead us through to the other side and teach us how to be superheroes. We just had each other.

Those who are born mutants have it really rough: the modern world wasn't made for the likes of us. The mainstream's waters choke us and make us gag. Modern institutions and industrial standardization feel particularly cold and heartless to us because our spirits are so wild. We see the end of the world in flashing billboards and clear-cut forests. We feel the pain of others like it's our own. We can't hold down regular jobs or make regular friends. We're told we're diseased and sick and need to be medicated for our entire lives or else horrible things will happen. There is no place for us except in institutions or out on the street. We're outcasts. And we gravitate towards other outcasts like ourselves.

People like us need community more than the normal ones. If we don't find strong communities we'll spend our lives feeling out of place, with a gnawing sensation that something is missing. If we're lucky, we find others like ourselves and manage to build our lives on the fringes of the mainstream, in our little enclaves. But even in our rebel communities, most of us don't know how to take care of each other. No one ever taught us how to get along with one another. We don't have guides or mentors. There is so much hidden knowledge that would make life easier for us, but many of us have no way to access that knowledge.

But that's where our dangerous gifts come in. One of the important lessons I learn over and over again in my life is that the people who can really understand and help me when I'm struggling with my madness are the ones who have had my same kind of problems and learned somehow to make it through. Being damaged and traumatized can be a dangerous gift if you figure out how to use it to help others come to terms with their own powers.

I'm one of those kids who got locked up in a psych hospital when I was a teenager because I didn't understand that I was different than most of the kids around me, that I had to take extra special care of myself to cultivate my powers and stay out of trouble. I really wish someone had been there to offer a little guidance, someone who had been through it before and understood what I was going through.

Our culture's version of guidance is to diagnose people as mentally ill, stick them on a bunch of anti-psychotic meds, and lock them up in the hospital. There are so many kids being locked up and given drugs because they don't fit into the narrow roles that the system lays out for them. And there's only so much time this can go on before the whole way our culture thinks about "mental illness" is dramatically discredited, falls apart, and melts down into something new. What's it going to look like when it happens?

I like to read the stories from indigenous cultures and imagine a different way: the way that shamans stay shamans is that they have to *shamanize*—they have to heal people with their powers, their dangerous gifts; they have to pass on the knowledge. That's what keeps them healthy. That's why I do the work that I do, because it keeps *me* healthy. It's very motivated by self-interest. If I want to survive in this world then I don't really have another choice: I have to figure out how to help other people who've been through what I've been through. I have to help weave, with words and ideas, the safety net to catch other people who fly too high, because it's going to be the same net that's going to catch me when I fall.

20. YOUR PHYSICAL BODY

The personal is political and the political personal. This is one of the essential notions of radical feminism. All this means is that we can see interlocking systems of oppression/privilege, systems of power that organize our economy, government, access to work, play out in our bodily experiences in the world. Whether it's emotional stress and violently enforced societal norms affecting your psyche or physical safety, or economic stress affecting your housing, nutrition, work, or ability to be provided for or provide for others, these life situations are deeply connected to racism, class structures, patriarchy, and capitalism. And your story, your experience is truth and knowledge you can draw on to understand the world.

The way you feel when you wake up in the morning, your body image, the expectations others have of you, your nutrition, your ways of coping with stress, the effect of stress on the body, your health and models for treating illness and pain, your very concept of self-care, are affected by interlocking systems of oppression. In recognizing this, you are also recognizing that your body is a site for revolutionary and radical action. When you choose to say, "fuck your 'norms,' what I am is beautiful, I deserve good things in life, I want to strive to nourish my body and self, I care about my family, my community, my parents are affected by all this violence too, and I am going to figure out how to treat my body well and learn about coping with stress in good ways," that is a act of defiance to an exploitative system that demands your compliance in being abused and abusing yourself.

But what has this got to do with your physical body, your flesh and blood and bone and hair? What does this feminist rant have do with you? We know you experience stress from wanting to fit in, that you have done some kind of harm to your body to cope with stress or expectations to fit in (dieting, over-exercise, abusing drugs/alcohol, not caring, hurting yourself). We have all gone through that. People call it "being a teenager." Developing a self-awareness and generosity towards yourself can be a real act of resistance—not just in implication, but in the act itself.

If you're going to be a force for good in this world, thinking every day about how to be healthy, about taking good care of yourself and the people around you, really is thinking about what a better world could and should look like.

OTHER STUFF TO CHECK OUT:

- **HEY, FAT CHICK** (online)

- "**HURTING YOURSELF**" (zine)

- **A PEOPLE'S HISTORY OF SPORTS**, Dave Zirin

- **BODY DRAMA**: Real Girls, Real Bodies, Real Issues, Real Answers, Nancy Amanda Redd

- **OUR BODIES, OURSELVES**, Boston Women's Health Book Collective

- **IN DEFENSE OF FOOD**: An Eater's Manifesto, Michael Pollan

- **HEALING WITH WHOLE FOODS**: Asian Traditions and Modern Nutrition, Paul Pitchford

- **YOGA**: The Spirit and Practice of Moving into Stillness, Erich Schiffmann

- **WILD FERMENTATION**, Sandor Ellix Katz

- **CALIBAN AND THE WITCH**, Silvia Federici

- **THE BREATHING BOOK**: Vitality & Good Health Through Essential Breath Work, Donna Farhi

ALEXIS PAULINE GUMBS, PhD, is a queer black troublemaker, a black feminist love evangelist, and the founder of the Eternal Summer of the Black Feminist Mind and co-creator of the Mobile Homecoming Experiential Archive project.

Because self-love is hairy.

From about middle school up into the beginning of college, my own hair was my mortal enemy. More intimate, pernicious, and persistent than the externalized racism and sexism I experienced as a black girl in white-dominated schooling environments was the internalized shame I projected onto my hair and its all-over wrongness.

I wanted space alien hairless skin, smooth and plastic. I wanted the hair on my head to calm the heck down, which should have been totally different. I thought. Invaded at every pore. Imagine. I went behind my mother's back to shave my legs before I was allowed. I stole her Nair to try to eradicate the peach fuzz on my upper lip. I used her tweezers to try to shape the bushy eyebrows that had already had their own bald spots since I was born. I put duct tape on my arms to try to rip the hair out. And then pubic hair? How dare my body betray me into animal. How dare my body betray me with hair.

Maybe it was because I became a black feminist. Maybe it was because I made it my personal political job to love myself the best I could. Maybe I got used to being the gorgeous manifestation of life that I am. Maybe I just eventually forgot about Barbies.

What I know is this: If I was able to teach my 11, 14, 17-year-old self about love and full acceptance of her body, I would ask her to ask a whole bunch of other people about grace with scoliosis, and fifty names for booty, and gender as a performance or a practice towards transformations. But I would have focused on one piece.

I would have told her about hair. That it's okay to have it. It's okay to hide in it. It's okay to hate it. It's okay to change it. If I was there to go to high school with her again, I would tell her that hair knows what it wants to do and is harder to control than your untame-able spirit. I would tell her that the person whose hair she wants to have wants hers. I would say that beauty salons and barbershops are places to listen to stories that have been told before, that might not be true, but are worth noticing. I would remind her that beauty salons and barber shops and bathroom mirrors and sleepover makeovers are places to listen to yourself when your self says "this won't change anything." I would have told her that there was nothing wrong with the hair or lack of hair on your head. I would have told her that touching your hair with your fingertips is like new years eve for your pores. I would have told her celebrate how life happens again and again. All over.

BEN HOLTZMAN edited *Sick: A Compilation Zine on Physical Illness* (Microcosm Publishing, 2009). His work has appeared in *Upping the Anti, Left History, Space and Culture, Radical Society,* and the collections *Constituent Imagination* and *Uses of a Whirlwind.*

"Communities of care," "healthy movements," "support networks"—these weren't concepts I began to engage with seriously until after my teenage years. Until then, I did a pretty crummy job of supporting at least a few friends when they needed it.

My thinking about support began to shift as I became friends with a beautiful person struggling with severe colitis. Our conversations helped me to understand how support could ameliorate the difficulties of living with a serious physical health issue, how young people struggling with illness could be isolated by their friends, and how there often is a disconnect on the radical left between our concern for the state of the world and the compassion we extend to our friends and allies.

These issues became even more tangible for me when I was diagnosed with cancer in my early twenties. Thankfully, my family and many friends rallied with support (for which I will be forever grateful), but other friends and people with whom I was organizing did not know how to respond and, in some cases, did not respond at all. I'm sure that many had not needed to think about how to respond to a peer having a serious illness before my diagnosis. I think many felt it was somehow better to withdraw rather than to potentially say or do something "wrong."

As I recovered from cancer, I began compiling a zine on physical illness. Contributions came from people dealing with a wide variety of conditions who were most often in their late teens and twenties and involved in radical politics and subcultures. While the "call for submissions" asked generally for writings on "experiences living with physical illness," the vast number of submissions mentioned support, most commonly in reference to not-adequate care and understanding from those around them. Clearly, the experience of being a young person and having a health crisis compounded by a lack of support—if not abandonment—from friends is far from uncommon. This can be more terrifying than the illness itself.

Though it can seem daunting, support can come in simple and seemingly insignificant ways: sharing some heartfelt words, attentive listening, or offering help with necessary tasks such as accompanying the person to the doctor or cooking a meal. Thankfully, for anyone interested in learning more, there are a growing number of resources aimed at helping people understand better how to provide support around illness (as well as other circumstances in which support is often needed).

Though support is not always easy or intuitive, it is critical not to retreat from friends, allies, and loved ones just when they need us most. Practices are crucial to creating more sustainable and healthy movements and ultimately moving us towards a more caring world. Just as critically, they help us to provide essential enrichment to friends, loved ones, and political allies in their struggles.

KALAMITY HILDEBRANDT is an anti-oppression activist living in unceded Coast Salish Territories (Vancouver, B.C.). They reject the "oppression Olympics" in all its forms, and embrace the idea that in order to overcome any one system of oppression we need to understand and resist them all. They are one of the founders of Fat Panic! Vancouver.

Activists question. We demand that society justify itself, and when it can't, we demand social change. Yet most of us still accept mainstream messages about fat people without any question at all. Fat or not, most of us have been convinced that, at least when it comes to this issue, the mainstream has it right.

We are told: Fat=Bad. Fat=Stupid. Fat=Lazy. Fat=Ugly. Fat=Unhealthy. We not only fail to question these stories, but we take these myths and we use them in our activism. Fat means bad/ugly/lazy/stupid so when we want to trash the police we use the image of a fat doughnut-eating cop. When we want to point out the problems of capitalism and Western overconsumption, we use graphics of some fat person eating the planet, or a fat CEO crushing the poor.

But, most cops aren't fat.

In countries like Canada and the USA the thinnest people are wealthy white folks, and the people most likely to be fat are poor, including Indigenous populations and some communities of Colour.

Being fat isn't inherently unhealthy.

That last bit probably sounds sketchy... but what if it's true? When fat activists or non-fat allies bring up sizeism, the usual response is a cry of "fat=unhealthy!" as if *that* settled *that*.

In fact, it settles nothing at all. Sure, it is worth talking about fat and health, but it is important to realize that this knee-jerk response to calls for an end to fat oppression is misguided because it distracts us from the real issue.

The issue is this: Fat oppression is *oppression*, and nothing justifies oppression.

Whether we are talking ableism, colonialism, or any of the many systems of inequity currently fucking with us, oppression is about systemic power imbalance, and it is always destructive and dehumanizing. Fat oppression is no different.

People who are considered "too fat" face social exclusion, discrimination in every area of life including education, employment, and access to health care, harassment and violence on the streets and in our homes, damaged self-esteem and increased rates of troubled eating and suicidal thinking, especially among youth. And because everything is interconnected, sizeism both supports and magnifies the harm of other oppressions like sexism, trans-oppression, racism, and classism.

As an added bonus, capitalism has made good use of the fear potential in fat oppression, and has convinced huge numbers of non-fat people to spend millions in panicked efforts to avoid becoming fat.

Those of us who think this state of affairs is bullshit are banding together—"enlarging" the resistance you might say.

Want to join us? Start here, whether you are fat or not:

> Your body is not your enemy.
> There is no wrong way to have a body.**
> Nothing justifies oppression. Ever.

Start there, and then keep on asking questions. After all, that is what activists do.

**Thank you to Hanne Blank—www.hanneblank.com/blog/2011/06/23/real-women/

ANA AMBROZ lives in Slovenia and just turned 16 this month. In her free time she mostly draws and her signature names are usually Annchyka123 (which is also her deviantArt username) or LoopyGc.

BUFFIE IRVINE is a non-fat ally and one of the founders of Fat Panic! Vancouver. An Indigenous activist of Gitxan and Coast Salish ancestry, Buffie works to end violence in all its forms, including anti-fat violence.

Fat Panic! Vancouver · Resisting Hate Since 2010

Hey, Activists!
Fat Kitty Says...

© Annchyka123

DON'T BLAME THE FAT CATS. BLAME CAPITALISM!

When you use "fat" to symbolize western over-consumption, corporate greed, capitalism or imperialism you dehumanize fat people and ignore the fact that in countries like Canada, the USA and Britian, the people most likely to be fat come from low income communities, including indigenous communities and communities of Colour. Remember: All systems of oppression intersect and support each other. You can't undermine "the system" by indulging in anti-fat prejudice. Check yourself.

JOE BIEL is the author of *beyond resistance and community, make a zine, bipedal, by pedal*, and *the scorcher*. He is the director of the documentaries *$100 & a tshirt, aftermass*, and *if it ain't cheap it ain't punk*. He founded microcosm publishing in 1996.

"Your thirties are all about the dealing with ignoring your health in your twenties." I said to my tattoo artist through laughter.

"It also doesn't have to be that way," she said, over the needle in my arm.

I was putting out feelers to compare others' experiences to my own. After fifteen years of an ungodly list of symptoms and medications, I was trying to distill what was going on and deal with it. I was diagnosed with an auto-immune condition, most likely Lupus.

If you've watched *House*, you know an auto-immune condition is when your white blood cells attack your healthy body. The same thing can be caused by certain food intolerances, like when I eat wheat or corn. Eating sugar feeds infections that can sneak in while this war is being waged in my guts.

Typically these kinds of problems—and undoubtedly in my case—are caused by overexposure to certain foods during your teenage years. It's easy to subsist on a diet of lots of wheat—pizza, toast, bagels, sandwiches, cereal, and pasta. But with some label inspection, the problem becomes more insidious. Most foods at the grocery store are processed or packaged with some form of wheat or corn. Or corn is made into corn syrup or high fructose corn syrup and used as a cheap sweetener for pop, candy bars, cereal, salad dressings, "fruit juices," and even marinara sauce.

Worse yet, most wheat or corn in these products is genetically modified and the results of that are not yet determined. But the last few years have yielded about ten times as many cases of known intolerance, particularly to wheat gluten, than we've seen before. And that will likely get worse.

So it's crushing to see teenagers munching down on a lunch of cookies and coffee, because I know the rest of the story.

An intolerance is particularly evil because it doesn't show up on allergy tests. And the more you eat of something, the more intense your reactions become. Until you can't help but notice and make changes.

With this in mind, I present the simplest solution: Cooking will allow you to know what you are eating and will allow you to produce better food than most restaurants. The most basic, yet obvious secret, is to work with raw materials. Start with brown rice, the vegetables you like, nuts or peanut butter, potatoes, beans—fresh food. Make your own sauces. Suffer a few failures in the name of development.

And don't get me wrong—eat some brownies and pasta in your life, just don't make it every meal.

There's a world worth impacting and it's a lot easier to do when you are strong and healthy.

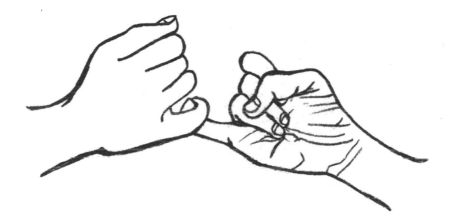

Image by aly de la Cruz

FIONA DE BALASI BROWN has a complicated heart (but don't we all?). Her vivid life has been coloured by experience with the "healthcare" system and, while in many respects she feels independent of those experiences, she can't deny that the hue of her day to day has been deeply affected. She wishes to thank the system for painting her with such violence as to highlight, of necessity, her passions for real health care and food as medicine.

Environmental Degradation

my body
has been invaded so many times and so
deeply
that now the slightest prick
makes me ache with 17 years of pain.
17 years of violation
my body on probation
not quite free
never autonomous
not quite mine.
they don't tell me what to expect
what tools
what tests
what trauma they intend to pull from my
veins
which places will hurt
for days.
code words
for rape
assault i must be grateful for
thank the state
every time i don't pay for the needles
the poisons.
my awareness tells me i'm privileged
my body knows this isn't right.
this 'healing' from harm
this system designed to keep us alive
rather than letting us live.
if we'd opted out
there would have been social workers calling.
parents legitimate fear
i could have been taken away.
why now do i return, legal?
willfully subject myself to this prescribed violence
sterile stupidity
i am afraid
it has dripped into me

inability to trust inner wisdom
wisdom of the land
our bodies, like lands
are victims of colonization.
i do not claim to be native to this place
i am a settler
but i am native in this body
and in domination
exploitation
civilization
no home is left unburned.
i cannot return
dependent
they put my home on the grid, and there
are
6.5 years of electricity left.
but like the land
my body
has its own energy sources
and my natural resources will not
be drained
without a fight.

MANISHA SINGH is an educator, activist, artist, and yoga teacher who received her doctorate in communication from Simon Fraser University. Her academic work explores seed and food sovereignty, Gandhian thought, social movement theory, and the biodiversity and cultural value of indigenous knowledge. She also coordinates the Purple Thistle Centre's Dream Seeds project.

As newborns, totally free of language, concepts, and memories, to fog up our sense of things, we feel our parents, our siblings, and ourselves as just one great living being… though each of us exists within a totally different physical body.

We easily can lose this sense of wholeness in a world that destroys love.

As children and as youth, we are immensely benefited if we have experiences that awaken this sense of wholeness, that feeling of being connected to the starry night sky, and all sentient beings in a deeply loving way.

One day we may awaken to the realization that life in this physical body is extremely short, and that we need to cultivate unconditional love for our bodies—repositories of the stardust and infinity poured into them.

Because we live in a time when we need to shower the earth with love. Loving our bodies is intimately connected to loving the earth.

Embracing the wisdom of one's body, born of this love, is connected to embracing the wisdom of the earth and working with its natural capacity to heal.

With the awareness that the earth and our bodies have this capacity to heal, it's possible to serve our own deep need, our community's, and the earth's need to heal, in the most profound of ways.

This calls for initiative on the part of radicalized youth, to fall deeply in love with your own body and with the earth's.

In service of the need to heal our bodies and the earthly body of the infinite, we may need to find healing arts which speak to our own hearts, both to improve our own lives and to be part of the radical healing and radical change needed at this time.

For me, the science and art of yoga, from Ancient India, calls to my heart and with years of practice, has become a way of life. The word Yoga comes from the Sanskrit word *yuj*, which means to yoke or join. The seminal text that codifies the ancient knowledge of yoga, *The Yoga Sutras of Patanjali*, defines yoga as the ability to focus the mind without distraction. To achieve a profound integration of mind, body, and spirit that is the essence of yoga, this text offers numerous methods including *yamas* and *niyamas* (lifestyle practices), asana (postures), *pranayama* (breath work), and meditation.

297

Yoga has offered an ethical guide to living, which starts with acting nonviolently or with loving kindness towards all sentient beings. *Ahimsa*, the Sanskrit word for nonviolence also means not bringing harm to ourselves. A yogic lifestyle includes committing to truth in word and thought and achieving an alignment between speech and action. Yogis also commit to not stealing, to faithfulness, to sustainability—taking only that which is necessary, to cleanliness, to acceptance of what we have been given and what things happen to us, to practice, to self inquiry, and to dedicating the fruits of our actions to the liberation and happiness of all sentient beings.

For me, yoga spoke to my body, heart, and mind. In the beginning I was drawn to this way of life because my father was a yogi and because I was able to connect to my ancestral culture heritage through this gateway, but really it was because yoga is a dance with my spirit, that also opens up the truth of my body and heightens my devotion to this beautiful earth.

It is for you also to find and feel what way is good for you, to ultimately create the change that you dream of.

As radicalized youth, you are radicalized artists, creating realities you believe will more deeply honor the whole. Investigate and explore your body, heart, and mind. This type of work will support your life.

> **DANNY McGUIRE** worked as a strength trainer at The University of Victoria under the head strength and conditioning coach for Pacific Sport, Tyler Goodale. He is currently working as a firefighter for the City of Surrey, and in 2013 he will be a competitor in bodybuilding at the World Police Fire Games is Belfast. He continues to be active in the strength training, yoga, outdoor sports, and the raw food community.

So you are thinking about getting fit? Here's what I wish someone had told me before I started:

I wish someone had told me that people were going to try to hijack my body—that the same assholes who manufactured the current wars, restless legs syndrome, the banking bailouts, and reality TV were going to try color my idea of what personal health is and how to achieve it. Crash diets, ephedrine, whey protein powder loaded with synthetics, toxic fitness centers crammed wall to wall with self-hatred, aggression, and thinly veiled narcissism—these are just a few of the hallmarks of a poisonous body cult that has taken the beautiful notion of personal health and transmuted it into a noxious byproduct of the dominant culture infused by a new classism: who can conform most closely to the fitness celebrity models in *Men's Health* and *Maxim*?

So you want to bypass all this and get fit without the help of a $70 an hour trainer? Here's the goods. If you really want to boil it down to its essence, I think there are four components: diet, stretching, strength training, and cardio.

★ Let's start with **Diet**. Michael Pollan wasn't wrong when he said eat whole foods, mostly vegetables. I would add that your body will naturally regulate the balance of carbs, protein, fats, calories, etc., so don't get swept up in counting grams of each or total calories—that'll suck and it's fucking boring. As for supplements, unless you are actually, genuinely, severely deficient in some area, you don't need them if you're eating whole, natural foods.

★ On to **Stretching**. Just because dorks in $200 capris are doing yoga doesn't mean you shouldn't. Yoga is amazing and you don't have to pay to go to an expensive yoga studio. There is tons of free yoga with instruction online.

★ **Strength Training** can be all kinds of fun and you should be able to do it all your life no matter what your physical condition. You can do it in a gym or on your own, lifting weights, practicing circus tricks, at home, or anywhere really. But when building strength make sure you do it right: it's easy to get hurt or turn yourself off. Get a friend or the internet to show you good form and don't worry about numbers (how much you lift or how many reps you do), just get your muscles moving and working hard.

★ **Cardio** is pure simplicity: run, cycle, jog, surf, skate, walk, play sports, swim, hike, fuck and play. Do what makes you happy and gets your heart rate up. Do it as often and for as long as feels good.

So, if you can synthesize the big 4: **stretching, cardio, diet, and strength training**, you've got the basis to move forward and get to know your own body in a healthy and vibrant way that'll give you the platform from which to take your next steps confidently, on your own terms.

GACHING KONG works as an acupuncturist and community researcher in Victoria, BC. As a settler with Chinese-Irish-English roots, her biggest passion is the cross-cultural medicine exchange at her affordable acupuncture clinic at the Victoria Native Friendship Centre. If you ask her on any given day, she'll say she ended colonization yesterday, even though she knows it's not over yet. She's working on it.

What Healers Wore

Jesus wore dresses and a loin cloth as panties.
Jesus performed faith healings
on naked blind beggars,
mismatched schizophrenics
and half-dressed prostitutes.
He was a philosopher who seldom made sense
but somehow the backwords got in your spirit
Reminded you who you really were
and what you really was.
He told us of big stories jogging in our veins,
Break dancing in our spirits
in Air Jordans and other ordinary runners.

Buddha wore saffron robes and no shoes or socks.
He talked the opposite of what he said
'til our heads turned round the right way.
Buddha poured our spirits a long bath
of hot breath and aromatherapy oils.
Said the body only needs three things—
compassion, joy and equanimity—
and told us to wear our feet like diamonds
and our eyes like stars
and our hands like truth.
So we take ourselves apart
and back together again
into an emptiness that is really full.

Only heroes and service providers wear capes
and sometimes suits over jeans
and hipsacks filled with needles and bandaids.
I wore all these things when he walked in
with shoes too small
and scabs growing through his soles.
My cape blew in my eyes
as I held my nose and called the street nurse.
Risked my job, broke the policies
to get him in a cab and into detox.
This outfit so tight and hot and uncomfortable.
And though I got the lecture,
no one ever mentioned my name.
I'd trade for robes and dresses and bare feet
so that I never have to wear that outfit again.

21. OUTRO: GETTING OLDER

One of the core arguments of this book is that leading a radical life doesn't have to be boring, dogmatic, or dreary: you can hang on to your best values and still have a really fun, creative, and fulfilling life. And we don't mean that just for when you're young—we're arguing that a radical, political life is a desirable way to roll and that you can stay solid for all your days.

And we know that's possible because we have had the pleasure of meeting so many fantastic, sharp, thoughtful, revolutionary people of all ages. Some of the people we know who have challenged us with the most creative, innovative ideas we have ever encountered are a lot older than us. Getting old does not have to mean getting dull. It doesn't have to mean giving up. It doesn't have to mean moving to the suburbs and buying a minivan. It doesn't have to mean getting tired and cynical. It doesn't have to mean constantly reminiscing about the old days. We know that because there are so, so many rad older folks out there.

So we asked some folks who are no longer young adults to offer their opinions about getting older and how they have aged and kept their best values and beliefs alive. We asked them what they would say to teenagers on this from the perspective of a few years down the road.

"You are what you do. If you do boring, stupid monotonous work, chances are you'll end up boring, stupid and monotonous. Work is a much better explanation for the creeping cretinization all around us than even such significant moronizing mechanisms as television and education."

—Bob Black

OTHER STUFF TO CHECK OUT:

- **MIRRORS**, Eduardo Galeano

- **A PEOPLE'S HISTORY OF AMERICAN EMPIRE**: A Graphic Adaptation, Howard Zinn and Paul Buhle (text) & Mike Konopacki (text & illus.)

- **HOW TO BE A HELP INSTEAD OF A NUISANCE**: Practical Approaches to Giving Support, Service, and Encouragement to Others, Karen Kissel Wegela

- **LIVING IN LIBERATION**: Boundary Setting, Self Care & Social Change, Cristien Storm

- **TRAUMA STEWARDSHIP**: An Everyday Guide to Caring for Self While Caring for Others, Laura Van Dernoot Lipsky and Connie Burk

- **THE GIVING TREE**, Shel Silverstein

- **MISS RUMPHIUS**, Barbara Cooney

- **WILFRID GORDON MCDONALD PARTRIDGE**, Mem Fox

- **LETTERS TO A YOUNG POET**, Rainer Maria Rilke

GUSTAVO ESTEVA is an independent writer and grassroots activist. Author of more than 30 books and scores of articles, he writes regularly in *La Jornada*, a leading Mexican newspaper, and occasionally in *The Guardian*. He was an advisor to the Zapatistas in their negotiations with the government. In Oaxaca, where he lives, Gustavo participates in the Centro de Encuentros y Diálogos Interculturales and Universidad de la Tierra en Oaxaca, of which he is a founding member.

"To change the world is very difficult, perhaps impossible. What is feasible is to create a whole new world."

We loved this statement when Subcomandante Marcos made it in 1996, at the very end of the Intercontinental Encounter for Humanity and against Neoliberalism convened by the Zapatistas in the Lacondon Jungle. But then we thought: beautiful, but too romantic, too idealistic… Months, even years passed, before we discovered how pragmatic this statement is.

The education system is not delivering: it does not prepare people for life and work. But you can spend your whole life trying to change it and end as a footnote in a text book. People are instead escaping from the system. Like babies, who learn to think or to talk without schools or teachers through a positive and loving interaction with others, people are transforming learning and studying into a leisurely activity of free people.

The health system is a complete mess. After the most important reform in 50 years, Americans still have the most expensive and inefficient health system of the world. People are thus escaping from professional control and reclaiming alternative ways of healing, applying their wisdom and autonomy to feel well and be healthy.

Some people are afraid of hunger, others afraid of eating, observes the Uruguayan poet Eduardo Galeano. A billion people cannot put enough food in their bellies and those "well-fed" are eating junk or poison served in their plates by the corporations. But people are now defining by themselves what they want to eat and trying to produce it, through initiatives like urban agriculture, CSAs and many others.

In replacing nouns—education, health, food—with verbs—learning, healing, eating/cultivating—people reclaim their autonomous capacity to again take control of their own lives.

The time has come for such peaceful and democratic revolution. "The world we know will be destroyed," warned Subcomandante Marcos in April 2011. Increasingly aware that the current crises are bringing the world to the point of collapse, ordinary men and women are taking initiative. Disenchanted with formal democracy ("My dreams don't fit into your ballot-box," said the *indignados* in Spain; "we want real democracy"), and disenchanted with capitalism and socialism, common people are creating a whole new world in the belly of the old. This is not an individual endeavor… but does not require masses. A few friends may start what soon can become an avalanche of transformations.

> **TASNIM NATHOO** lives in Vancouver, BC where she enjoys reading stories where good things happen and frequently ponders the interconnections between personal and social transformation.

Char didn't really know what to expect when the revolution finally arrived. She'd been preparing for it for quite some time. At first, she'd been hyper alert, always keeping an eye out for warning signs of its imminent arrival. But while there were clear signs of good things brewing, she'd become used to the idea that this was going to be a quiet revolution—slow, steady, gentle, but truly transformative. She'd even considered the possibility that the revolution might gather speed and strength throughout her lifetime, and then burst full force in her children's lifetimes, or possibly even her grandchildren's.

So she began to make preparations of a different sort: a pillow book. In times past, a pillow book was a record of truths, observations, and advice to the next generation. It was something to be left under the pillow of those who would need it—a compilation of thoughts so profound they were almost taboo and could not be spoken in the light of day.

She started by writing down the story of her mother's family. It was a story of class struggle, religious persecution, and of dreams of a new life in a young country. She couldn't say much about her father's family—too much had been lost. Her father had been raised in an urban landscape of concrete and hard work and competition. His was a wisdom of sweat, perseverance, and dreams of a better world for all.

She began to consider what she would tell her children of her own life. Would they understand that the revolution was fueled equally by silent contributions like hers as it was by vocal protests and political acts? Would they see that a movement was really made up of ordinary individuals making choices with their hearts and conscience? That a revolution could only be sustained by those who carried dreams in their hearts, no matter what they might look like to others?

Char told stories about all the women she knew—mothers, grandmothers, aunts, sisters—who knew that the next generation needed to be healthy. She told stories of people working to heal themselves, working to heal the past, so the future could be created free of old hurts. She wrote of people creating alternatives—sometimes successfully, sometimes not—but still trying.

Mostly, she wrote of times past when people had forgotten that the revolution must be for all. She wrote of the revolutions that had failed because the leaders had tried to decide what was best for others. After all, all revolutions had to start from within: with inner knowing, culminating in small acts that grew into a force of their own.

Char was very old when the revolution arrived. She prayed fervently that she had done enough to prepare those who would come after her. As she closed her eyes to sleep on that first night of joy and freedom, she remembered the old pillow book she had written. And she knew that this revolution belonged to all who had dreamed of a better world. She reached her hand under her pillow and knew that when she woke, she would begin to write another pillow book—this time of a very different kind. She breathed out a little sigh and fell into a deep contented sleep.

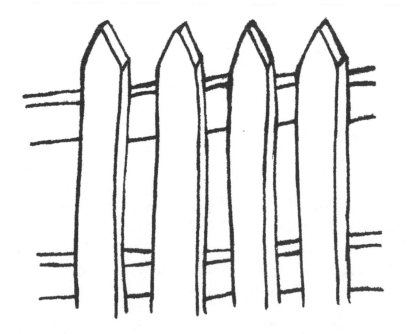

Image by aly de la Cruz

ADRIENNE MAREE BROWN is a facilitator, writer, doula, singer, artist, and science fiction scholar living in Detroit. She works with the Food Justice Task Force, Digital Justice Coalition, and Allied Media Projects locally, and the Engage Network nationally. She worked with US Social Forum, The Ruckus Society, and the League of Pissed Off Voters before coming to Detroit.

I wish i had known the power of curiosity. i used to feel so fierce all the time, righteous with knowledge. now i see curiosity as a more powerful and revolutionary characteristic than any other. holding out the space to have a question, to be outside the system that presumes to know everything, that has given me so much space to learn.

i wish i knew how amazing my parents are. all i could think about at that time in my life was how different i was from them, how no one could possibly understand me. but i wasn't so complicated. the unconditional love they showed me during that time still shocks me when i reflect on it.

i wish i had known that my body was beautiful, and that i had power over my body. by the time i was 15 i thought that power had been taken from me, forever, and i thought that my body was only ugly or dangerous.

i wish i had known what a fleeting gift health was, and that every day was a chance to be healthy and to be healing.

i wish i had known that you really don't know who is going to live, and who is going to die—you don't know how long you have with people. you have to love people all the time with all the love you want to give them for a lifetime.

i wish i had known how unnecessary college was. i loved it—but it was the community, the social justice work, and being in ny, that i loved. i didn't need to worry so much about grades, that hasn't mattered.

i wish i had known that gossip, negativity, and to a large extent critique eat at your soul. and you have to feed your soul—that's where peace and joy come from. compassion, love, curiosity, friendship, honesty—these things feed your soul, or as my mentor grace lee boggs says, "grow your soul."

i wish i had known there is no reconciling with capitalism. it is a failed system. begin practicing cooperative ways of living and being immediately. compost, use consensus, share leadership, recycle, be a self-aware member of a cooperative society, live it into being.

i wish i had known that if any little voice tells you it's not right, you have to listen, you have to amplify that voice within yourself.

i wish that i had known that the only person i could ever truly change is myself.

and finally, i wish i had known that whatever i knew then, that was just fine.

DAN CHODORKOFF is a cultural anthropologist who lives in Vermont. He is a lifelong activist, educator, and writer who cofounded the Institute for Social Ecology His novel, *Loisaida*, was recently published by Fomite Press.

Nothing sadder than an aging radical? Hardly. A lifetime commitment to social change is one of the most important choices an individual can make. It may not lead to great riches, popular acclaim, or other forms of conventional success, but it will result in a well-spent life, rich in relationships, understanding, and meaningful work. Be prepared for ridicule, rejection, antipathy, and even hatred from the powers that control the dominant culture, but all should be borne with pride. In a world ruled by money and dominated by self-interest, life-long radicals are a rare breed, and maintaining one's beliefs, and developing a critique of domination over a lifetime requires a certain kind of tough mindedness. Make no mistake, even in the most discouraging of times (and we are currently living in the most discouraging time I have ever experienced) there is a crucial need for people to speak truth to power, and to engage in active resistance to the evils of domination, exploitation, and ecological destruction.

My personal journey in a range of radical movements (anti-war, civil rights, radical ecology, grassroots community development, counter institution building, etc.), has evolved through several stages. I began as an anti-war activist and organizer while still in high school in the mid-1960s and continued to develop my understanding when I was in college through my involvement with SDS (Students for a Democratic Society). Later, while I continued to learn and work through the insights offered by anarchism by involvement with a range of activist groups, I also co-founded the Institute for Social Ecology (ISE) , a project that encompasses a radical approach to education in both formal degree-granting studies and popular education, with an emphasis on a radical, critical, and reconstructive praxis. My work for the ISE, which I served as Director for 32 years, led me to define myself primarily as an educator who tried to teach other educators, activists, and organizers about radical social change from the perspective of social ecology. After my retirement from the ISE, I continued to try to work with these same ideas through my writing. My recently published novel, *Loisaida*, explores aspects of anarchism and social ecology on New York's Lower East Side. I believe that fiction has the potential to bring these ideas to a wider audience than that which reads theoretical and scholarly work. The core of my beliefs has changed little over my 45+ years of radicalism, though I hope I have developed a deeper and more nuanced understanding, which can help others achieve the revolution I will probably never live to see.

In my life I have been inspired by the openness, energy, fervor and commitment of young people, and I have also drawn a great deal of inspiration from my elders, and learned from their lifetimes of commitment. People like Dave Dellinger, a WWII war resister and lifelong non-violent activist well into his nineties; Grace Paley, a great writer, feminist and peace activist until the day she died in her eighties; my mentor, Murray Bookchin, an activist and social theorist who wrote twenty-five books over the course of his life on radical themes ranging widely from radical ecology to revolutionary history. I was also privileged to know several old timers from the Yiddish Anarchist movement, going back to the days of Emma Goldman. These people were my teachers and informed my understanding of what it means to make a real commitment to revolutionary social change.

I will never forget meeting, in 1975, Daniel Guérin, the great French libertarian socialist, author of the classic works *Fascism and Big Business, and Anarchism: Theory and Practice*, who, in his eighties helped to found the French Gay Liberation Movement. We spent a fascinating afternoon together when he was (I believe) ninety years old, before he addressed a major conference in New York. I remember he ended his speech that night on the failure of the May/June revolt in Paris in '68, with his index finger pointing in the air insisting that "next time we will make la Revolución."

"Anarchism is not a romantic fable but the hardheaded realization, based on five thousand years of experience, that we cannot entrust the management of our lives to kings, priests, politicians, generals, and county commissioners."

—Edward Abbey

ONE CRIMETHINC EX-WORKER–CrimethInc. is a revolutionary secret society dedicated to overthrowing capitalism, abolishing the state, and defending spaces of mutual aid and autonomy. Visit www.crimethinc.com for more info.

I wish I'd known that what I needed to do to prepare for my future was not to build up a résumé, but to focus on the things I loved. I wish I'd known earlier that I would dedicate my life to music, writing, and rebellion instead of some miserable career, so I could have taken them more seriously than test scores or obedience. I wish I'd known that the whole idea of making progress along a standardized track towards the future was bullshit, that there was no future waiting ahead for any of us except what we built ourselves. I could have gotten started building mine earlier and saved myself a lot of trouble.

I wish I'd taken myself more seriously. I thought I had to get older before I could do anything that mattered. But young people have always been at the forefront of everything revolutionary, be it music or art or overthrowing governments. Arthur Rimbaud was a teenager when he wrote the best poetry ever composed in French; Joan of Arc saved France from the British at the same age. Most of the fighters in the Warsaw Ghetto Uprising were teenagers, just like the guerrillas who fought against the dictators in Latin America. Older people are usually invested in the status quo, however fucked up it is, and afraid to challenge it. When things change, it's mostly young people who make it happen.

I wish I'd known how trivial the threat of punishment was compared to the danger of not doing what I believed in. I wish I'd known that if I was going to break the little rules I might as well break the big ones. I wish I'd been more ambitious—I could have found more people to rebel with. The adults around me were just as scared and confused as I was—they had no idea what was going on.

Parents, teachers, and police pretend they're confident and in control, but they suffer from this social order even more than kids do. Their only hope is that you'll come up with something better and make it a reality.

HACK + SMASH

Image via crimethinc.com

MAIA RAMNATH wears many hats, including writer, teacher, activist, aerialist/dancer/choreographer, and Institute for Anarchist Studies board member. She lives in New York City.

Do you ever write journals and stop to wonder why you're doing it, who it is you're writing to? Once while cleaning up I came across some old journals, stuff I'd written more than 20 years ago. Though she didn't know it at the time, Past-me had plainly written this to Future-me. She cast her bottled message into the space-time tides because she had to, so she didn't burst, not knowing if anyone would ever receive it. Well, I received it. This was hard, because it re-activated old pains, shames, and griefs. But it was also a beautiful shock to realize that Now-me is actually who I always was, before life distorted everything and made me forget; and that if 10- or 12-year-old me had met 30-something me, she would have been astonished and delighted. Astonished because she had never imagined such a way of being was even an available option; and delighted because I think that once she had gotten over her incredulity and resistance, she might have hoped to be something like me when she grew up. (Of course, once she got to know me better, she would have realized that I fell a bit short of the ideal she had suddenly fixed on—but maybe once her disappointment wore off, she would have relented, because at least I keep trying.)

Many of you, I suspect, are a lot further along than I was at your age, in terms of both social consciousness and self-awareness; figuring out stuff about what's wrong with the world, and what you might be able to do about that. You may already know everything Now-me has to offer. Nevertheless, if I met up now with Past-me—odd, stubborn kid that she was—here are some things I would tell her.

★ When you're miserable, make the frame bigger. Get perspective. Sometimes taking action on something bigger than you makes your own problems, well, not go away, but at least not seem so big and painful.

★ Always pay attention. Don't take anything for granted, as a given, as just the way things are. Ask questions. Be critical. But also choose your battles.

★ Don't be afraid of solitude, or ashamed of it, if that's where you feel happy and restored. Don't let anyone make you feel like a loser for that. Know you can be emotionally self-sufficient and true to your own beliefs. But don't be isolated either. Keep in mind the risks of removing yourself from circuits of activity and community. Especially if you want to make change happen. You can't do it alone; it requires exponential synergy. So, seek the company of people who inspire and challenge you: politically, intellectually, artistically. Those are people who will make you excited to try to be even better at manifesting your own ideals.

★ If you feel alienated, keep in mind the problem is probably not you. As they say, being totally well-adjusted in a fucked-up world is a sign of mental illness. Seek community so you know you're not delusional, and so that together you can weave resistance and alternatives: to intervene in, not just escape from, the society that feels so alienating and wrong.

★ Purity is impossible. Context is complex. Nothing is without compromise. Sometimes it helps to think about the net amount of good that you do over time, rather than the absolute amount of bad in an isolated situation. I'm not saying choose the lesser of evils, I'm just saying don't beat yourself up for negotiating among contradictions.

★ Be healthy. Take care of yourself. Your body and mind are no less part of a holistic system than any other element of the planet, so respect them as such. But neither are they the center of this system, or the most important part. There are far worse things than discomfort and inconvenience, so do push yourself if there are worthwhile reasons.

★ Radicalism is a long-term commitment; there have to be ways to do it over a lifetime. This means that barring burn-out, or sell-out, or annihilation in a blaze of glory, there have to be manifestations appropriate to all stages of life. Having a kid, or a job, or other responsibilities, or going to school, may all be part of this journey, as much as those moments where you're more free to put everything on the line. So be patient: life is long enough, hopefully, to do a lot of stuff in its time.

Of course, that's what Now-me would say to Past-me. But who does Now-me listen to? Well, you see, there's this really badass old woman that lives in my head. She is creative, strong, fearless, and principled and she hangs out at street protests in a badass old lady bloc with Patti Smith, Nawal El Saadawi, and the ghost of Rosa Luxemburg. Of course, I usually don't listen to her—that is, I hear her; I'm just not yet capable of doing what she says. I'm not ready. But I can still hope to be like her when I grow up.

MIKE DAVIS is a geezer radical in San Diego, CA who writes books, including *City of Quartz*, *Magical Urbanism*, *Planet of Slums*, and *In Praise of Barbarians*. He's also the founder and only member of the organization "White Guys in Pickup Trucks Against White Guys in Pickup Trucks."

Conversations between generations are governed by an iron law: the older crew struggles for decades to achieve a wisdom that, when it actually arrives, is largely irrelevant to the changed life situation of its children or grandchildren.

I'm not talking, of course, about skills that have eternal shelf-life like child-rearing, big game hunting, or successfully organizing a strike (listen to your grandparents), but the contention that youth should be obedient to the political experience of its self-nominated elders.

What a silly and arrogant assumption.

We Sixties kids, after all, are the ones who left you—forty-five years later—the responsibility of saving the planet from global warming and terminal inequality. It's a nice inheritance and if I were you, I probably wouldn't trust anyone over 12.

But if I could, I would introduce you to my radical elders. Indeed it breaks my heart that you will never know of those extraordinary rebels, their names usually uncarved in granite or footnoted in history books, who shook the earth to its foundations in the early twentieth century.

Wobblies, feminists, Communists, pacifists, anarchists, and Black nationalists—not always patient but sharing the irony and sense of humor that keeps you alive in a freezing Alberta boxcar, an Alabama prison cell, or a trench in Spain.

Frank Spector was one of my favorite heroes. An old Bolshevik (literally), he had been sent to San Quentin in 1930 for leading an uprising of farm workers in California's Imperial Valley. He was also a master of the killing joke.

We worked in the same leftwing bookstore, and I was always trying to mine insight from his adventures. One day, I asked him about San Quentin.

"Of course, kid, if you're a serious revolutionary, count on going to prison someday."

I gulped.

Frank was built like a Russian bear with a magnificent leonine head. He could have been a statue at Stalingrad.

"Don't worry," he chuckled. "I'll give you a secret for surviving capitalist dungeons."

He scribbled on a sheet of paper for about five minutes.

He handed it to me and I read intently.

Milk? Squeeze through cotton? An incomprehensible set of instructions.

"Frank, is this a weird recipe for making a bomb?"

"No, stupid, it's the directions for how to make yogurt in your socks."